J.K. LASSER'S™

HOW TO
PROTECT YOUR
RETIREMENT
SAVINGS FROM THE
IRS

Seymour Goldberg, CPA, MBA, JD

IDG BOOKS WORLDWIDE

IDG Books Worldwide, Inc.
An International Data Group Company
919 East Hillsdale Boulevard
Suite 400
Foster City, CA 94404

J.K. Lasser is a trademark of Macmillan General Reference USA, Inc., a wholly owned subsidiary of IDG Books Worldwide, Inc.

Publisher's Note: *How to Protect Your Retirement Savings from the IRS* is published in recognition of the great need for useful information regarding the income tax laws for the millions of men and women who must fill out returns. We believe the research and interpretation by the J.K. Lasser Institute™ of the nation's tax laws to be authoritative and of help to taxpayers. Reasonable care has been taken in the preparation of the text. Taxpayers are cautioned, however, that this book is sold with the understanding that the publisher and the contributors are not engaged in rendering legal, accounting, or other professional services herein. Taxpayers with specific tax problems are urged to seek the professional advice of a tax accountant, lawyer, or preparer.

The publisher and contributors to this book specifically disclaim any responsibility for any liability, loss, or risk (financial, personal, or otherwise) that may be claimed or incurred as a consequence, directly or indirectly, of the use and/or application of any of the contents of this book.

IDG Books Worldwide, Inc. does not attest to the validity, accuracy or completeness of this information. Use of a term in this book should not be regarded as affecting the validity of any trademark or service mark.

For general information on IDG Books Worldwide's books in the U.S., please call our Consumer Customer Service department at 800-762-2974. For reseller information, including discounts and previous sales, please call our Reseller Customer Service department at 800-434-3422.

J.K. Lasser Editorial and Production
Kathy Nebenhaus, Publisher, Lifestyle Group
Cindy Kitchel, Associate Publisher, Lifestyle Group
Elliott Eiss, Member of the New York Bar, Editorial Director of the J.K. Lasser Institute
Brice Gosnell, Managing Editor
Michelle Patterson, Marketing Director
Rebecca Cremonese, Senior Production Manager
George McKeon, Designer
Arun Das, Production Editor and Copyeditor
Eric Brinkman and Marie Kristine Parial-Leonardo, Layout
Judith McMullen, Proofreader
Helen Chin, Indexer

ISBN 0-02-862796-2

Manufactured in the United States of America
10 9 8 7 6 5 4 3 2 1

CONTENTS

Chapter Two

When Must You Begin Minimum Distributions from Your Retirement Plan?   33

Chapter Three

Choosing Your Spouse as Your Designated Beneficiary   58

C H A P T E R   F O U R

C H A P T E R   F I V E

Chapter Six

If Your Beneficiary Is Older or Is No More Than Ten Years Younger Than You   157

Chapter Seven

The Estate as Beneficiary of IRA or Qualified Plan   184

Chapter Ten

Appendix A

Appendix B

APPENDIX C

APPENDIX D

About the Author

Seymour Goldberg is an attorney and a certified public accountant. He is the senior partner in the law firm of Goldberg & Goldberg, P.C., in Garden City, New York, and has been practicing law since 1966.

Mr. Goldberg spends a great deal of his time in the areas of estate planning, estate taxation, and retirement distribution planning. He is professor emeritus at Long Island University. Mr. Goldberg has conducted workshops on retirement distribution planning throughout the United States. He was formerly associated with the Internal Revenue Service.

Mr. Goldberg is the recipient of outstanding discussion leader awards from both the American Institute of Certified Public Accountants and the Foundation for Accounting Education. He has been quoted extensively in the *New York Times*, *Wall Street Journal*, *Forbes*, *Money Magazine*, and the *Boardroom Reports Tax Hotline*. He has also been interviewed by CNN, CNBC, and WCBS. Mr. Goldberg has taught many continuing professional education courses on taxation and pension at the state and national level and has taught continuing legal education courses for the New York State Bar Association.

INTRODUCTION

THIS BOOK COVERS THE NEW LAW CHANGES UNDER THE SMALL BUSINESS JOB PROTECTION ACT OF 1996, THE TAXPAYER RELIEF ACT OF 1997, AND THE IRS RESTRUCTURING AND REFORM ACT OF 1998. AN ENTIRE CHAPTER HAS BEEN ADDED ON THE NEW ROTH IRA TO HELP YOU THROUGH THE ROTH IRA RULES. SAMPLE BENEFICIARY FORMS AND ELECTIONS FORMS ARE ALSO INCLUDED.

As the population of the United States ages, the need for retirement distribution planning becomes vital. Many taxpayers have accumulated a significant amount of assets in retirement-type accounts during their working careers through their participation in qualified corporate plans, Keoghs, 401(k) plans, 403(b) plans, IRAs, and other similar plans. Since the primary purpose of your retirement assets is to provide you with an adequate nest egg during your golden years, you should know the rules governing these assets since they may be your main source of support. Unfortunately, many individuals with considerable retirement plan assets are unaware that substantial tax burdens may await them or their beneficiaries when distributions commence.

There are many IRS rules applicable to distributions from retirement plan accounts. Some rules apply while you are alive and other rules are triggered on your death. If you have a working knowledge of these rules then both you and your family can take advantage of them in a manner that can result in a substantial tax savings for everyone. The goal of this book is to help you understand the distribution rules for IRAs and employer retirement plans so that you can maximize their tax-saving potential and avoid unexpected tax burdens for yourself and your heirs. By knowing these rules you can save yourself and your family a great deal of money.

This book is written in question-and-answer format. The questions and answers emphasize not only the many IRS rules but also tax-planning strategies and income tax–deferral techniques. For example, several chapters in this book emphasize techniques in passing your retirement assets to children and grandchildren in order to preserve the tax deferred growth of your retirement assets for decades after your death. Another chapter deals with preserving your retirement assets for your surviving spouse, explaining what your spouse must do after you pass away in order to further protect your retirement assets for the family.

The questions in this book are based on real-world situations. The answers are based upon the author's actual experiences as well as his analysis of IRS rules. In many cases, detailed computations are provided to illustrate in dollars-and-cents how the distribution rules apply in actual situations (computations are based on the IRS Life Expectancy Tables in effect as of December 1998). Special emphasis is placed on IRA distribution planning. Although the required distribution rules for qualified employer plans and IRAs generally are the same, distributions from qualified employer plans are frequently transferred to IRAs, requiring the IRA owner to take tax-planning steps.

Do not consider this book or the forms included in this book as a substitute for a professional advisor. Your professional advisor—whether an accountant, attorney, or financial planner—must be involved in creating and implementing your retirement distribution plan. Your professional advisor can also keep you informed about changes in the tax laws that could affect the distribution rules and planning techniques described in this book.

CHAPTER ONE

Tapping Your Retirement Plan Assets Without Penalty Before Age 59½

The advantage of being able to accumulate tax-free earnings within an employer retirement plan or IRA has a downside. Because the plan funds are intended to be used for retirement, you do not have free access to your own account when you are under age $59^1/_2$. In some cases, access to your money is restricted or even prohibited. In other cases, access is allowed, but at the cost of a tax penalty.

Age $59^1/_2$ may seem to be an arbitrary point for determining retirement plan access, but nevertheless, Congress has chosen $59^1/_2$ as a key dividing-line age for retirement plan distributions.

If you have contributed to an employer retirement plan, you may find that you are not allowed to make withdrawals before age $59^1/_2$ from your account, unless you meet stringent tests for "hardship" withdrawals, or you have made after-tax contributions to the plan. A loan may be available where an outright withdrawal is not.

Where withdrawals are allowed before age $59^1/_2$, they generally are subject to a 10 percent early distribution tax penalty, in addition to the regular income tax on the withdrawal. There are exceptions to the 10 percent penalty, but they are limited.

The amount of the early-distribution penalty is increased from 10 percent to 25 percent for distributions from a Simple IRA within the first two years of commencing participation in the Simple IRA. A Simple IRA is a plan set up by employers who in the prior year had 100 or fewer employees.

The tax law does not restrict direct access to an IRA before age $59^1/_2$, but distributions from an IRA are subject to the 10-percent early-distribution penalty, unless a penalty exception applies.

The questions and answers in this chapter will explain the tax law restrictions on distributions before age $59^1/_2$, including the early-distribution penalty and the exceptions to the penalty. Some penalty exceptions apply to IRAs as well as to employer plans. Some exceptions allowed for IRA distributions do not apply to employer plans, and an important separation from service exception applies only to employer plans.

The Taxpayer Relief Act of 1997 (1997 Act) eliminated certain penalties involving retirement assets as of January 1, 1997. The 1997 Act eliminated the 15-percent penalty tax on excess distributions as well as the 15-percent penalty tax on excess accumulations. For tax years after December 31, 1997, the 1997 Act expanded the exceptions to the 10-percent early-distribution penalty for IRA distributions. The 1997 Act permits penalty-free withdrawals from IRAs to include distributions for first-time homebuyer expenses and for higher-education expenses.

Under the IRS Restructuring and Reform Act of 1998 (1998 Act), hardship distributions that are made after December 31, 1998, may not be rolled over to an IRA.

RESTRICTIONS ON 401(K) AND 403(B) PLAN WITHDRAWALS

Before age $59^1/2$, it is difficult to obtain an in-service distribution from a 401(k) or 403(b) plan because of restrictions on withdrawals of pre-tax salary-reduction contributions. Hardship distributions are available in limited circumstances. Loans, subject to limitations, generally are available for any purpose.

ALLOWABLE DISTRIBUTIONS AND LOANS: QUESTIONS 1.1–1.5

QUESTION 1.1: James Smith has made salary-reduction contributions to his company's 401(k) plan for 10 years. He is age 52 and would like to withdraw $30,000 from his account to purchase a principal residence. Will he be able to make the withdrawal?

ANSWER: No, unless he is disabled or qualifies for a hardship distribution. Distributions of elective salary deferrals (pre-tax contributions) from a 401(k) plan generally may be made only upon reaching age $59^1/2$, becoming permanently disabled, showing financial hardship, or separating from service.

If James had made any after-tax contributions to the plan, these could be withdrawn without restriction if permitted under the terms of the plan.

CASE STUDY
Questions 1.2–1.8 illustrate how financial hardship may allow a distribution before age 59^1/$_2$.

QUESTION 1.2: What would James have to show to qualify for a hardship withdrawal?

ANSWER: For a hardship withdrawal, IRS regulations require there to be an "immediate and heavy" financial need. Nontaxable loans, if permitted under the plan, must be made before a hardship withdrawal will be allowed. A hardship withdrawal may include pre-tax salary deferrals, but investment earnings credited after the 1988 plan year may *not* be included.

Qualifying financial need can be to buy a principal residence (excluding mortgage payments); pay previously incurred medical expenses for you, your spouse, or your dependents; tuition-related fees and room and board for the next 12 months of post-secondary education for you, your spouse, or your dependents; preventing eviction or mortgage foreclosure; or funeral expenses for a family member.

In general, the employee must agree to suspend contributions to the plan for 12 months after taking a hardship withdrawal.

QUESTION 1.3: If James qualifies for a hardship withdrawal, is it tax-free?

ANSWER: No, a hardship distribution is taxable, and because James is under age 59^1/$_2$, he will also be subject to the 10-percent penalty; *see* the discussion of the penalty later in this chapter.

By law, hardship distributions made after 1998 are *not* eligible for rollover and thus are not subject to the 20 percent mandatory withholding that applies to eligible rollover distributions. However, to give employers time to adapt to the new law, the IRS allowed employers the option of treating hardship distributions made during 1999 as eligible rollover distributions under the prior law rules. Even if the employer elected to apply the new law and not allow direct rollover treatment (plan-to-plan) for a 1999 hardship distribution, employees who received such distributions could make a personal rollover within 60 days.

QUESTION 1.4: Alice Craig has made salary-reduction contributions to a 403(b) annuity contract at the university where she works. She is age 50 and wants to make a withdrawal to pay for her daughter's college expenses. Is she subject to restrictions similar to James's?

ANSWER: Yes. Distributions of pre-tax salary-reduction contributions before age 59$^{1}/_{2}$ from a 403(b) annuity are allowed only for hardship, permanent disability, or separation from service. Hardship rules are the same as for 401(k) plans as discussed in the answers to Questions 1.2 and 1.3.

QUESTION 1.5: If James decided to take a loan from his 401(k) plan account, how much could he borrow without being subject to tax?

ANSWER: The maximum amount that can be borrowed without tax is the lesser of (1) 50 percent of the total account balance, or (2) $50,000.

    In a case where there were other loans within the prior 12-month period, the $50,000 amount would have to be reduced by the outstanding loan balance on the date of the new loan and also by the excess of the highest outstanding loan balance during the 12-month period ending on the day before the new loan over the outstanding balance on the date of the new loan.

WHEN DOES THE EARLY-DISTRIBUTION PENALTY APPLY?

The 10-percent penalty for distributions before age 59$^{1}/_{2}$ applies in addition to regular income tax on a taxable distribution. For Simple

IRA distributions within the first two years, the penalty increases to 25 percent.

QUESTION 1.6: Does the 10-percent early-distribution penalty apply to distributions from all retirement plans?

ANSWER: The 10-percent penalty applies to early distributions from all "qualified retirement plans." This includes IRAs, simplified employee pensions, pension plans, profit-sharing plans, stock bonus plans, 401(k) plans, annuity plans, and 403(b) tax-sheltered annuity contracts.

As previously noted, if the distribution from a Simple IRA is received within the first two years of plan participation, the penalty increases to 25 percent.

QUESTION 1.7: Carol Jones attains age 59 on January 15, 2000, and 59¹/₂ on July 15, 2000. If Carol receives a distribution of $10,000 from her IRA on July 14, 2000, is she subject to a 10-percent early-distribution penalty?

ANSWER: Yes, assuming she does not qualify for one of the penalty exceptions discussed in this chapter. She is subject to a 10-percent early-distribution penalty of $1,000, equal to 10 percent of the $10,000 distribution, because she received a distribution prior to attaining age 59¹/₂. If Carol is in the 28-percent tax bracket she will pay $2,800 in income tax (28 percent of $10,000) plus $1,000 for the early-distribution penalty. Distributions received on or after July 15, 2000, would not be subject to the early-distribution penalty because Carol will then be at least 59¹/₂ years old.

QUESTION 1.8: James is a participant in a 401(k) plan. He is age 52 and receives an in-service hardship distribution from his 401(k) plan in the amount of $30,000 in order to purchase a principal residence. Is James subject to an early-distribution penalty?

ANSWER: Yes. The 10-percent early-distribution penalty is applicable to this hardship distribution. The penalty is $3,000, equal to 10 percent of the $30,000 distribution.

QUESTION 1.9: What are the exceptions to the 10-percent early-distribution penalty?

ANSWER: The 10-percent early-distribution penalty does not apply to distributions that are

1. used to pay medical expenses exceeding 7.5 percent of adjusted gross income, or in the case of an IRA, used to pay medical insurance premiums after becoming unemployed;

2. rolled over or directly transferred to another qualifying retirement plan;

3. received from a former employer after separating from service after age 55;

4. received after becoming permanently disabled;

5. part of a qualifying series of substantially equal payments;

6. made on account of an IRS levy if the distribution is made after December 31, 1999;

7. received from an IRA and used to pay qualifying higher-education expenses or first-time homebuyer expenses.

These exceptions are discussed in the following sections.

PENALTY EXCEPTION FOR MEDICAL EXPENSE PAYMENTS

Part or all of a distribution received from a qualified employer plan or from an IRA may avoid the 10-percent early-distribution penalty if substantial medical expenses are incurred. A person receiving unemployment benefits may be able to avoid the penalty to the extent that medical insurance is paid for.

QUESTION 1.10: Karen Lane withdraws $3,000 from her IRA in 1999 and has $5,000 of unreimbursed medical expenses in the

same year. She is age 50 at the time of the distribution. Is the IRA distribution subject to a 10-percent penalty?

ANSWER: Whether the penalty applies depends on the amount of Karen's adjusted gross income. The penalty does not apply to the extent that her qualified medical expenses exceed 7.5 percent of her 1999 adjusted gross income. This excess equals the amount of medical expenses that Karen could claim as itemized deductions on her 1999 return. If her adjusted gross income is $30,000, she could claim medical expenses of $2,750 as itemized deductions, the excess of $5,000 over $2,250 (7.5 percent of $30,000). Whether Karen in fact itemizes deductions on her return or instead claims the standard deduction, $2,750 of the $3,000 distribution is exempt from the 10-percent penalty. The 10-percent penalty would apply only to the $250 balance ($3,000-$2,750), Thus, she would owe a $25 penalty. The penalty is in addition to regular federal income tax on the entire $3,000 distribution.

If Karen's adjusted gross income were $50,000, her deductible medical costs would be only $1,250 ($5,000-$3,750; equal to 7.5 percent of $50,000). In that case, the 10-percent penalty would not apply to $1,250 of her distribution. The remaining $1,750 ($3,000-$1,250) would be subject to the 10-percent penalty.

QUESTION 1.11: Sam Thomas at age 53 receives a $3,000 hardship distribution from his 401(k) plan in 1999 to pay medical expenses. Does the penalty exception discussed in Question 1.10 apply to his distribution?

ANSWER: Yes. The penalty exception applies to this hardship distribution to the extent that Sam had medical expenses in excess of 7.5 percent of his adjusted gross income, following the same computation as in the answer to Question 1.10.

The exception for medical expenses exceeding 7.5 percent of adjusted gross income also applies to other qualified retirement plans, such as profit-sharing plans and 403(b) tax-sheltered annuity plans, that are mentioned in the answer to Question 1.6 as being subject to the 10-percent penalty.

QUESTION 1.12: My 40-year-old son-in-law recently lost his job and is receiving unemployment benefits from the state. He has to pay medical insurance premiums and is considering making a withdrawal from his IRA to cover the cost. Would the withdrawal be exempt from the early-distribution penalty?

ANSWER: A penalty exception applies to the extent that your son-in-law pays medical insurance in the year of the distribution for himself, his spouse, and his dependents, and the following conditions are met:

1. The IRA distribution is made after unemployment compensation has been received for 12 consecutive weeks under any state or federal law;

2. The IRA distribution is in the year of the unemployment compensation or in the following year, but no later than 60 days after new employment.

   Self-employed individuals: This medical insurance exception for the unemployed also applies to self-employed individuals who would have received unemployment compensation but for the fact that the individual is self-employed.

Rollovers and Direct Transfers Not Subject to Pre-59^1/$_2$ Penalty

A qualifying rollover of a distribution from an employer plan to another employer plan, or to an IRA, avoids tax on the distribution and also the 10-percent penalty for early distributions. Rollovers from one IRA to another are also tax-free and penalty-free. A direct transfer from one IRA to another IRA is also tax-free and not subject to the 10-percent early-distribution penalty.

QUESTION 1.13: Carol Jones receives an IRA distribution of $5,000 on February 1, 1999, when she is age 58. She rolls over $5,000 into another IRA on March 15, 1999. Is Carol subject to a 10-percent early-distribution penalty?

ANSWER: No. The 10-percent early-distribution penalty is not applicable if Carol rolls over the $5,000 IRA distribution into another IRA within 60 days from the date of receipt of the distribution. The 10-percent early-distribution penalty is based upon the amount reported as taxable income on the recipient's income tax return. If the IRA distribution is timely rolled over, then it is not subject to federal income tax and therefore will not be subject to the 10-percent early-distribution penalty.

QUESTION 1.14: If Carol had timely rolled over to another IRA only $2,500 of the $5,000 IRA distribution in Question 1.13, what would the tax and penalty be?

ANSWER: Because $2,500 was not timely rolled over, $2,500 would be taxable to Carol. She would also pay a penalty of $250, equal to 10 percent of the $2,500 taxable distribution.

QUESTION 1.15: How often can you roll over distributions received from one IRA to another IRA?

ANSWER: According to the IRS you can receive a distribution from one IRA and roll over all or part of it into another IRA only once in any one-year period.

QUESTION 1.16: If you are under age 59¹/₂ and have more than one IRA, can you receive and roll over a distribution from each IRA during a given one-year period without being subject to the 10-percent early-distribution penalty?

ANSWER: The law is not clear on the subject. However, the IRS in Publication 590 and in Letter Ruling 8731041, dated May 6, 1987, has taken a liberal position and states that the one-year rule applies separately to each IRA that is maintained by an individual.

IRS Publication 590 provides as follows:

You can take (receive) a distribution from an IRA and make a rollover contribution (of all or part of the amount received) to another IRA only once in any one-year period. The one-year period begins on the date you receive the IRA distribution, not on the date you roll it over into another IRA.

This rule applies separately to each IRA you own. For example, if you have two IRAs, IRA No. 1 and IRA No. 2, and you roll over assets of IRA No. 1 into a new IRA No. 3, you may also make a rollover from IRA No. 2 into IRA No. 3, or into any other IRA, within one year after the rollover distribution from IRA No. 1. These are both rollovers because you have not received more than one distribution from either IRA within one year. However, you cannot, within the one-year period, again roll over the assets you rolled over into IRA No. 3 into any other IRA.

If any amount distributed from an IRA was rolled over tax-free, later distributions from that IRA within a one-year period will not qualify as rollovers. They are taxable and may be subject to the 10-percent tax on premature distributions.

QUESTION 1.17: If you receive a distribution from an IRA, may you roll it back into the same IRA within the 60-day period instead of into a new IRA?

ANSWER: Yes. The IRS issued Letter Ruling 9010007, dated December 14, 1989, which stated the following:

IRA distributions are tax-free in the year of distribution if the rollover rules are met. As long as the IRA distribution is redeposited into the same or another qualifying IRA within 60 days of receipt of the distribution, such distribution would constitute a qualified rollover.

The letter ruling also stated the following:

The individual may make such a rollover of a distribution only once a year.

QUESTION 1.18: Instead of receiving a distribution from my IRA and making a rollover within 60 days, can't I switch IRA investments by asking one IRA trustee to make a direct transfer to another IRA trustee?

ANSWER: Yes. By authorizing a direct transfer of your IRA, you can make a tax-free transfer without having to handle the funds yourself. A direct transfer also has this advantage: You are not subject to the once-a-year limitation on rollovers (Questions 1.15 and 1.16).

If you are under age 59^1/$_2$, the 10-percent early-distribution penalty does not apply to a direct transfer because there is no taxable distribution.

CASE STUDY
Questions 1.19–1.21 illustrate options for handling a lump-sum distribution upon separation from service.

QUESTION 1.19: Arthur Anders leaves his job with XYZ Corporation in 2000 at age 52 and joins another company. He is entitled to a $100,000 lump-sum distribution from his 401(k) plan account at XYZ Corporation. Can Arthur avoid the 10-percent early-distribution penalty on the lump sum by making a rollover?

ANSWER: Yes, a direct rollover can avoid both tax and penalty. To avoid 20-percent withholding, Arthur should instruct the XYZ Corp. plan administrator to make a "direct rollover" to an IRA that he designates, or to the plan of his new employer.

If the distribution is paid to Arthur, 20 percent will be withheld. Arthur could then make a rollover within 60 days to an IRA or another employer plan, but an amount equal to the withheld portion must be included in the rollover for the distribution to be completely tax-free. If Arthur rolled over less than the total distribution before withholding, the portion not rolled over will be taxable, and also be subject to the 10-percent penalty.

QUESTION 1.20: How would Arthur report the lump-sum distribution in Question 1.19 if he instructs the plan administrator to make a direct rollover to an IRA?

ANSWER: A direct rollover of the $100,000 lump sum to an IRA or another employer plan will be reported to Arthur and the IRS on Form 1099-R, although the transfer is not taxable. On Form 1099-R, $100,000 will be shown as the gross distribution, and distribution code G will be used. There would not be any withholding. On his tax return, Arthur would report $100,000 on the line for total pensions and annuities and then enter zero on the line for the taxable amount.

QUESTION 1.21: How would Arthur report the distribution in Question 1.19 if he received the distribution, was subject to 20-percent withholding, and then completed a rollover himself within the 60-day rollover period?

ANSWER: If Arthur received the distribution himself, 20-percent withholding will apply. The plan will pay him $80,000 and withhold a tax of $20,000. If Arthur rolls over $100,000 to an IRA within 60 days, the entire rollover is tax free. On his tax return, he would then report $100,000 on the line for total pensions and annuities and zero as the taxable amount. However, if Arthur rolled over less than $100,000 within the 60-day period, the amount not rolled over would be reported on his tax return as the taxable amount. The $20,000 of withheld taxes is entered as a tax payment on the line of his return for federal income tax withholdings.

Note on withholding: The 20-percent withholding rule does not apply to IRAs. It applies to distributions from qualified employer plans and 403(b) arrangements that are eligible for rollover. IRA distributions payable on demand are subject to withholding at a flat 10-percent rate, but you can elect to completely avoid withholding on Form W-4P.

DISTRIBUTION TO EMPLOYEE UPON SEPARATION FROM SERVICE AFTER AGE 55 EXEMPT FROM THE PENALTY

For employees who retire or leave their job after reaching age 55 but before age 59¹/₂, a special exception to the 10-percent early-distribution penalty applies to distributions from the employer's plan, as discussed in the next series of questions.

QUESTION 1.22: What does "separation from service" mean?

ANSWER: The term *separation from service* includes all reasons for ending the employment relationship. For example, you have separated from service if you have retired, have left a company for another job, are disabled, or were fired.

QUESTION 1.23: Ralph Peters is age 55 in 2000. He is a participant in the XYZ Corporation Profit-Sharing Plan. Pursuant to the provisions of the plan, Ralph receives a within-service distribution of $10,000 in 2000 from the profit-sharing plan. Ralph has not separated from service with the employer. Ralph does not roll over the distribution into an IRA. Is Ralph subject to the 10-percent early-distribution penalty on this $10,000 distribution?

ANSWER: Yes. The 10-percent early-distribution penalty applies because Ralph did not separate from service with the employer. The penalty of $1,000 (10 percent of $10,000) is in addition to the regular income tax on the $10,000 distribution.

QUESTION 1.24: If Ralph had retired, would he have avoided the early-distribution penalty?

ANSWER: If Ralph retired after attaining age 55 and then received the distribution of $10,000, the 10-percent early-distribution penalty would not apply.

QUESTION 1.25: Will the XYZ Corporation Profit-Sharing Plan withhold taxes from Ralph's distribution?

ANSWER: Yes. Under the law, the plan administrator or plan trustee must withhold $2,000, 20 percent of the plan distribution of $10,000.

The withholding requirement applies whether or not Ralph is separated from service.

QUESTION 1.26: How can Ralph avoid the 20-percent withholding of $2,000 described in your answer to Question 1.25?

ANSWER: Ralph may request the plan trustee to make the $10,000 check payable to Ralph's IRA. This is called a *direct rollover*. On a direct rollover, the 20-percent withholding requirement is eliminated.

QUESTION 1.27: If Ralph separates from service at age 55 and arranges a direct rollover to an IRA as suggested in Question 1.26, can he withdraw the $10,000 check from the IRA without being subject to the 10-percent early-distribution penalty?

ANSWER: Not before age 59^1/$_2$. The age 55 separation-from-service exception is not applicable to distributions from an IRA. Once the funds are received in Ralph's IRA, a distribution from that IRA is subject to the IRA distribution rules. Unfortunately, distributions from an IRA after age 55 and prior to age 59^1/$_2$ are subject to the 10-percent early-distribution penalty, unless an exception applies, although a distribution from the employer's plan after age 55 would qualify for the separation-from-service exception.

QUESTION 1.28: What should Ralph do if he needs the distribution from the profit-sharing plan in 2000 and does not wish to pay the 10-percent early-distribution penalty?

ANSWER: Ralph must request a $10,000 distribution (see Question 1.24) which will be subject to the 20-percent withholding tax of $2,000. He will avoid the 10-percent early-distribution penalty because he is age 55 and has separated from service with his employer. Ralph will receive a net check of $8,000 from the plan, but he will report $10,000 on his income tax return for the calendar year 2000 as a plan distribution and receive a federal withholding tax credit of $2,000.

QUESTION 1.29: Jack Marshall works for ABC University and is a participant in a 403(b) annuity contract. If he separates from service at age 56, may he receive distributions from the annuity contract without being subject to the 10-percent early-distribution penalty?

ANSWER: Yes. A 403(b) annuity contract is a qualified retirement plan subject to the 10-percent penalty rules and the penalty exceptions. If Jack separates from service after reaching age 55, then the distributions from the annuity contract are not subject to the 10-percent early-distribution penalty.

QUESTION 1.30: Melanie Miller, at age 56, separates from service with her employer in 2000. Can she tap her IRA in 2000 without being subject to the 10-percent early-distribution penalty?

ANSWER: No. The separation-from-service rule does not apply to distributions that are made to Melanie from her IRA. The fact that she separated from service with her employer has no bearing on the tax treatment of distributions from her IRA. Distributions received by Melanie from her employer plan would not be subject to the 10-percent penalty based on the age 55 separation-from-service exception.

QUESTION 1.31: How would Melanie be taxed if she received a $16,000 net distribution (after $4,000 of federal withholding)

from her employer's plan after separating from service and in the same year she withdrew $15,000 from her IRA?

ANSWER: Assuming Melanie does not roll over any part of the $16,000 net distribution, she would have to report as income on her federal tax return a taxable distribution of $20,000, the amount of the lump sum prior to withholding. Melanie received the net check of $16,000 after the distribution of $20,000 was reduced by a 20-percent federal withholding of $4,000. The $20,000 distribution from the qualified plan is not subject to the 10-percent early-distribution penalty under the separation-from-service exception.

The $15,000 distribution from the IRA is taxable and also is subject to a 10-percent early-distribution penalty of $1,500 because the separation-from-service exception does not apply to IRA distributions.

THE DISABILITY EXCEPTION TO THE PENALTY

The disability exception applies to distributions from IRAs as well as from qualified employer retirement plans.

QUESTION 1.32: James Allen maintains an IRA that has an account balance of $50,000. He becomes permanently disabled in 1999, at age 54. James needs funds and would like to take $10,000 from his IRA in 2000. May he receive $10,000 from his IRA in 2000 and not be subject to the 10-percent early-distribution penalty?

ANSWER: Yes. One of the exceptions to the 10-percent early-distribution penalty is for a distribution that is made as a result of being permanently disabled within the meaning of the Internal Revenue Code. The distributions are, however, subject to regular income tax.

QUESTION 1.33: What is the definition of disabled under the law?

ANSWER: Under the Internal Revenue Code an individual is considered disabled

> *... if he or she is unable to engage in any substantial gainful activity by reason of any medically determinable physical or mental impairment which can be expected to result in death or to be of long-continued and indefinite duration. An individual shall not be considered to be disabled unless he furnishes proof of the existence thereof in such form and manner as the Secretary may require.*

QUESTION 1.34: Assume that Martin Jones is receiving Social Security disability benefits. Can Martin withdraw distributions from his IRA at age 54 without being subject to the 10-percent early-distribution penalty?

ANSWER: Maybe, if he meets the Internal Revenue Code definition of disability. According to the IRS and the United States Tax Court, Martin must provide medical evidence that his physical condition precludes him from engaging in substantial gainful activity and can be expected to result in death or to be of long-continued or indefinite duration. This definition is not the same as the requirement for receiving Social Security disability benefits.

QUESTION 1.35: Fran Davis is age 52 and employed by the ABC Corporation. The ABC Corporation maintains a defined benefit pension plan. Fran becomes permanently disabled at age 52 and is entitled to a pension of $100 per month. Is Fran subject to the 10-percent early-distribution penalty on her pension?

ANSWER: No. A distribution to Fran before she reaches age $59^1/2$ from the ABC Corporation's defined benefit plan on the basis of her permanent disability is exempt from the 10-percent early-distribution penalty.

QUESTION 1.36: A taxpayer, age 50, is under medical treatment for a physical or mental illness. Until the treatment is completed, his ability to earn a living is diminished. Are current distributions from his IRA automatically exempt from the 10-percent early-distribution penalty?

ANSWER: No. According to the United States Tax Court and the IRS regulations, the impairment must be expected to last for an indefinite period and must be irremediable. An impairment that is remediable is not a disability under the tax law. According to the IRS regulations, an individual is not considered disabled if with reasonable effort the impairment can be diminished to the extent that the individual may engage in his customary or any comparable substantial gainful activity.

QUESTION 1.37: Al Bryant is age 54 and permanently disabled. His IRA in 1999 amounts to $50,000. He would like to withdraw distributions from his IRA from time to time over the next few years as he needs funds. May he withdraw funds from his IRA at random without being subject to the 10-percent early-distribution penalty?

ANSWER: Yes. According to the IRS in Letter Ruling 9318043 dated February 11, 1993, a disabled taxpayer may withdraw funds from the IRA in unequal, nonperiodic payments and will not be subject to the 10-percent early-distribution penalty.

THE SUBSTANTIALLY EQUAL PAYMENT EXCEPTION TO THE 10-PERCENT EARLY-DISTRIBUTION PENALTY

After separation from service, distributions taken from an employer plan as part of a series of substantially equal payments are not subject to an early-distribution penalty, regardless of your age. Similarly, there is no penalty on IRA withdrawals that qualify under the substantially equal payment test.

QUESTION 1.38: How does an employee satisfy the substantially equal payment test?

ANSWER: The law requires that distributions to a former employee who has separated from service be "part of a series of substantially equal periodic payments (not less frequently than annually) made for the life (or life expectancy) of the employee or the joint lives (or joint life expectancies) of such employee and his or her designated beneficiary." The age of the employee does not matter.

QUESTION 1.39: Has the IRS established any ground rules on how the substantially equal payment test applies?

ANSWER: Yes. The IRS issued Notice 89-25, dated March 20, 1989, on how to apply the substantially equal payment test. The IRS permits the substantially equal payment rule to be satisfied under one of the following three methods:

Method 1—Uses a life-expectancy approach. This method divides the account balance by the applicable life expectancy, which is found in IRS tables (see Question 1.45). This is the same life-expectancy approach used under the IRS's minimum required distribution rules for those over age $70^{1}/_2$, discussed in Chapter 2.

Method 2—Uses an amortization approach. This method computes equal payments using the same life expectancy as under Method 1 and a reasonable rate of interest.

Method 3—Uses an annuity approach. This method computes payments using the annuity factor from the UP 1984 mortality table and a reasonable rate of interest.

QUESTION 1.40: Does the substantially equal payment rule apply to distributions from an IRA?

ANSWER: Yes. IRS Publication 590 states in part as follows:

You can receive distributions from your IRA that are part of a series of substantially equal payments over your life (or your life expectancy) or over the lives of you and your beneficiary (or your joint life expectancies) without having to pay the 10-percent additional tax, even if you receive such distributions before you are age 59 1/2. You must use an IRS approved distribution method and you must take at least one distribution annually for this exception to apply.

QUESTION 1.41: If you wish to tap your IRA before age 59¹/₂ under the substantially equal payment rule, must you separate from service with your employer?

ANSWER: No. The law does not require that you, as an IRA owner, separate from service with your employer in order to use the substantially equal payment rule.

QUESTION 1.42: Which of the three methods should an IRA owner under age 59¹/₂ use in order to satisfy the substantially equal payment rule?

ANSWER: The amortization method (Method 2) is probably the easiest to work with. It is similar to the fixed payments that one makes on his or her home mortgage. The factors that go into the computation of the annual payments are principal, interest rate, and period of time.

AMORTIZATION METHOD: QUESTIONS 1.43–1.51

QUESTION 1.43: Can you illustrate how the amortization method works?

ANSWER: The IRS in Notice 89-25, dated March 20, 1989, illustrates the amortization method and states the following:

> *Payments will be treated as substantially equal periodic payments if the amount to be distributed annually is determined by amortizing the taxpayer's account balance over a number of years equal to the life expectancy of the account owner or the joint life and last survivor expectancy of the account owner and beneficiary (with life expectancies determined in accordance with proposed section 1.401(a)(9)-1 of the regulations) at an interest rate that does not exceed a reasonable interest rate on the date payment commences. For example, a 50-year-old individual with a life expectancy of 33.1, having an account balance of $100,000, and assuming an interest rate of 8 percent, could satisfy (the substantially equal payment rule) by distributing $8,679 annually, derived by amortizing $100,000 over 33.1 years at 8 percent interest.*

QUESTION 1.44: Does the IRA owner using the amortization method described above have a choice of using a single life-expectancy table or a joint life-expectancy table?

ANSWER: Yes. IRS Notice 89-25 permits the IRA owner to select which life-expectancy table to use.

QUESTION 1.45: Where are the IRS life-expectancy tables found?

ANSWER: The IRS regulations have tables that are based upon a single life expectancy or a joint life expectancy. These tables are reproduced in the Appendix. The tables are from section 1.72-9 of the IRS regulations. Table V of the regulations is used for a single life expectancy and Table VI of the regulations is used for a joint life expectancy. IRS Publication 590 refers to Table V of the regulations as Table I, and Table VI of the regulations as Table II. In the Appendix of this book are Tables I and II from Publication 590.

QUESTION 1.46: What interest rate is used under the amortization method?

ANSWER: According to the IRS, an interest rate that does not exceed a reasonable rate of interest on the date payment commenced should be used. The IRA owner could, for example, use 120 percent of the long-term applicable federal rate. Alternatively, he or she may ask a local bank what the fixed rate is for a long-term mortgage and use that rate. The IRS has been flexible in terms of rates that may be used by IRA owners.

QUESTION 1.47: How do the life-expectancy tables work?

ANSWER: According to the IRS, if a single life expectancy is used then the life expectancy of the IRA owner is based upon the IRA owner's attained age as of his or her birthday in the calendar year in which distributions commence. If a joint life expectancy is used then the life expectancy of the IRA owner and his or her beneficiary would be based upon their attained ages as of their birthdays in the calendar year in which distributions commence.

For example, if Jack Adams, an IRA owner, is age 49 on his birthday in 2000, has no beneficiary, and commences IRA distributions in 2000 under the amortization method, then he must use a 34-year single life expectancy for purposes of determining the amount of the annual payments. If you check IRS Table I in the Appendix, you will see that 34 years is the life expectancy of a 49-year-old person; the table is used by men and women.

If Jack has designated his wife, Mary, age 48 in 2000, as his beneficiary and commences distributions, then he may use a joint life expectancy of 40.7 years for purposes of determining the amount of the annual payments. The joint life expectancy of 40.7 years is shown in IRS Table II in the Appendix, in the column where ages 49 and 48 intersect.

QUESTION 1.48: Assume that Jack is eligible to use either a single life expectancy or joint life expectancy in 2000 in order to

calculate the annual payments. He uses a single life-expectancy table in 2000. May Jack switch to the joint life-expectancy table in 2001?

ANSWER: No. Under the amortization method, once the amount of the annual payments has been established, it cannot be changed. It is similar to payments on a fixed-rate mortgage, which becomes fixed for the duration of the mortgage.

QUESTION 1.49: If the amortization method is selected, may the IRA owner receive monthly or quarterly payments?

ANSWER: Yes. However, a reasonable interest rate (see Question 1.46) must be used to reflect the frequency of payments.

QUESTION 1.50: Assume that Marvin Bardiner is age 52 in 2000 and has four separate IRAs in his name. He would like to currently tap only one of his IRAs and take advantage of the substantially equal payment rule. May he receive distributions from only one IRA and satisfy the substantially equal payment rule?

ANSWER: Yes. The IRS has issued several letter rulings that indicate that each IRA stands on its own and that the law does not require that IRAs be aggregated in order to calculate a series of substantially equal payments.

QUESTION 1.51: If Marvin uses the amortization method (see Method 2 under Question 1.39) in calculating his substantially equal payments from IRA No. 1, must he use the same method if he decides to tap IRA No. 2 prior to age 59$^{1}/_{2}$?

ANSWER: No. Each IRA stands on its own. If Marvin decides to tap another of his IRAs before age 59$^{1}/_{2}$, any one of the three methods discussed in Question 1.39 can be used with respect to distributions from that IRA. The fact that Marvin tapped IRA

No. 1 prior to age 59¹/₂ does not mean he must tap any other IRA prior to age 59¹/₂.

MODIFYING A SCHEDULE OF PAYMENTS: QUESTIONS 1.52–1.54

QUESTION 1.52: Assume that Marvin, age 52, uses the amortization method and a single life expectancy of 31.3 years in calculating his annual payments from IRA No. 1. If Marvin commences distributions from IRA No. 1 at age 52 under the substantially equal payment rule, must he continue to receive payments over a 31.3-year period?

ANSWER: No. IRS Publication 590 states that the substantially equal payments must continue for at least five years or until an individual reaches age 59¹/₂, whichever is the longer period. Because Marvin commenced his substantially equal payments at age 52, he must continue to receive such payments until he attains age 59¹/₂. See Question 1.55 for calculating the five-year period.

QUESTION 1.53: What happens if Marvin in 2006 at age 58 voluntarily decides to discontinue receiving his payments from IRA No. 1?

ANSWER: As discussed in Question 1.52, payments must continue under the substantially equal payments rule for a minimum of five years or until you are age 59¹/₂, whichever is the longer period. Here, the longer period ends when Marvin attains age 59¹/₂. The act of discontinuing the payments before the end of this minimum period is deemed to be a modification of the amortization method and triggers the 10-percent early-distribution penalty. According to the law, Marvin's tax for the year 2006, the year in which the modification takes place, is increased by the amount of the 10 percent early-distribution

penalty that would have been paid on the early distributions if
the substantially equal payment rule was not applicable.

**QUESTION 1.54: How much would Marvin's penalty be under the
facts of Question 1.53?**

ANSWER: Assume that Marvin was required to receive $10,000 per
year from IRA No. 1 under the amortization method (Method 2
under Question 1.39). He would have received the following
amounts:

MARVIN'S AGE	YEAR	AMOUNT RECEIVED FROM IRA NO.1
52	2000	$10,000
53	2001	10,000
54	2002	10,000
55	2003	10,000
56	2004	10,000
57	2005	10,000
58	2006	-0-
		$60,000

Because Marvin voluntarily discontinues the receipt of annual payments from IRA No. 1 in 2006, he must pay an additional
10-percent early-distribution penalty to the IRS with his income
tax return for 2006. The penalty is $6,000, which is equal to 10

percent of all the amounts received by Martin before age 59^{1}/$_{2}$. In addition, he must pay interest on the $6,000 early-distribution penalty on a retroactive basis.

QUESTION 1.55: Assume that Marvin's brother Gregory is age 56 in 2000 when he decides to tap his IRA on a monthly basis starting on July 1, 2000. He uses the amortization method (see Method 2 under Question 1.39) until he attains age 59^{1}/$_{2}$ in 2003 and then voluntarily stops receiving distributions from his IRA. Has Gregory's voluntary act in 2003 triggered an early-distribution penalty?

ANSWER: Yes. Gregory's act of voluntarily ceasing distributions from his IRA in 2003 constitutes a modification of the amortization method. Because the modification takes place before the close of the five-year period beginning with the date of the first payment, Gregory is subject to the early-distribution penalty on all distributions he received prior to age 59^{1}/$_{2}$. The voluntary modification in this case should not have taken place prior to July 1, 2005, because the close of the five-year period is June 30, 2005.

EFFECT OF DISABILITY OR DEATH: QUESTIONS 1.56–1.61

QUESTION 1.56: If Marvin died at age 58 in the calendar year 2006, would the $6,000 early-distribution penalty described in your answer to Question 1.54 be applicable?

ANSWER: No. The law states that if the substantially equal payments are subsequently modified as a result of death, then the additional early-distribution penalty is not applicable.

QUESTION 1.57: If Marvin becomes permanently disabled at age 58 in the calendar year 2006, would the $6,000 early-distribution penalty described in your answer to Question 1.54 be applicable?

ANSWER: No. The law states that if the substantially equal payments are subsequently modified as a result of disability, then the additional tax is not applicable.

QUESTION 1.58: If Marvin became temporarily disabled at age 58 in the calendar year 2006, would the $6,000 additional tax described in your answer to Question 1.54 be applicable?

ANSWER: The law does not define the word "disability" in the context of a subsequent modification of the substantially equal payment rule, but it is obvious that a permanent type of disability would be necessary in order to avoid the $6,000 additional tax.

QUESTION 1.59: If an IRA owner age 50 dies and the death benefits from the IRA are paid to his estate, will the estate be subject to the 10-percent early-distribution penalty?

ANSWER: No. IRA death benefits payable to an estate are exempt from the 10-percent early-distribution penalty.

QUESTION 1.60: If Craig, an IRA owner age 60, dies and has the death benefits of his IRA payable to his son Joseph, age 30, will Joseph be subject to the 10-percent early-distribution penalty?

ANSWER: No. IRA death benefits that are payable to a designated beneficiary are exempt from the 10-percent early-distribution penalty. The age of the beneficiary is not important. The law states that the 10-percent early-distribution penalty is not applicable to death benefits that are paid to a beneficiary.

QUESTION 1.61: Assume that in Question 1.60, Craig died at age 58. Will his son, Joseph, be subject to the 10-percent early-distribution penalty?

ANSWER: No. The fact that the IRA owner was under age $59^1/2$ at the time of his death does not change the rule that the beneficiary is not subject to the 10-percent early-distribution penalty.

CASE STUDY
Questions 1.62–1.63 illustrate the substantially equal payment penalty exception for employees.

QUESTION 1.62: Carter is a participant in the XYZ Inc. section 401(k) plan. On January 20, 2000, he terminates his employment with his employer at age 53. He elects a method of distribution from the section 401(k) plan that is in the form of substantially equal payments. His first distribution starts in the calendar year 2000. Is the distribution from the section 401(k) plan that is made to Carter in the calendar year 2000 subject to the 10-percent early-distribution penalty?

ANSWER: No. The substantially equal payment exception applies to distributions from qualified plans as well as IRAs.

QUESTION 1.63: Assume the facts in question 1.62, except that Carter receives a lump sum distribution (subject to the 20-percent withholding requirements) during the calendar year 2000. Is the lump sum distribution to Carter from the section 401(k) plan in the calendar year 2000 subject to the 10-percent early-distribution penalty?

ANSWER: Yes. Carter would be exempt from the 10-percent early-distribution penalty if he was age 55 or older in the year he separated from service with the employer; see Question 1.22. Because he is age 53 in the calendar year 2000, he does not qualify for this penalty exception. Obviously, a lump-sum distribution does not qualify under the substantially equal payments exception.

PENALTY EXCEPTION FOR HIGHER-EDUCATION EXPENSES

QUESTION 1.64: Is an IRA owner subject to the 10-percent early-distribution penalty if funds are withdrawn to pay for a child's college expenses?

ANSWER: The penalty does not apply to the extent that you have qualifying higher-education expenses in the year you receive an IRA distribution.

QUESTION 1.65: What are qualified higher-education expenses for purposes of the exception from the 10-percent early-distribution penalty for IRA distributions?

ANSWER: Qualified higher-education expenses means tuition, fees, books, supplies and equipment required for enrollment or attendance and room and board at a post-secondary educational institution. Amounts withdrawn from the IRA are not subject to the 10-percent penalty to the extent that in the year of distribution, the taxpayer pays qualified higher-education expenses of the taxpayer, the taxpayer's spouse, or any child or grandchild of the taxpayer or taxpayer's spouse.

QUESTION 1.66: Does the 10-percent early-distribution penalty apply to an employee's hardship withdrawal from a 401(k) plan that is used to pay higher-education costs?

ANSWER: Yes. The penalty exception for qualified higher expenses applies only to IRAs, not to distributions from employer plans.

PENALTY EXCEPTION FOR FIRST-TIME HOMEBUYER EXPENSES

QUESTION 1.67: Is there a penalty exception for distributions used to buy a house?

ANSWER: There is a penalty exception for IRA distributions used for qualifying first-time homebuyer expenses. The exception does not apply to employer plan distributions.

QUESTION 1.68: What are first-time homebuyer expenses for purposes of the exception from the 10-percent early-distribution penalty for IRA distributions?

ANSWER: Qualified first-time homebuyer distributions are withdrawals of up to $10,000 during the individual's lifetime that are used within 120 days of the distribution to pay costs (including reasonable settlement, financing, or other closing costs) of acquisition, constructing, or reconstructing the principal residence of a first-time homebuyer who is the individual, the individual's spouse, or a child, grandchild, or ancestor of the individual or individual's spouse. If more than $10,000 of a distribution is used to pay first-time homebuyer expenses, the penalty applies to the excess over $10,000. Once the limit is exceeded, you may not claim the penalty exception for any other home purchase.

QUESTION 1.69: Who is considered to be a first-time homebuyer?

ANSWER: A first-time homebuyer is an individual who has not had an ownership interest in a principal residence during the two-year period ending on the date of acquisition of the principal residence to which the withdrawal relates. The homebuyer's spouse also must meet this two-year test as of the date the contract is entered into or construction commences.

QUESTION 1.70: What is the date of acquisition for purposes of the two-year rule described in question 1.68?

ANSWER: The date of acquisition is the date the individual enters into a binding contract to purchase a principal residence or begins construction or reconstruction of such a residence.

QUESTION 1.71: What happens if there is a delay or cancellation of the purchase or construction of the residence?

ANSWER: If the 120-day rule cannot be satisfied due to a delay or cancellation of the purchase or construction of the residence, all or part of the amount of the IRA distribution may be recontributed to an IRA prior to the end of the 120-period without adverse tax consequences.

Penalty Exception for IRS Levy Added by 1998 IRS Restructuring Act

QUESTION 1.72: Did the IRS Restructuring and Reform Act of 1998 (1998 Act) add an additional exception to the 10-percent early-distribution penalty?

ANSWER: Yes. An additional exception applies to distributions from any employer sponsored plan or an IRA that is made on account of an IRS levy. It applies to distributions made after December 31, 1999.

CHAPTER TWO

WHEN MUST YOU BEGIN MINIMUM DISTRIBUTIONS FROM YOUR RETIREMENT PLAN?

The longer you can keep funds in your IRA or employer plan without withdrawing them, the more money you can accumulate tax-free for your retirement years and, ultimately, for your heirs. However, the tax law does not allow you to indefinitely delay the start of distribution.

When you reach age 70¹/₂, you must begin to receive minimum annual distributions from your traditional IRAs. The IRS has established a series of complex rules for determining the minimum amount you must receive each year. Penalties can be imposed by the IRS if the rules are not followed.

These minimum distribution requirements apply to owners of traditional IRAs and to the designated beneficiaries of a Roth IRA after the Roth IRA owner's death. You do not have to take distributions from your Roth IRA at any time; see Chapter Ten for Roth IRA rules.

Before 1997, the age 70¹/₂ beginning date rules also applied to qualified employer plans. However, under current law, the required beginning date for employees (except 5-percent owners) who continue to work beyond age 70¹/₂ is April 1 of the calendar year following the calendar year in which the employee retires. So as not to hurt employees who were near age 70¹/₂ when the law was changed, the IRS has taken the position that the new rule may not be applied unilaterally by an employer unless the employee attains age 70¹/₂ after December 31, 1998, and the employer makes certain amendments to the employer sponsored plan; see the answer to Question 2.3.

In general, the minimum amount that you must withdraw each year is based upon your life expectancy or the life expectancy of you and your beneficiary. Your choice of beneficiary and distribution method will affect not only your required minimum distribution, but also the amounts that your beneficiaries will have to receive—and pay tax on—after your death. This chapter will introduce you to the minimum distribution requirements. Subsequent chapters will highlight the specific rules that apply when your designated beneficiary is your spouse (Chapter 3); a child, grandchild, or other beneficiary who is more than 10 years younger than you (Chapter 4); or other adult beneficiary (Chapter 6).

Minimum Distribution Basics

The following series of questions and answers provides an introduction to the required minimum distribution rules.

QUESTION 2.1: What type of retirement accounts are subject to the required minimum distribution rules?

ANSWER: Distributions from qualified plans such as 401(k) plans or profit-sharing plans, simplified employee pension plans, qualified annuity plans, traditional individual retirement accounts (but *not* Roth IRAs during your lifetime), individual retirement annuities, 403(b) tax-sheltered annuity contracts, and certain deferred compensation plans of state and local governments and tax exempt organizations are subject to the required minimum distribution rules. The rules also apply to Keogh accounts or simplified employee pension plans maintained by self-employed individuals.

QUESTION 2.2: Why are the required minimum distribution rules so important?

ANSWER: The required minimum distribution rules are important because you can be subject to a tax penalty if you fail to receive the required minimum annual distributions. Understanding the IRS distribution rules will help you avoid these penalties. In addition, understanding these rules can be an important element of your income-tax and estate-tax planning. For example, you may want to preserve your retirement plan assets as much as possible for your beneficiaries by minimizing the required minimum distributions you must receive and extending the period over which the assets may continue to grow tax-free within the retirement plan. You may accomplish these goals by becoming familiar with the required minimum distribution rules discussed in this book and applying them to your particular situation, with the help of your professional advisor where appropriate.

QUESTION 2.3: What is the required beginning date for minimum distributions from an IRA?

ANSWER: The required beginning date for traditional IRA distributions is April 1 of the calendar year following the calendar year in which you reach age $70^{1}/2$.

The required minimum distribution rules do not apply to your Roth IRAs during your lifetime.

QUESTION 2.4: What is the required beginning date for minimum distributions from a qualified employer plan?

ANSWER: Before 1997, the IRA required beginning date discussed in the answer to Question 2.3 also generally applied to employees, even if they were still working. However, after December 31, 1996, a new rule applies to employees, other than 5-percent owners, who continue to work beyond the year in which they reach age 70^1/2. For employees other than 5-percent owners, the required beginning date is April 1 of the calendar year following the *later* of (1) the calendar year in which the employee attains age 70^1/2, or (2) the calendar year in which the employee retires.

For example, assume that employee John Jones (not a 5-percent owner) attains age 70^1/2 during 2000 and continues to work for the employer until he retires in 2002. His required beginning date will be April 1, 2003. To protect older employees who were relying on an age 70^1/2 distribution option when the law was changed, the IRS by regulation prohibited employers from unilaterally changing an age 70^1/2 option if the employee reached age 70^1/2 before 1999. In other words, such employees may have anticipated being able to begin withdrawing funds from the plan starting April 1 of the calendar year following the calendar year in which they reached age 70^1/2. The IRS allows an age 70^1/2 distribution option to be taken away from such employees only with the consent of the employee and if married, the consent of the employee's spouse.

However, the IRS regulations allow employers to unilaterally amend a plan document to eliminate an age 70^1/2 distribution option for employees (other than 5-percent owners) who reached age 70^1/2 in 1999 or a later year; proper notice of the amendment must be provided by the employer to the employees. With such an amendment, the employer may prohibit in-service distributions to employees (other than 5-percent owners) who continue working past age 70^1/2. The required beginning date for such employees would be April 1 of the calendar year following the calendar year in which the employee retires.

Employees who participate in a 403(b) tax-sheltered annuity plan of a public school system or tax-exempt organization may be subject to a special rule if they have a pre-1987 account balance. The IRS stated in Letter Ruling 9345044, dated August 16, 1993, if the issuer or custodian of a section 403(b) contract maintains records that enable it to identify the value of the account balance under the section 403(b) account as of December 31, 1986, then distributions of that pre-1987 balance do not have to begin until the employee or retired employee attains age 75.

QUESTION 2.5: When is an employee considered to be a 5-percent owner of a business and what is the required beginning date for such owners?

ANSWER: An employee is considered to be a 5-percent owner if at any time on or after age 66$^{1}/_{2}$, the employee directly or indirectly owns more than 5 percent of the stock of the corporation, or if the employer is not a corporation, the plan participant directly or indirectly owns more than 5 percent of the capital or profits interest in the employer.

For such 5-percent owners, the required beginning date for distributions from the employee's plan is April 1 of the calendar year following the year in which age 70$^{1}/_{2}$ is attained. Also see questions 2.46–2.50.

DISTRIBUTIONS BEFORE REQUIRED BEGINNING DATE: QUESTIONS 2.6–2.10

QUESTION 2.6: On June 1, 2000, Martin Mitchell will attain age 64. He has an IRA that has in excess of $250,000 and would like to withdraw approximately $10,000 from it in each of the next three years. May Martin do so without being subject to any IRS penalties?

ANSWER: Yes. All he should be concerned about is paying the income taxes on the distributions from his IRA. Because he has attained age 59$^{1}/_{2}$, he is not subject to the 10-percent early-distribution penalty described in the previous chapter. Because he has not yet attained age 70$^{1}/_{2}$, the amounts he withdraws are not subject to the required minimum distribution rules.

QUESTION 2.7: Once Martin takes the $10,000 distribution from his IRA at age 64, must he continue to do so for each year after reaching age 64?

ANSWER: No. Because Martin has not attained his required beginning date, he is free to take distributions from his IRA at age 64 or in later years before the required beginning date without regard to the minimum distribution rules. Until he reaches his required beginning date, he does not have to take any further distributions if he does not want to.

QUESTION 2.8: When does Martin reach his required beginning date?

ANSWER: Based upon existing law, Martin's required beginning date is April 1 following the calendar year in which he attains age $70^{1}/_{2}$. Assume Martin is age 64 on June 1, 2000. He is therefore age 70 on June 1, 2006, and age $70^{1}/_{2}$ on December 1, 2006. Martin's required beginning date is April 1, 2007.

QUESTION 2.9: If Martin dies prior to his required beginning date of April 1, 2007, what distribution rules are applicable to his IRA beneficiary?

ANSWER: Specific death benefit distribution rules are applicable. Those rules depend upon who the beneficiary is and whether or not the five-year rule or the life-expectancy exception to the five-year rule applies. It also depends on whether or not a surviving spouse is involved, because a surviving spouse is eligible to create a spousal rollover IRA. If Martin's beneficiary were his wife, she would have the options discussed in Chapter 3. If Martin's beneficiary were his child, grandchild, or other beneficiary, either the life-expectancy or the five-year method would be used by the beneficiary, as described in Chapter 8.

QUESTION 2.10: If Martin is alive on his required beginning date of April 1, 2007, how will he determine the amount that he must receive as a required minimum distribution from his IRA?

ANSWER: The following information is necessary in order to determine the amount that Martin must receive as a required minimum distribution from his IRA:

a. The distribution calendar year that is involved in the computation;

b. The IRA balance as of the valuation date;

c. His age;

d. His designated beneficiary's age;

e. Whether the designated beneficiary was timely selected;

f. Whether the recalculation method is applicable;

g. Whether the term-certain method is applicable;

h. Whether the hybrid method is applicable;

i. Whether the Minimum Distribution Incidental Benefit Requirement (MDIB Requirement) is applicable.

The terms used in (a)–(i) are explained throughout this book.

CASE STUDY
Questions 2.11–2.15 illustrate when Martin must begin to receive required minimum distributions from his IRA.

QUESTION 2.11: What is Martin's first distribution calendar year?

ANSWER: The first calendar year for which a distribution is required is called the first distribution calendar year. Martin's required beginning date is April 1, 2007, but his first distribution calendar year is 2006. The year 2006 is the calendar year in which Martin attains age 70¹/₂.

QUESTION 2.12: Must Martin receive his required minimum distribution for the calendar year 2006 in 2006?

ANSWER: No. Martin may receive his required minimum distribution for the calendar year 2006 by no later than April 1, 2007, the required beginning date. The IRS rules permit a distribution for the individual's first distribution calendar year to be made by no later than his required beginning date.

QUESTION 2.13: May Martin receive his required minimum distribution for the first distribution calendar year 2006 in 2006?

ANSWER: Yes. Martin may receive his required minimum distribution for the first distribution calendar year 2006 in 2006.

QUESTION 2.14: May Martin receive his required minimum distribution for the first distribution calendar year 2006 partially in 2006 and partially in 2007?

ANSWER: Yes. He can allocate his required minimum distribution for his first distribution calendar year 2006 in any manner he wishes provided that it is completely paid by no later than his required beginning date of April 1, 2007. Thus, Martin may receive his required minimum distribution for his first distribution calendar year 2006 between the period commencing January 1, 2006, and ending April 1, 2007. Distributions will be taxable in the year Martin receives them.

QUESTION 2.15: Must Martin receive his required minimum distribution for his second distribution calendar year 2007 in 2007?

ANSWER: Yes. The required minimum distribution for all subsequent distribution calendar years after the first distribution calendar year must be received by no later than December 31 of that distribution year. Thus, required minimum distributions for his second distribution calendar year and years thereafter must be received on or before December 31 of such distribution calendar year.

LIFE-EXPECTANCY METHODS

The following questions and answers illustrate how your choice of life-expectancy method affects the minimum distributions you must receive.

QUESTION 2.16: Assume that Martin is single. Over what period of time may Martin receive required minimum distributions from his IRA?

ANSWER: Martin may receive his required minimum distributions from his IRA over a period that does not exceed his single life expectancy, or over a period that does not exceed the joint life expectancy of Martin and his designated beneficiary.

QUESTION 2.17: How is Martin's single life expectancy determined?

ANSWER: From IRS life-expectancy tables. In the Appendix we include the single life-expectancy table found in IRS Publication 590, which the IRS refers to as Table I.

In section 1.72-9 of the Income Tax Regulations, this table is included, but it is labeled as Table V.

QUESTION 2.18: What age does Martin use when applying the IRS life-expectancy table?

ANSWER: Martin's life expectancy is based upon his attained age as of his birthday in his "first distribution calendar year" (Question 2.11)—the calendar year he attains age 70$^{1}/_{2}$.

Assume Martin will be age 70 on June 1, 2006, and age 70$^{1}/_{2}$ on December 1, 2006. In the calendar year 2006, Martin's attained age is age 70. Therefore, age 70 is Martin's attained age for purposes of looking up his life expectancy in the IRS table.

As shown in the Appendix, IRS Table I from Publication 590 provides that an individual age 70 has a 16-year single life expectancy.

QUESTION 2.19: If Martin uses a single life-expectancy table, must he receive required minimum distributions from his IRA for his life expectancy of 16 years?

ANSWER: No. The law allows Martin to accelerate the distributions from his IRA from time to time, so all withdrawals may be completed before 16 years.

QUESTION 2.20: If Martin wants to use the joint life-expectancy method instead of the single life-expectancy method, and his beneficiary is his sister Sara, who will be age 64 on her birthday in 2006, how would he determine their joint life expectancy?

ANSWER: Joint life expectancy is determined under IRS Table II from IRS Publication 590, which is shown in the Appendix. In section 1.72-9 of the Income Tax Regulations, this same table is included, but it is labeled as Table VI.

Using their attained ages of 70 and 64 in 2006, Martin's first distribution calendar year, Table II in the Appendix shows that Martin and Sara have a joint life expectancy of 23.7 years.

QUESTION 2.21: Martin has been told that there are two methods under which he may receive distributions from his IRA based

upon his single life expectancy or joint life expectancy with his sister Sara. What are the two methods that may be used in calculating his required minimum distributions from his IRA?

ANSWER: The law generally permits Martin to receive his required minimum distributions from his IRA under the term-certain method, the recalculation method, and the hybrid method. The hybrid method is a combination of the term-certain method and the recalculation method. It is a complex method that requires the use of a specialist.

Under the term-certain method, the initial single or joint life expectancy used by Martin would be reduced by one in each subsequent year. Under the recalculation method, Martin's initial life expectancy would be refigured for each year based upon his attained age in that year. The life expectancy of a spousal beneficiary may also be recalculated, but the life expectancy of a nonspouse beneficiary may not be recalculated. A nonspouse beneficiary is required to use the term-certain method.

Examples of these methods are provided in this book.

QUESTION 2.22: Is it more advantageous to use the term-certain method or the recalculation method?

ANSWER: In general terms, the recalculation method allows you to take smaller required minimum distributions. This is because life expectancy is reduced each year by less than one under the recalculation method, while under the term-certain method life expectancy is reduced by a full year.

However, where minimum distributions are based on joint life expectancy, the term-certain method, besides being easier to apply, is generally more advantageous to the beneficiary following the IRA owner's death. This is because under the term-certain method, the beneficiary may spread out distributions over the balance of the initial term-certain joint life expectancy. Under the recalculation method, the life expectancy of a recalculating owner is reduced to zero in the year following the year of the owner's death. As a result, distributions to the beneficiary must then be based solely on the beneficiary's remaining life expectancy. Similarly, if the beneficiary were the owner's spouse whose life expectancy was being recalculated, and the spouse died first, the owner's single life expectancy would have to be used to determine the required minimum distributions for years following the year of the spouse's death.

Examples comparing the two distribution methods are provided throughout this book.

ELECTING THE TERM-CERTAIN METHOD: QUESTIONS 2.23–2.28

QUESTION 2.23: Assuming the owner of an IRA would like to elect the term-certain method of distribution, is that method always available?

ANSWER: No. The IRA plan document must be consulted in order to determine whether or not the term-certain method is available. A number of financial institutions have distribution forms that permit the IRA owner to elect the term-certain method or the recalculation method. However, many financial institutions do not have election forms. If the financial institution permits the term-certain method to be elected but does not have an election form, then the IRA owner must create his or her own election form. The election must be made by no later than the IRA owner's required beginning date.

QUESTION 2.24: Do some financial institutions use words other than "term certain" that are the equivalents of the meaning of the words "term certain"?

ANSWER: Yes. Some institutions may use such terms as

a. fixed period;

b. fixed period of time;

c. nonrecalculation method;

d. once computed;

e. election out of the recalculation method;

f. election not to refigure life expectancy;

g. declining years.

QUESTION 2.25: What does the IRS say about whether or not an IRA owner may elect the term-certain method?

ANSWER: The IRS states that the IRA plan document must be examined in order to determine whether or not you may elect to use the term-certain method. The IRS does not use the words "term-certain," but uses equivalent language such as "election not to recalculate life expectancy."

QUESTION 2.26: Assume that a term-certain method is available under the terms of the IRA plan document. What does the IRS say about the mechanics of making the term-certain election?

ANSWER: Unfortunately, the IRS guidelines on how the election is to be made are general in nature. The IRS states that the election must be made by the IRA owner by no later than the IRA owner's required beginning date. In addition, according to the IRS the election is irrevocable as of the IRA owner's required beginning date.

QUESTION 2.27: Assume that the IRA owner wishes to make the term-certain election with respect to his or her IRA. What action should be taken in order to protect the IRA owner against an IRS challenge at a later date?

ANSWER: The IRA owner should make a written election with the IRA institution by no later than his or her required beginning date. The written election should be sent to the appropriate responsible person at the IRA institution by certified mail, return receipt requested. In order to avoid a technical problem, the election should be sent to the IRA institution well in advance of the required beginning date so that it is received by the IRA institution no later than the required beginning date. It may be advisable to send two copies of the written election to the IRA institution. The IRA owner should request that the IRA institution acknowledge the election by returning the second copy to the IRA owner. A copy of both the forwarding letter and the written election, together with the acknowledged copy of the election, should be retained in a permanent file. The written election should indicate the following:

1. The name of the IRA owner;

2. The name of the IRA financial institution;

3. The account number of the IRA;

4. An indication that the term-certain method is being elected in calculating his or her required minimum distributions;

5. A statement by the IRA owner that his or her life expectancy shall not be recalculated and that the spouse's life expectancy shall not be recalculated if the spouse is the designated beneficiary;

6. A statement that the term-certain method shall be irrevocable and binding for the first distribution calendar year and all subsequent years;

7. The signature of the IRA owner and the date he or she signed the election.

QUESTION 2.28: Assume that the IRA institution plan document permits the term-certain election. Further assume that the financial institution has its own election form that contains some basic information such as the name of the IRA owner, the name of the IRA financial institution, and the account number of the IRA. The form further states that the IRA owner may check either a box that states that the term-certain method is

applicable or another box that states that the recalculation method is applicable. The form must be signed and dated by the IRA owner. Assume that the IRA owner fills out the form properly, signs and dates it, checks the term-certain box, and sends it back to the IRA institution by no later than his or her required beginning date. Has the IRA owner made a valid written election of the term-certain method?

ANSWER: Probably. The IRS does not indicate how the election should be made or upon whom the election should be served. In the absence of any court decision, regulation, or ruling to the contrary, the above action by the IRA owner should be sufficient to demonstrate that a term-certain election has been made. The IRS is interested in the IRA owner's timely decision to make an election. The actions by the IRA owner are clear evidence of his or her intention to make a term-certain election. The IRS would have to permit the maximum term period to be used in this situation, because the IRS has not issued any guidelines on what should be contained in the election or the mechanics of making the election.

CASE STUDY
Questions 2.29–2.38 illustrate how Martin would figure his required minimum distributions using the term-certain method and his single life expectancy.

QUESTION 2.29: Assume Martin reaches age 70 on June 1, 2006, and 70$\frac{1}{2}$ on December 1, 2006. He elects the term-certain method. His estate is the beneficiary of his IRA. Can you show what life expectancy he would use to figure his required minimum distributions each year?

ANSWER: Martin would use his single life expectancy of 16 years to figure his required minimum distributions. Life expectancy is based upon Martin's attained age of 70 as of his birthday in 2006, the year in which he reaches age 70$\frac{1}{2}$. As shown in the Appendix, IRS Table I (Publication 590) provides a 16-year life expectancy for a 70-year-old individual.

The following schedule reflects the application of the term-certain method over a 16-year period:

AGE	DISTRIBUTION YEAR	CALENDAR YEAR	REMAINING TERM-CERTAIN PERIOD
70	1	2006	16
71	2	2007	15
72	3	2008	14
73	4	2009	13
74	5	2010	12
75	6	2011	11
76	7	2012	10
77	8	2013	9
78	9	2014	8
79	10	2015	7
80	11	2016	6
81	12	2017	5
82	13	2018	4
83	14	2019	3
84	15	2020	2
85	16	2021	1
86	17	2022	0

QUESTION 2.30: Assume that Martin's IRA balance as of December 31, 2005, is $96,000. How much is Martin's required minimum distribution that is attributable to his first distribution calendar year 2006?

ANSWER: $6,000. Martin's first distribution calendar year is 2006. The year 2006 is the year he attained age 70^1/2. In order to determine his required minimum distribution for the first distribution calendar year 2006, he must use the value of his IRA balance as of the end of the prior year, which is then divided by the appropriate life expectancy that is applicable to the first distribution calendar year 2006. The account balance as of December 31, 2005, of $96,000 is divided by 16 years, which is the life expectancy of Martin in the first distribution calendar year 2006. The result is $6,000.

QUESTION 2.31: Must Martin receive the required minimum distribution of $6,000 that is attributable to his first distribution calendar year 2006 by December 31, 2006?

ANSWER: No. The law states that he may receive his required minimum distribution for his first distribution calendar year of 2006 by no later than his required beginning date, which is April 1, 2007. His required beginning date, as you may recall, is April 1 of the calendar year following the calendar year in which he attained age 70^1/2. He attained age 70^1/2 in 2006.

QUESTION 2.32: Assume that Martin received his $6,000 required minimum distribution for his first distribution calendar year 2006 on October 31, 2006. Further assume that his account balance in his IRA as of December 31, 2006, is $96,700, taking into account earnings during 2006 and the $6,000 distribution. How much must Martin receive during the second distribution calendar year 2007 under the term-certain method in order to satisfy the required minimum distribution rules for the year 2007?

ANSWER: $6,446.67. The calendar year 2007 is Martin's second distribution calendar year. He must receive his required minimum distribution for his second distribution calendar year by December 31, 2007.

In order to determine his required minimum distribution for the calendar year 2007, the value of his account balance as of December 31, 2006, must be divided by the appropriate life expectancy that is applicable to the calendar year 2007. The balance of $96,700 is divided by 15 years, which is Martin's remaining life expectancy under the term-certain method as of the second distribution calendar year 2007. The result is $6,446.67.

QUESTION 2.33: Assume that Martin received his required minimum distribution of $6,000 for his first distribution calendar year 2006 on March 31, 2007. Further assume that Martin's IRA balance as of December 31, 2006, is $104,000. How much must Martin receive during the calendar year 2007 in order to satisfy the required minimum distributions for the second distribution calendar year 2007?

ANSWER: $6,533.33. The IRS has a special rule that is only applicable if any portion of a distribution that is attributable to a first distribution calendar year is paid in the second distribution calendar year by the required beginning date. Based upon this rule, the actual balance in the IRA as of December 31, 2006, is reduced by $6,000, because that amount is attributable to the first distribution calendar year and was paid in the second distribution calendar year on March 31, 2007, which is not later than the required beginning date of April 1, 2007.

The actual account balance of $104,000 on December 31, 2006, is hypothetically reduced by $6,000 to $98,000. The hypothetical account balance of $98,000 is divided by 15 years, which is the life expectancy of Martin as of the second distribution calendar year 2007. The result is $6,533.33, the amount Martin must receive for the second distribution calendar year 2007. It must be received by Martin by no later than December 31, 2007. Martin reports both the $6,000 distribution and the $6,533.33 distribution, for a total of $12,533.33, on his Form 1040 for the calendar year 2007.

QUESTION 2.34: Assume the same facts as in Question 2.33 except that Martin receives a distribution of $7,000 on March 31, 2007. How much must Martin receive during the calendar year 2007 in order to satisfy the required minimum distribution rules?

ANSWER: Martin must receive a total of $12,533.33 during the calendar year 2007. This is computed as follows: $7,000 was received on March 31, 2007, of which $6,000 is applicable to the first distribution calendar year 2006 and the excess of $1,000 is applied towards the required minimum distribution of $6,533.33 for the second distribution calendar year 2007. In addition, Martin must receive the balance of $5,533.33 for the second distribution calendar year 2007 by no later than December 31, 2007.

QUESTION 2.35: If Martin's required minimum distribution for 2006 is $6,000 and he receives a $7,000 distribution on March 31, 2007, and $5,533.33 by December 31, 2007, does he have to report the entire distribution on his Form 1040 for the calendar year 2007?

ANSWER: Yes. The entire amount received by Martin in the calendar year 2007 must be reported on his federal tax return for 2007.

QUESTION 2.36: Assume the same facts as in Question 2.34 except that Martin receives a distribution of $17,333.33 on March 31, 2007. Is Martin entitled to a credit of $5,000 against his required minimum distribution for his third distribution calendar year 2008?

ANSWER: No. If an IRA owner receives a distribution in a given distribution calendar year that exceeds the required minimum distribution for that calendar year, he or she may not receive a credit for the additional distribution against the required minimum distribution for a subsequent year. There is a limited exception for the first distribution calendar year that was previously discussed.

The $17,333.33 that Martin received on March 31, 2007, would satisfy the $6,000 required minimum distribution for the first distribution calendar year 2006 and the $6,533.33 required minimum distribution for the calendar year 2007. The fact that he received an additional distribution of $5,000, whether by accident or design, does not result in a credit towards his required minimum distribution for his third distribution calendar year 2008.

However, the entire distribution of $17,333.33 (which includes the additional $5,000 distribution) on March 31, 2007, does reduce the IRA balance as of December 31, 2007. This has the indirect effect of reducing the amount of the required minimum distribution for the third distribution calendar year 2008 and all years thereafter.

QUESTION 2.37: Martin timely elected a 16-year term-certain period in which to receive his required minimum distributions from his IRA. May Martin accelerate distributions from his IRA from time to time?

ANSWER: Yes. If Martin elects to receive his required minimum distributions over a 16-year term-certain period, he can accelerate distributions from his IRA from time to time. The IRS is not concerned about Martin receiving more than his required minimum distributions from his IRA.

QUESTION 2.38: If Martin determines that he must receive a $6,000 distribution for his first distribution calendar year of 2006, should he defer taking the distribution until the beginning of 2007?

ANSWER: Martin has the option of receiving the $6,000 IRA distribution with respect to his first distribution calendar year 2006 at any time between the period January 1, 2006 and April 1, 2007. For tax purposes, he may prefer to receive the $6,000 distribution in 2007 instead of in 2006. However, if he defers the entire amount to 2007, he will have two IRA distributions to report in 2007. Martin must receive his IRA distribution for his second distribution calendar year 2007 by December 31, 2007.

PENALTY FOR INSUFFICIENT DISTRIBUTIONS AFTER THE REQUIRED BEGINNING DATE

The following questions and answers explain the penalty that the IRS may impose if the required minimum distribution for a year is not received.

QUESTION 2.39: If Martin must receive a required minimum distribution of $6,000 from his IRA for his first distribution calendar year 2006, but in December 2006 he receives only $4,000, may the IRS assess a penalty against Martin?

ANSWER: No penalty will be imposed if the required $2,000 balance is received by April 1, 2007, Martin's required beginning date. If the balance is not received by April 1, 2007, the IRS may assess a penalty equal to 50 percent of the insufficient distribution for the first distribution year of 2006. Thus, if the remaining $2,000 were not timely received, the penalty would be $1,000.

QUESTION 2.40: May the IRS waive the $1,000 penalty described in the previous question?

ANSWER: Yes. Martin must prove to the IRS that the shortfall was due to reasonable error and that reasonable steps are being taken to remedy the shortfall.

QUESTION 2.41: Assume that Martin timely made a term-certain election based upon his single life expectancy. Further assume

that Martin dies on July 1, 2010, before receiving his required minimum distribution of $7,000 from his IRA for that calendar year. Is Martin's IRA beneficiary subject to an IRS penalty of $3,500 based upon the fact that Martin failed to receive his required minimum distribution of $7,000 for his fifth distribution calendar year 2010?

ANSWER: No. The death of Martin prior to the end of the calendar year 2010 is obviously reasonable cause, and the IRS would not assess a penalty against Martin's beneficiary. However, Martin's beneficiary should request the $7,000 required minimum distribution from Martin's IRA for the calendar year 2010 within a reasonable period of time after discovering that Martin failed to receive his required minimum distribution of $7,000 for his fifth distribution calendar year 2010.

QUESTION 2.42: Assume that Martin died on July 1, 2010, before receiving his required minimum distribution of $7,000 from his IRA for the fifth distribution calendar year. Martin's estate is his IRA beneficiary and the insufficient distribution is discovered by the executor of Martin's estate in 2011. Assume that the required minimum distribution that Martin would have received in 2011 had he lived would have been $7,200. What action should the executor of Martin's estate take in order to avoid any IRS penalties?

ANSWER: The executor of Martin's estate should take a total distribution of $14,200 from Martin's IRA during the calendar year 2011. The executor should take the required minimum distribution of $7,000 attributable to the fifth distribution calendar year 2010 as soon as possible during 2011. The required minimum distribution of $7,200 attributable to the sixth distribution calendar year 2011 must be received by Martin's executor from Martin's IRA by no later than December 31, 2011. Such action by Martin's executor during 2011 should eliminate any IRS penalty with respect to the $7,000 shortfall for the fifth distribution calendar year 2010.

QUESTION 2.43: Assume the same facts as Question 2.42. Also assume that the executor of Martin's estate wishes to avoid paying income taxes on the estate income tax return on the entire $14,200 that he must receive from Martin's IRA during 2011. The estate has additional income, all of which is tax exempt. What options are available to the executor of the estate of Martin in order to save income taxes for the estate?

ANSWER: The professional advisor to Martin's estate should suggest to the executor that the estate of Martin select a fiscal year so that the entire $14,200 is not received in one tax year. The estate is subject to high federal income tax rates at relatively low levels of estate taxable income. It is important to minimize taxable income where possible because a significant portion of estate taxable income is subject to a 39.6 percent federal income tax rate. In addition, the estate may be subject to state income taxes as well. It is possible to have the $7,000 IRA distribution attributable to the calendar year 2010 received in one fiscal year of the estate and the $7,200 IRA distribution attributable to calendar year 2011 received in another fiscal year of the estate through proper planning.

In addition, distributions if timely made by Martin's executor to the beneficiaries of Martin's estate will shift the income tax burden from the estate to the beneficiaries of the estate. This should be done if the beneficiaries of the estate are in a lower income tax bracket than the estate. Generally, most beneficiaries are in a lower income tax bracket than the estate.

REQUIRED DISTRIBUTIONS TO 5-PERCENT OWNER OR SELF-EMPLOYED INDIVIDUAL

The following questions and answers discuss the penalty rules that apply to the self-employed individuals or 5-percent owner of a business.

QUESTION 2.44: Jack owns 5 percent of the stock of a corporation. The other shares are owned by unrelated stockholders. The corporation maintains a qualified profit-sharing plan. Is Jack considered to be a 5-percent owner of the corporation for purposes of the required minimum distribution rules?

ANSWER: No. According to the law a 5-percent owner is someone who owns more than 5 percent of the stock of the corporation.

QUESTION 2.45: Assume that Jack owns 6 percent of the stock of a corporation. Jack attains age 70^1/$_2$ in the calendar year 2000. Jack participates in a qualified corporate profit-sharing plan. What is Jack's required beginning date?

ANSWER: Because Jack is considered to be 5-percent owner of the corporation, his required beginning date with respect to distributions from the qualified corporate profit sharing plan is April 1, 2001, the year after the year (2000) in which he attains age 70^1/$_2$.

QUESTION 2.46: Assume that Marvin has a 5-percent partnership interest in a law firm partnership. All the other partners are unrelated. The law firm maintains a qualified pension plan. Marvin participates in the qualified plan. Is Marvin considered to be a 5-percent owner of the partnership for purposes of the required minimum distribution rules?

ANSWER: No. If the employer is not a corporation, a 5-percent owner is an individual who owns more than 5 percent of the capital or profits interest in the employer. Marvin does not own more than 5 percent of the capital or profit interest in the law firm.

QUESTION 2.47: Assume that Marvin has a 5-percent partnership interest in a law firm partnership and his son has a 1-percent

partnership of the capital or profits interest in the same partnership. Marvin participates in the partnership's qualified pension plan. Is Marvin considered to be a 5-percent owner of the partnership for purposes of the required minimum distribution rules?

ANSWER: Yes. Marvin is deemed to own his son's partnership interest in the partnership. Therefore Marvin is considered to be a 5-percent owner in the partnership.

QUESTION 2.48: Assume for the purposes of question 2.47 that Marvin attains age 70^{1}/$_{2}$ in the calendar year 2000. Marvin participates in the law firm's qualified pension plan. What is Marvin's required beginning date?

ANSWER: Because Marvin is considered to be a 5-percent owner of the partnership, and he is age 70^{1}/$_{2}$ in the calendar year 2000, his required beginning date with respect to distributions from the qualified pension plan is April 1, 2001.

QUESTION 2.49: Janet is a sole proprietor who maintains a qualified profit-sharing plan. She attains 70^{1}/$_{2}$ in the calendar year 2000. What is Janet's required beginning date?

ANSWER: Because Janet is the 100-percent owner of the sole proprietorship, her required beginning date with respect to distributions from the qualified profit sharing plan is April 1, 2001. She is age 70^{1}/$_{2}$ in the calendar year 2000 and her required beginning date is April 1 of the following year (2001).

QUESTION 2.50: To figure her minimum required distributions, does Janet (Question 2.49) apply the life-expectancy methods for IRAs discussed earlier in this chapter?

ANSWER: Yes. The same life-expectancy rules, including the use of the term-certain, the recalculation method, and hybrid method, apply to qualified plans as well as IRAs.

CHAPTER THREE

CHOOSING YOUR SPOUSE AS YOUR DESIGNATED BENEFICIARY

Tax planning and estate planning are crucial when you select a designated beneficiary. If your spouse is the designated beneficiary of a qualified plan, a 403(b) annuity contract, or a traditional IRA, then both you and your spouse must become familiar with the special distribution rules discussed in this chapter.

The tax law favors spousal beneficiaries with tax-savings opportunities not available to other beneficiaries. For example, the restrictive life-expectancy "MDIB" rules that apply to younger beneficiaries (see Chapter 4) do not apply to spousal beneficiaries. The life expectancy of a spousal beneficiary may be recalculated annually but not that of other beneficiaries. After the owner's death, a surviving spouse is the only beneficiary that may roll over the deceased's account to an IRA in the survivor's own name.

If you are married and do not plan to select your spouse as the designated beneficiary of your IRA or qualified plan death benefits, be aware that many qualified plans require that the surviving spouse receive all or at least a portion of the plan death benefits. However, a spouse may waive his or her rights to these plan death benefits. IRAs are not subject to spousal rights under the federal law. However, state law may grant the surviving spouse certain rights to IRA death benefits.

YOUR FIRST REQUIRED MINIMUM DISTRIBUTION

The following questions and answers highlight the rules that apply when you name your spouse as your designated beneficiary and you must start to receive required minimum distributions at your required beginning date.

QUESTION 3.1: Frank Wagner has an IRA at the ABC Bank. His 70th birthday is on March 15, 1999, and he attains age 70¹/₂ on September 15, 1999. His wife, Cathy, the designated beneficiary of his IRA, is age 67 on November 15, 1999. When must Frank receive his first required minimum distribution from his IRA?

ANSWER: The first year for which Frank must receive a minimum distribution, his "first distribution calendar year," is 1999—the calendar year in which he attains age 70¹/₂. However, for the first distribution calendar year, the tax law allows extra time to take the required minimum distribution. Frank must receive his required minimum distribution for his first distribution calendar year 1999 by no later than April 1, 2000. Frank's required beginning date is April 1, 2000.

QUESTION 3.2: If Frank wants to base his required minimum distributions on his joint life expectancy with Cathy, what should he do?

ANSWER: Frank must select Cathy as his designated beneficiary by his required beginning date of April 1, 2000, in order to base his required minimum distributions on their joint life expectancy.

QUESTION 3.3: How is the joint life expectancy of Frank and Cathy determined?

ANSWER: The joint life expectancy of Frank and Cathy is based upon their attained ages in the year that Frank reached age $70^{1}/_{2}$. Frank attained age $70^{1}/_{2}$ on September 15, 1999. Frank is age 70 and Cathy is age 67 in 1999. Under the IRS joint life-expectancy Table II shown in the Appendix of this book, the joint life expectancy of a 70-year-old and a 67-year-old is 22 years.

QUESTION 3.4: Assume that Frank timely selected his wife, Cathy, as the designated beneficiary of his IRA. How much is Frank's required minimum distribution for his first distribution calendar year 1999?

ANSWER: Frank must divide his IRA balance as of the end of the year prior to the first distribution calendar year by his and Cathy's joint life expectancy. Because 1999 is the first distribution calendar year, the account balance as of December 31, 1998, must be used. Assume Frank's IRA balance on December 31, 1998, is $100,000.

Frank's required minimum distribution for his first distribution calendar year 1999 is $4,545.45. This amount is determined as follows:

Frank's IRA balance as of December 31, 1998:	Divided by the joint life expectancy of Frank and Cathy for the calendar year 1999:	Required minimum distribution for the calendar year 1999:
$100,000.00	÷22 years	$4,545.45

For the year 1999 Frank must receive a minimum of $4,545.45 to satisfy the IRS rules. He may of course withdraw more than that. Whatever he receives from the IRA will be taxable in the year of receipt.

QUESTION 3.5: May Frank receive his required minimum distribution for his first distribution calendar year 1999 in 1999?

ANSWER: Yes. Frank may receive his required minimum distribution for his first distribution calendar year in 1999. He may receive it at any time during the period between January 1, 1999 and April 1, 2000. Frank's required beginning date is April 1, 2000.

QUESTION 3.6: Assume that Frank has other IRAs as well as a profit-sharing plan account under his employer's plan. Frank is not a 5-percent owner of his employer's corporation. He is not retired and intends to work for several more years. The profit-sharing plan is on a calendar-year basis. Does Frank have to receive a required minimum distribution from each of these arrangements by his required beginning date of April 1, 2000?

ANSWER: Perhaps. Frank must receive required minimum distributions for the year 1999, his first distribution calendar year, with respect to his IRAs. Frank must compute a required minimum distribution based upon the account balance of each IRA as of December 31, 1998, following the steps shown in Question 3.4. However, the required minimum distributions from all of the IRAs may be received from any one IRA or any combination of

IRAs, as Frank prefers. Under the new IRS rule described in the answer to Question 2.4, Frank may not be required to receive a required minimum distribution from his employer's profit-sharing plan by April 1, 2000, if the plan is timely amended to provide for this new rule.

TERM-CERTAIN METHOD

The following questions and answers explain how election of the term-certain method affects the calculation of required minimum distributions from an IRA. Also see the Answers to Questions 2.21–2.28 for issues to consider in choosing the term-certain method.

QUESTION 3.7: Assume that the IRA plan document permits Frank to elect the term-certain method of calculating his required minimum distributions for him and his wife. What term-certain period is applicable to Frank if Cathy has been timely selected as his designated beneficiary?

ANSWER: Frank may elect a term-certain period based upon his and Cathy's joint life expectancy as determined in the calendar year 1999.

Based upon an initial joint life expectancy of 22 years (see Question 3.3) in 1999, the term-certain period used to calculate the required distribution for each distribution calendar year will be 22 years for 1999 (first distribution calendar year) and then it will decrease by one each year—from 22 to 21 to 20 to 19 and so on.

The mechanics of electing the term-certain method were discussed in Questions 2.23–2.28, in Chapter 2. A joint term-certain election is permissible in most IRA plan documents.

QUESTION 3.8: Assume that Frank timely selected Cathy as his designated beneficiary and timely elected the term-certain method of calculating his required minimum distributions. Assume that Cathy dies in the calendar year 2006. The calendar year 2006 is

Frank's eighth distribution calendar year. May Frank continue to use the balance of the initial term-certain period of 22 years in determining his required minimum distributions?

ANSWER: Yes. If the IRA owner timely elects a term-certain method of calculating his required minimum distributions, that method will survive the death of the designated beneficiary. If Cathy dies during the term-certain period Frank can still continue to use the balance of the initial term-certain period. Thus, Frank will determine his required minimum distribution for his ninth distribution calendar year 2007 by dividing his IRA balance as of December 31, 2006, by 14 years, the unused balance of the initial 22-year term-certain period. Frank can still continue to use the balance of the term-certain period for all later years as well. Upon his subsequent death his beneficiary can still continue to use the balance of the term-certain period. A partial listing of the term-certain period follows.

TERM-CERTAIN	YEAR	PERIOD
First distribution calendar year	1999	22
Second distribution calendar year	2000	21
Third distribution calendar year	2001	20
Fourth distribution calendar year	2002	19
Fifth distribution calendar year	2003	18
Sixth distribution calendar year	2004	17
Seventh distribution calendar year	2005	16
Eighth distribution calendar year	2006	15
Ninth distribution calendar year	2007	14

QUESTION 3.9: Assume that Frank timely selected Cathy as his designated beneficiary and timely elected the term-certain method of calculating his required minimum distributions. Also assume that he did not specify the term-certain period in his election with the IRA institution. May Frank use the 22-year term-certain period?

ANSWER: Yes. The IRS does not require that the term-certain period be spelled out. It may be best to spell it out but it is not a legal requirement. The 22-year period based upon Frank and Cathy's joint life expectancy would be automatically available.

QUESTION 3.10: Assume that Frank timely selected Cathy as his designated beneficiary and timely elected the term-certain method of calculating his required minimum distributions. Also assume that Frank dies on August 1, 2004, having already received his required minimum distribution for the calendar year 2004. The calendar year 2004 is Frank's sixth distribution calendar year. Assume that Cathy survives Frank. May Cathy receive distributions from Frank's IRA for the balance remaining in the initial term-certain period, which is 16 years?

ANSWER: Yes. Cathy may receive the balance in Frank's IRA over 16 years, the balance of the initial 22-year term-certain period.

SPOUSAL IRA ROLLOVER IF ACCOUNT OWNER DIES DURING TERM-CERTAIN PERIOD: QUESTIONS 3.11–3.24

QUESTION 3.11: Assume the same facts in Question 3.10, except that Cathy was advised shortly after Frank's death to create a spousal IRA rollover account. Should Cathy make the rollover?

ANSWER: Yes. There is an advantage in making the spousal rollover. By rolling over the account to a new spousal IRA rollover account in her own name, Cathy can select her own designated beneficiary. This may allow Cathy to spread out distributions from the spousal IRA rollover account over a period that is longer than 16 years, the balance of Frank's initial term-certain period.

QUESTION 3.12: Does Cathy's age at the time of Frank's death bar her from creating a spousal IRA rollover account?

ANSWER: No. According to the IRS, the fact that Cathy has passed her required beginning date does not prevent her from creating a spousal IRA rollover account.

QUESTION 3.13: Assume the same facts in Question 3.10 and that Cathy was advised shortly after Frank's death to create a spousal IRA rollover account. Cathy creates a spousal IRA rollover account on September 1, 2004. Cathy is age 72 on November 15, 2004. Cathy immediately selects her son, Thomas, as the designated beneficiary of her spousal IRA rollover. Thomas is age 40 on April 15, 2004. Must Cathy receive a required minimum distribution during the calendar year 2004 from this new spousal IRA rollover account that she created in the calendar year 2004?

ANSWER: No. According to the IRS, if the IRA owner in the calendar year of death received his or her required minimum distribution, then the designated beneficiary need not receive a required minimum distribution in the same calendar year that the IRA owner died.

QUESTION 3.14: Assume that Frank timely selected Cathy as his designated beneficiary and timely elected the term-certain method of calculating his required minimum distributions. Also assume that Frank died on August 1, 2004, before he received his required minimum distribution of $10,000 for the calendar year 2004. Cathy would like to create a spousal IRA rollover in

the calendar year 2004 of Frank's entire account balance of $110,000. May Cathy create a spousal IRA rollover of $110,000?

ANSWER: No. The IRS does not permit Cathy to roll over a required minimum distribution. Cathy may create a spousal IRA rollover to the extent of $100,000, not $110,000. She must report the required minimum distribution of $10,000 as income in 2004. Cathy should not roll over Frank's IRA into her own preexisting IRA.

QUESTION 3.15: If before his death in 2004 Frank receives his required minimum distribution for 2004 and Cathy creates a spousal IRA rollover account on September 1, 2004, when does Cathy have to commence her required minimum distributions from her spousal IRA rollover account?

ANSWER: The IRS recognizes that Cathy has already attained her required beginning date as of the date of the creation of the spousal IRA rollover account in the calendar year 2004. Based on these facts, she must commence her required minimum distribution from her spousal IRA rollover account in the calendar year following the year of her spousal rollover. Cathy must commence her required minimum distributions from her spousal IRA rollover account during the calendar year 2005.

QUESTION 3.16: If Cathy creates a spousal IRA rollover account as discussed in Question 3.13, and names her son, Thomas, as beneficiary, how is Cathy's life-expectancy factor for her spousal IRA rollover account for the calendar year 2005 determined?

ANSWER: Cathy is age 73 in the calendar year 2005, and Thomas, the designated beneficiary of the spousal IRA rollover account, is age 41 in the calendar year 2005. Because Cathy has passed her required beginning date and has a nonspouse designated beneficiary who is more than 10 years younger than she, then

Cathy is subject to the special MDIB rules discussed in Chapter 4. Under the MDIB rules, Thomas's actual age may not be used during Cathy's lifetime to determine joint life expectancy. Instead, Thomas, during Cathy's lifetime, is considered to be 10 years younger than Cathy. As a result, Cathy must use ages 73 (her age in 2005) and 63 (Thomas's deemed age under MDIB rules) when looking up their joint life expectancy in the IRS tables. As shown in the table in Appendix A, the joint life expectancy for a 73-year-old and 63-year-old is 23.5 years. For the calendar year 2006, Cathy must use age 74 (her age in 2006 and 64—Thomas's deemed age under MDIB rule).

The IRS has a special table as shown in the Appendix that automatically calculates the joint life expectancy based upon a nonspouse designated beneficiary who is more than 10 years younger than the IRA owner. The table can be found in Appendix A of this book; it is from IRS Publication 590, Appendix E. It is called the Table for Determining Applicable Divisor for MDIB (Minimum Distribution Incidental Benefit).

The MDIB rule is not applicable in calendar years after Cathy's subsequent death. The age of Thomas is taken into account in calendar years after Cathy's death. This is explained in Chapter 4.

The special MDIB rule is not considered to be a recalculation method or a term-certain method. It is considered to be a special computation.

QUESTION 3.17: How much is Cathy's required minimum distribution from the spousal IRA rollover account for the calendar year 2005?

ANSWER: Assuming that the value of the spousal IRA rollover account balance at the end of 2004 is $105,000, Cathy's required minimum distribution for the calendar year 2005 year would be $4,468.09. This amount is determined as follows:

Cathy's spousal IRA rollover account balance as of December 31, 2004:	Divided by the applicable divisor for the calendar year 2005:	Required minimum distribution for the calendar year 2005:
$105,000	÷23.5 years	$4,468.09

QUESTION 3.18: Based upon the fact that at the time of Frank's death he has passed his required beginning date and Cathy has passed her required beginning date, when should Cathy select the designated beneficiary of her spousal IRA rollover account?

ANSWER: Based upon the fact that Frank died after his required beginning date, Cathy should select the designated beneficiary of her spousal IRA rollover account as soon as possible in order to reduce her required minimum distributions and provide for an extended payout for her designated beneficiary.

According to the IRS, because Frank died after his required beginning date and Cathy had passed her required beginning date when she created the spousal IRA rollover account in the calendar year 2004, then Cathy must select the designated beneficiary of her spousal IRA rollover account prior to December 31, 2005. This is prior to the last day of 2005, the year in which she must commence her required minimum distributions from the spousal IRA rollover account that she established during the calendar year 2004. If Frank had died prior to his required beginning date, then Cathy should create the spousal IRA rollover account as soon as possible for tax and estate planning purposes and select a designated beneficiary of the spousal IRA rollover account.

Timing is a crucial issue because if Cathy should die before she consummates the spousal IRA rollover and if the recalculation method is applicable, then under the recalculation method Frank's entire IRA balance must be paid to Cathy's estate by December 30 of the calendar year following the year of her death. However, if Cathy immediately creates a spousal IRA rollover account and selects her son, Thomas, as the designated beneficiary of the spousal IRA rollover account, she could compute her required minimum distribution using the MDIB rules discussed in Question 3.16 and Chapter 4. If Frank had elected the term-certain method and Cathy dies before creating the spousal IRA rollover, then her estate may receive the required minimum distributions for the balance of the term-certain period. The recalculation method is discussed in Questions 3.25 through 3.35.

QUESTION 3.19: Is there any other reason that Cathy should select a designated beneficiary of her spousal IRA rollover account as soon as possible?

ANSWER: Yes. Upon Cathy's subsequent death, her designated beneficiary, Thomas, for example, may take advantage of the extended payout rules discussed in Chapter 4 that are available to a nonspouse designated beneficiary who is more than 10 years younger than the IRA owner. If Cathy should die or become incompetent before she selects the designated beneficiary of her spousal IRA rollover account, then her estate becomes the beneficiary of her spousal IRA rollover account and the entire IRA balance generally would have to be paid to her estate by December 30 of the calendar year following the year of Cathy's death under the recalculation method, unless the term-certain method was applicable.

In the case of incompetence, her legally appointed guardian could arrange for the spousal rollover and selection of beneficiaries with court approval.

QUESTION 3.20: May Cathy establish more than one spousal IRA rollover account?

ANSWER: Yes. Upon Frank's death, Cathy may establish more than one spousal IRA rollover account and select a different designated beneficiary for each spousal IRA rollover account.

QUESTION 3.21: If Cathy creates more than one spousal IRA rollover account, must she receive her required minimum distributions from each IRA?

ANSWER: No. The IRS permits Cathy to receive her total required minimum distribution from her IRAs for a particular calendar year from any IRA or combination of IRAs that she wishes.

QUESTION 3.22: Assume that Cathy has one regular IRA and one spousal IRA rollover account. Assume that during a given calendar year she must receive $2,500 as a required minimum distribution from the regular IRA and $5,000 as a required minimum distribution from her spousal IRA rollover account. May she receive the entire $7,500 from either IRA?

ANSWER: Yes. The IRS permits Cathy to receive the $7,500 required minimum distribution for the given calendar year from any IRA she wishes. She may allocate the distribution entirely to one IRA or partially to one IRA and partially to the other IRA. These IRA distributions need not be allocated in any specific manner.

QUESTION 3.23: If under the facts of Question 3.11, Frank dies and Cathy decides to create a spousal IRA rollover account, but Cathy dies before she can establish the account, would the executor of her estate be able to set up the spousal IRA rollover account?

ANSWER: No. Only a surviving spouse can create a spousal IRA rollover. An executor has no authority under the tax law to do so.

QUESTION 3.24: If Frank timely elected the term-certain method and after his death Cathy dies before she can establish a spousal rollover account, may Cathy's estate receive the balance in Frank's IRA over 16 years, the remaining balance of the initial 22-year term-certain period?

ANSWER: Yes. Because the spousal IRA rollover was never made, Cathy's estate may continue to use the remaining 16-year period in determining its required minimum distributions from Frank's IRA.

RECALCULATION METHOD

The following questions and answers explain how required minimum distributions are calculated by a married IRA owner under the recalculation method of determining life expectancy. The advantages and disadvantages of the recalculation method mentioned in the Answer to Question 2.22 are illustrated in this section.

QUESTION 3.25: What is the recalculation method?

ANSWER: The recalculation method allows the IRA owner who has timely selected a spousal designated beneficiary to use the spouse's attained age as of his or her birthday in each year when looking up their joint life expectancy in the IRS tables. The effect of this "recalculation" is that joint life expectancy decreases by less than one in each succeeding year.

QUESTION 3.26: Assume that an IRA owner selects his or her spouse as the designated beneficiary by no later than the required beginning date. Also assume that under the IRA plan document, the recalculation method of determining life expectancy is the default option if another method is not elected. Would this default option apply to both the IRA owner and his or her spouse as the designated beneficiary?

ANSWER: Yes. If the IRA owner timely selected his or her spouse as the designated beneficiary and fails to elect out of the recalculation method by the required beginning date, then the recalculation method is applicable to both the IRA owner and the designated spousal beneficiary under the default option.

QUESTION 3.27: How does an IRA owner determine whether or not the default option of the recalculation method is applicable?

ANSWER: The majority of IRA plan documents state that unless the IRA owner elects out of the recalculation method by his or her required beginning date, the recalculation method applies as the default option.

QUESTION 3.28: Does the recalculation method apply to a non-spouse who is selected as the designated beneficiary?

ANSWER: No. A nonspouse designated beneficiary is not allowed to recalculate life expectancy. This is true even if the owner does recalculate. Where the owner does recalculate, a special hybrid method must be used to calculate joint life expectancy, as shown in Chapter 6.

QUESTION 3.29: Assume that Frank Wagner, an IRA owner, is age 70 on March 15, 1999, and age 70$^{1}/_{2}$ on September 15, 1999. Frank's required beginning date is April 1, 2000. His wife, Cathy, the designated beneficiary of his IRA, is age 67 on November 15, 1999. Frank elects to recalculate his and Cathy's life expectancy. Assume that Frank and Cathy are alive during the calendar years 1999 through 2009. Would you please show what life expectancy Frank would use for the calendar years 1999 through 2009 under the recalculation method in determining his required minimum distributions from his IRA?

ANSWER: The following schedule shows the life expectancy that Frank would use under the recalculation method through 2009, when he would be age 80.

RECALCULATION OF LIFE EXPECTANCY

FRANK'S AGE	CATHY'S AGE	CALENDAR YEAR	JOINT LIFE EXPECTANCY DISTRIBUTION YEAR	JOINT LIFE EXPECTANCY RECALCULATION METHOD
70	67	1999	1	22.0
71	68	2000	2	21.2
72	69	2001	3	20.3
73	70	2002	4	19.4
74	71	2003	5	18.6
75	72	2004	6	17.8
76	73	2005	7	17.0
77	74	2006	8	16.2
78	75	2007	9	15.4
79	76	2008	10	14.7
80	77	2009	11	14.0

QUESTION 3.30: Assume that Frank timely selected Cathy as the designated beneficiary of his IRA. Would you compare the life-expectancy period that Frank may use under the recalculation method with the life expectancy that may be used under the term-certain method during the calendar years 1999 through 2009?

ANSWER: The following schedule indicates the difference between the life expectancy that Frank would use during the calendar years 1999 through 2009 under each method.

As the schedule indicates, life expectancy is reduced more slowly under the recalculation method. As a result, slightly smaller annual distributions are required under the recalculation method than under the term-certain method.

RECALCULATION METHOD VS. TERM-CERTAIN METHOD

FRANK'S AGE	CATHY'S AGE	CALENDAR YEAR	DISTRIBUTION YEAR	JOINT LIFE EXPECTANCY TERM-CERTAIN METHOD	JOINT LIFE EXPECTANCY RECALCU-LATION METHOD
70	67	1999	1	22	22.0
71	68	2000	2	21	21.2
72	69	2001	3	20	20.3
73	70	2002	4	19	19.4
74	71	2003	5	18	18.6
75	72	2004	6	17	17.8
76	73	2005	7	16	17.0
77	74	2006	8	15	16.2
78	75	2007	9	14	15.4
79	76	2008	10	13	14.7
80	77	2009	11	12	14.0

QUESTION 3.31: Assume the facts in Question 3.29 except that Cathy dies in 2004. How does her death affect the life expectancy Frank must use under the recalculation method in figuring his subsequent required minimum distributions for the calendar years 2005 through 2009?

ANSWER: Because Cathy died in the calendar year 2004, her life expectancy under the recalculation method becomes zero in the calendar year after the year of her death. For 2004, the year of her death, Frank figures his required minimum distribution using a joint life expectancy of 17.8 years, the same as if Cathy were alive. In the year 2005, Frank must use only his own single life expectancy of 11.9 years. IRS Table I in the Appendix shows 11.9 years as the single life expectancy for an individual age 76.

For later years, here is the single life expectancy Frank would use:

FRANK'S AGE	CALENDAR YEAR	DISTRIBUTION YEAR	SINGLE LIFE EXPECTANCY
77	2006	8	11.2
78	2007	9	10.6
79	2008	10	10.0
80	2009	11	9.5

QUESTION 3.32: Assume the facts in Question 3.31 except that after Cathy's death, Frank names his son, Thomas, as the new designated beneficiary of his IRA. Does this change the answer to Question 3.31?

ANSWER: No. The recalculation method cannot be changed after the required beginning date. The substitution of a new designated beneficiary after the death of Cathy will not permit Frank to avoid the recalculation method.

Frank must continue to use his single life expectancy each year when figuring his required minimum distributions, regardless of whom he may name as the replacement beneficiary of his IRA.

QUESTION 3.33: Assume the facts in Question 3.29 except that a few days before Cathy's death, Frank changes the designated beneficiary of his IRA from Cathy to his son, Thomas. Will your answers to Questions 3.31 and 3.32 change?

ANSWER: No. The IRS position is that if you change your designated beneficiary after your required beginning date from an older to a younger designated beneficiary, you must continue to use the life expectancy of the original, older designated beneficiary. If Frank replaced Cathy with Thomas as his designated beneficiary, he would still have to treat Cathy as the designated beneficiary for purposes of calculating his required minimum distributions. After Cathy dies, her life expectancy under the recalculation method is reduced to zero in the calendar year following the year of her death, as explained in Question 3.31. The fact that Thomas was the designated beneficiary when Cathy dies does not change this result.

QUESTION 3.34: Assume the facts in Question 3.31 except that Frank names his estate as the beneficiary of his IRA after Cathy's death in 2004. Frank dies in 2007 after receiving his required minimum distribution for 2007. When must Frank's estate receive Frank's IRA balance?

ANSWER: Frank's estate must receive Frank's *entire* IRA balance by no later than December 30, 2008. Under the recalculation method Frank's life expectancy is reduced to zero in 2008, the calendar year following the year of his death. Cathy's life expectancy has already been reduced to zero in the calendar year 2005. According to the IRS, for any calendar year in which the last applicable life expectancy is reduced to zero, the entire IRA balance (including earnings or decreased by losses) must be distributed prior to the last day of such calendar year. Therefore, Frank's estate must receive the entire account balance between the period January 1, 2008, and December 30, 2008.

  The requirement in this example of an accelerated payout to the estate following the death of both recalculating spouses is a disadvantage of the recalculation method. The accelerated payout would not be required under the term-certain method; see Question 3.35.

QUESTION 3.35: Assume the facts in Question 3.34 except that Frank had timely selected the term-certain method of receiving his required minimum distributions from his IRA instead of the recalculation method. Also assume that Frank's IRA balance as of December 31, 2007, is $300,000. Must Frank's estate receive his entire IRA balance during the period January 1, 2008, through December 30, 2008?

ANSWER: No. Because Frank timely elected the term-certain method of receiving his required minimum distributions from his IRA, then his estate may succeed to the remaining period that is left in the initial term-certain period of 22 years. As of the calendar year 2008, the remaining term-certain period is 13 years (see answer to Question 3.30). During the calendar year 2008 the required minimum distribution that Frank's estate must receive is $23,076.92. This is determined as follows:

Frank's IRA balance as of December 31, 2007:	Divided by the remaining period left in the term-certain as of the calendar year 2008:	Required minimum distribution for the calendar year 2008:
$300,000.00	÷13 years	$23,076.92

Under the term-certain method the required minimum distribution for 2008 of $23,076.92 must be received by Frank's estate during the period January 1, 2008, through December 31, 2008.

Although the estate may receive distributions over the remaining 13-year term-certain period, the executor may choose to accelerate the distributions or assign the rights to the distributions to the heirs of the estate.

Hybrid Method

The following questions and answers discuss the use of the hybrid method of determining life expectancy when a spouse is the designated beneficiary of an IRA, qualified plan, or section 403(b) arrangement.

QUESTION 3.36: What is the hybrid method of determining life expectancy when a spouse is the IRA owner's designated beneficiary?

ANSWER: The IRA owner elects a method of calculating life expectancy that is a combination of the term-certain method and the recalculation method.

QUESTION 3.37: May the IRA owner elect the hybrid method?

ANSWER: Perhaps. The IRA institution may not permit the IRA owner to elect the hybrid method.

QUESTION 3.38: If the IRA institution permits the hybrid method, how does it work?

ANSWER: If the IRA owner is older than the spouse, then the IRA owner elects the recalculation method for himself or herself and the term-certain method for the spouse.

If the IRA owner is younger than the spouse, then the IRA owner elects the term-certain method for himself or herself and the recalculation method for the spouse.

QUESTION 3.39: What is the advantage of the hybrid method?

ANSWER: If both the IRA owner and spouse live beyond their joint term-certain life expectancy, then the hybrid method results in a longer payout period.

QUESTION 3.40: What is the disadvantage of the hybrid method?

ANSWER: If the IRA owner and spouse die prematurely and in the wrong sequence, then the hybrid method results in a shorter payout than the joint term-certain life expectancy. In addition, the hybrid method is complex and requires professional assistance.

LUMP-SUM DEATH BENEFITS PAID BY AN EMPLOYER PLAN TO SURVIVING SPOUSE

The following questions and answers discuss the tax planning options of a surviving spouse who is entitled to receive a lump-sum payment from a qualified employer retirement plan following the death of his or her spouse.

QUESTION 3.41: Ronald Kane is a participant in a qualified profit-sharing plan. His wife, Linda, is his designated beneficiary. The plan provides that a lump-sum distribution of his death benefits in the plan be paid to her within one year after his death. Ronald dies in 1999 at the age of 64. The lump sum is approximately $100,000. Linda is age 62 in 1999. What options are available to Linda?

ANSWER: Linda may receive a lump-sum distribution from the qualified plan and elect special averaging treatment or she may arrange for the plan's death benefits to be transferred directly to a brand new IRA that she establishes in her own name.

QUESTION 3.42: Why should Linda consider using special averaging treatment?

ANSWER: If Linda has substantial taxable income and is in a high tax bracket, special averaging can greatly reduce the tax liability on the lump-sum distribution. For example, if Linda is in the 31 percent tax bracket, the use of special averaging treatment will cut the income tax liability down to approximately 15 percent.

QUESTION 3.43: What type of special averaging treatment are we talking about?

ANSWER: For a plan participant born before 1936, there are two methods of calculating the income tax liability on a lump-sum distribution received before 2000 from a qualified plan. These methods are five-year special averaging treatment and 10-year special averaging treatment. Because Ronald Kane, the plan participant, was born before 1936, then Linda as his beneficiary may elect special 10-year averaging treatment using the 1986 federal tax rates, or, if more advantageous, five-year averaging using the federal income tax rates for single persons in 1999 when the distribution is received.

In taxable years beginning after December 31, 1999, five-year averaging will no longer be an option. The five-year method is repealed for years after 1999. However, 10-year averaging will still be available after 1999 for the beneficiary of a plan participant born before 1936.

If Ronald had not been born prior to 1936 and had died at or after age 59$\frac{1}{2}$, then his beneficiary could use five-year averaging in 1999 to compute the tax on the lump-sum distribution, but 10-year averaging is not allowed because he was not born before 1936. If Ronald had not been born before 1936 and had died prior to age 59$\frac{1}{2}$, then his beneficiary could not use five-year averaging or 10-year averaging.

Because five-year special averaging treatment is repealed for taxable years beginning after December 31, 1999, Linda, as Ronald's beneficiary, will not have the option of electing five-year averaging if she receives a lump-sum distribution after 1999 as a result of Ronald's death.

QUESTION 3.44: If Linda has the option to use either five-year special averaging treatment or 10-year special averaging treatment, which method should she use?

ANSWER: Because Ronald Kane was born before 1936, Linda may use 10-year averaging treatment or she may use five-year averaging. The tax liability is practically the same at the $100,000 level. The income tax on $100,000 under 10-year averaging is $14,471 and at five-year averaging is $15,000. The averaging computation is made on IRS Form 4972. For substantially larger distributions, five-year averaging may be advantageous; Linda should compute the tax under both methods on Form 4972.

SURVIVING SPOUSE'S ROLLOVER OPTION IF IRA OWNER DIES BEFORE REQUIRED BEGINNING DATE

If an IRA owner dies before the required beginning date, and his or her spouse is the designated beneficiary, then the surviving spouse has the option of rolling over the funds to one or more new IRAs in his or her name, as discussed in the following questions and answers.

QUESTION 3.45: Roger Smith is age 62 in 1999. He has an IRA with the XYZ bank that contains approximately $75,000. Jane Smith, his wife, is the designated beneficiary of Roger's IRA. Jane is age 60 in 1999. Assume that Roger dies in 2000. Jane does not need the income and would like to defer paying taxes on these funds at the present time. What options are available to Jane?

ANSWER: Jane may treat Roger's IRA as her own or she can be taxed under the designated beneficiary rules that are applicable to a surviving spouse.

QUESTION 3.46: Which approach is best for Jane?

ANSWER: As Jane does not have a current need for the funds from Roger's IRA, she should definitely treat the IRA as her own for estate and tax planning reasons. By treating the IRA as her own, Jane may name her own designated beneficiary; see Questions

3.11–3.24. If Jane were under age 59$^1/_2$ and she needed to withdraw funds from Roger's IRA, receiving distributions under the designated beneficiary rules may be advantageous; see Questions 3.54–3.77.

QUESTION 3.47: How does Jane make the IRA her own?

ANSWER: Jane may merely change the title of the IRA to her own name or request a distribution from the IRA institution and roll it over into a brand new spousal IRA rollover account in her name. A roll over to a new spousal IRA rollover must be completed within 60 days of the date that Jane receives the distribution from Roger's IRA.

QUESTION 3.48: Must Jane create only one spousal IRA rollover account?

ANSWER: No. Jane may roll over from Roger's IRA into as many spousal IRA rollover accounts as she wishes.

QUESTION 3.49: If Jane receives a distribution of Roger's IRA from the IRA institution, how does Jane create multiple spousal IRA rollover accounts?

ANSWER: Jane must complete the spousal rollover within 60 days from the date that she receives the initial distribution from her deceased spouse's IRA. Jane can deposit the funds that she receives from Roger's IRA into her own money market account. Then, within the 60-day period from the date that she receives the initial distribution from Roger's IRA, she can transfer the initial distribution amount into multiple spousal IRA rollover accounts.

QUESTION 3.50: Assume Jane receives the IRA death benefits from Roger's IRA and temporarily transfers these funds into her

money market account. **Assume she earns $500 on these funds while they are in the money market account. May she transfer these earnings into a spousal IRA rollover account?**

ANSWER: No. Only the initial amount she receives may be timely transferred into a spousal IRA rollover account. She may, of course, timely transfer the initial amount into more than one spousal IRA rollover account.

QUESTION 3.51: Are distributions from IRAs subject to the 20 percent federal withholding tax requirement?

ANSWER: No. Distributions from IRAs are not subject to the mandatory 20 percent withholding requirement that applies to distributions from a qualified employer plan.

IRA distributions are subject to withholding, generally at a 10 percent rate, but an election to avoid this withholding can be filed with the IRA trustee.

QUESTION 3.52: When should Jane consummate the spousal IRA rollover?

ANSWER: Jane should act promptly after Roger's death and create the spousal IRA rollover account(s). The reason that this prompt action is necessary is because only a surviving spouse can create a spousal IRA rollover account. If Jane should die before she creates the spousal IRA rollover, then her executor may not create the spousal IRA rollover account.

QUESTION 3.53: Why is it important that the surviving spouse act quickly in establishing the spousal IRA rollover?

ANSWER: Jane can use a spousal IRA rollover as a tool in her retirement distribution planning. Jane may create multiple spousal IRA rollovers and select a different member of the family as the designated beneficiary of each spousal IRA

rollover account. The life expectancy of the designated beneficiary as well as the income tax bracket of the designated beneficiary should be considered in order to maximize the tax benefits
of the spousal IRA rollover accounts.

SURVIVING SPOUSE'S OPTION TO RECEIVE IRA DISTRIBUTIONS AS BENEFICIARY IF OWNER DIES BEFORE REQUIRED BEGINNING DATE

If an IRA owner dies before his required beginning date and the surviving spouse elects not to treat the deceased spouse's IRA as his or
her own, then special rules for electing the life expectancy rule and
commencing distributions may be available, as discussed in the following questions and answers.

**QUESTION 3.54: Sheldon Madison was born on June 15, 1939. He
dies on August 10, 2000, at age 61. His wife, Darlene Madison,
is age 48 on January 20, 2000. Darlene is the designated beneficiary of Sheldon's IRA. What options are available to Darlene?**

ANSWER: Darlene has several options. She may treat Sheldon's IRA
as her own (see answer to Question 3.47) or she can be taxed
under the designated beneficiary rules that are applicable to a
surviving spouse.

**QUESTION 3.55: Darlene wants as much flexibility as possible in
being able to withdraw funds from Sheldon's IRA. Her primary
interest is in avoiding exposure to the 10-percent early-
distribution penalty. Should she consider receiving distributions
under the designated beneficiary rules instead of creating a
spousal IRA rollover account?**

ANSWER: Yes. Unless she qualifies for an exception to the 10-
percent penalty that was previously discussed in Chapter 1,

Darlene, who is age 48 when Sheldon dies, would be subject to the 10 percent early-distribution penalty if she created a spousal IRA rollover account and took withdrawals from the IRA before reaching age $59^{1}/_{2}$. However, if she withdraws funds from Sheldon's IRA under the designated beneficiary rules, the 10-percent penalty does not apply.

QUESTION 3.56: Assume that Darlene's date of birth is January 20, 1952. She will attain age $59^{1}/_{2}$ on July 20, 2011. May Darlene receive distributions from Sheldon's IRA as a designated beneficiary from time to time during the period between Sheldon's date of death of August 10, 2000, and July 20, 2011, without worrying about the 10-percent early-distribution penalty?

ANSWER: Yes. Because Darlene is receiving distributions from Sheldon's IRA in her capacity as a designated beneficiary, then she is not subject to the 10 percent early-distribution penalty if she receives IRA death benefits. It does not matter whether or not Darlene is under age $59^{1}/_{2}$ at the time she receives distributions from Sheldon's IRA in her capacity as a designated beneficiary.

QUESTION 3.57: Could Darlene elect to receive distributions from Sheldon's IRA for a number of years under the designated beneficiary rules in order to avoid the 10-percent early-distribution penalty and later roll over the account to an IRA in her own name?

ANSWER: Yes, Darlene may receive distributions before she attains age $59^{1}/_{2}$ from Sheldon's IRA as a designated beneficiary and avoid the 10-percent early-distribution penalty. She can at a later date create a spousal IRA rollover and treat the IRA as her own. There is no statute of limitations on the creation of a spousal IRA rollover account. However, she cannot rollover any required minimum distributions. If possible, a spousal IRA rollover should be created prior to the time that the designated beneficiary distribution rules are triggered under the five-year rule or the life-expectancy exception to the five-year rule, as discussed in Questions 3.58–3.63.

Alternatively, Darlene may decide to immediately use a split approach. For example, if Sheldon's IRA balance at the date of his death was $150,000, and Darlene wanted to withdraw $100,000 prior to the time she attained age 59^1/$_2$, Darlene could create a spousal IRA rollover for approximately $50,000 within a few months after Sheldon's death. This spousal IRA rollover account would not be subject to the designated beneficiary distribution rules that are applicable to a surviving spouse. The remaining $100,000 in Sheldon's IRA plus the earnings thereon would be subject to the designated beneficiary rules that are applicable to a surviving spouse. Darlene would therefore avoid the 10 percent early-distribution penalty on the distributions she receives prior to age 59^1/$_2$ under the designated beneficiary rules on the amount that she does not roll over.

QUESTION 3.58: Under the distribution rules for designated beneficiaries, what method would Darlene use to withdraw funds from Sheldon's IRA?

ANSWER: It depends on whether the IRA plan document requires the use of the so-called five-year rule. Under the five-year rule, the entire balance of a deceased IRA owner's account balance must be paid to the designated beneficiary by no later than December 31 of the fifth year following the year of the IRA owner's death.

However, under an exception to the five-year rule, the IRA plan document may allow the designated beneficiary to elect to receive required minimum distributions over his or her life expectancy. The following questions and answers illustrate how the life-expectancy method rules apply to a surviving spouse.

QUESTION 3.59: If an IRA owner dies before the required beginning date, and his or her surviving spouse is the designated

beneficiary of the IRA, may the IRA plan document provide that the life-expectancy exception to the five-year rule is automatic?

ANSWER: Yes. The IRA plan document may provide that the life-expectancy exception to the five-year rule is automatic if the IRA owner dies before the required beginning date, leaving a surviving spouse as his or her designated beneficiary.

QUESTION 3.60: If the IRA plan document is silent on whether or not the five-year rule is applicable to a surviving spouse who is the designated beneficiary, does the five-year rule apply?

ANSWER: No. According to the IRS, if the IRA plan document is silent, the life-expectancy exception to the five-year rule is automatic where the designated beneficiary is the surviving spouse.

QUESTION 3.61: Assume that Darlene does not intend to treat Sheldon's IRA as her own. Darlene would like to use the designated beneficiary rules that are applicable to a surviving spouse. If the life-expectancy exception to the five-year rule applies automatically to a surviving spouse under the IRA plan document, when must Darlene commence distributions from Sheldon's IRA under the designated beneficiary rules?

ANSWER: When an IRA owner dies before the required beginning date, a special distribution commencement date applies to a surviving spouse under the life-expectancy exception to the five-year rule. Distributions to Darlene must commence on or before the later of (1) December 31 of the year Sheldon would have reached age $70^1/_2$ had he lived or (2) December 31 of the year following the year of Sheldon's death.

Sheldon died in 2000. If Sheldon had lived he would have attained age $70^1/_2$ on December 15, 2009 (see Question 3.54). Darlene must therefore commence distributions from Sheldon's IRA as a designated beneficiary by no later than December 31, 2009, as this date is later than December 31, 2001 (December 31 of the year after 2000, the year of Sheldon's death).

QUESTION 3.62: Assume that Sheldon's IRA plan document permits Darlene to elect whether the five-year rule or the life-expectancy exception to the five-year rule is applicable. Assume that Darlene does not want to use the five-year rule. When must Darlene make the election out of the five-year rule so she can use the life-expectancy exception?

ANSWER: Special election rules apply to the surviving spouse. These rules are tied to the date of death of the IRA owner. Because Sheldon died on August 10, 2000, at age 61, then distributions to Darlene must commence by December 31, 2009; see the answer to Question 3.61. Darlene must elect out of the five-year rule by no later than the earlier of the December 31, 2009, commencement deadline, or December 31, 2005, the calendar year containing the fifth anniversary of Sheldon's death. The IRS allows Darlene to make the election out of the five-year rule by no later than the earlier date, which is December 31, 2005.

Therefore, in this case, Darlene's deadlines for electing the life-expectancy rule, and for actually commencing distributions under that rule, are not the same. The election must be made by December 31, 2005, but distributions do not have to start until December 31, 2009.

Had Darlene been a nonspouse designated beneficiary, the election out of the five-year rule would have to be made no later than December 31 of the calendar year following the year of the IRA owner's death. By that same December 31 date, a nonspouse designated beneficiary must receive the first required minimum distribution under the life-expectancy exception. See Chapter 8.

QUESTION 3.63: Assume that the terms of Sheldon's IRA plan document require Darlene to make an election out of the five-year rule in order to apply the life-expectancy exception. How does Darlene make the election out of the five-year rule?

ANSWER: Darlene should file a written election with the IRA institution that in essence states that she wishes to elect out of the five-year rule. The written election should be sent by certified mail, return receipt requested to the IRA institution. The written election should be made promptly after Sheldon's death on August 10, 2000. Darlene should not rely upon the extended dates for electing out of the five-year method as described in Question 3.62, because Darlene may forget to do it or be unable to make the election because of a physical or mental disability.

QUESTION 3.64: Assume that Darlene receives distributions from Sheldon's IRA in her capacity as a designated beneficiary and that the life-expectancy exception to the five-year rule applies. What life-expectancy table must Darlene use in determining her required minimum distributions from Sheldon's IRA?

ANSWER: Darlene must use the IRS single life-expectancy table under Table V of 1.72-9 of the Income Tax Regulations. This table, called Table I in IRS Publication 590, is shown in Appendix A of this book.

QUESTION 3.65: For purposes of figuring her first required minimum distribution from Sheldon's IRA, what is Darlene's life expectancy under the IRS single life-expectancy table?

ANSWER: Darlene must receive her first required minimum distribution from Sheldon's IRA by the end of 2009 (Question 3.61). If Darlene waits until 2009 to receive her first required minimum distribution, her age for purposes of determining her life expectancy is 57, her age on her birthday in 2009. As shown in Appendix A, Darlene has a single life expectancy at age 57 of 26.8 years. Darlene would use a single life expectancy of 26.8 years in calculating her required minimum distribution from Sheldon's IRA for 2009. She can, of course, receive distributions prior to the year 2009.

QUESTION 3.66: Assume that Sheldon's IRA balance as of December 31, 2008 is $200,000. What is the amount of Darlene's required minimum distribution in her capacity as a designated beneficiary for the calendar year 2009?

ANSWER: The amount of Darlene's required minimum distribution in her capacity as a designated beneficiary for the calendar year 2009 is $7,462.69. This is determined as follows:

Sheldon's IRA balance as of December 31, 2008:	Divided by the single life expectancy of Darlene for the calendar year 2009 which is 26.8 (Question 3.65):	Required minimum distribution for the calendar year 2009:
$ 200,000.00	÷$ 26.8	$7,462.69

QUESTION 3.67: Assume that Darlene withdrew $3,462.69 from Sheldon's IRA during the calendar year 2009 instead of $7,462.69. Can the IRS impose a penalty against Darlene for receiving less than the required amount?

ANSWER: Yes. Darlene's required minimum distribution for the calendar year 2009 is $7,462.69. Because she only received $3,462.69, she is subject to a 50-percent penalty on the shortfall of $4,000. The penalty for the failure to receive a required minimum distribution is 50 percent of the shortfall or $2,000 in Darlene's case.

QUESTION 3.68: May the IRS waive the $2,000 penalty discussed in Question 3.67?

ANSWER: Yes. The IRS may waive the 50 percent penalty if Darlene can prove to the IRS that she acted in a reasonable manner. In addition, as soon as she discovers the shortfall she must remedy the situation. If Darlene discovers the error in the calendar year 2010, she must immediately take an additional $4,000 distribution in the calendar year 2010 in addition to her required minimum distribution for the calendar year 2010.

QUESTION 3.69: Assume that Darlene withdraws $27,462.69 from Sheldon's IRA during the calendar year 2009 instead of the required minimum distribution of $7,462.69. Will Darlene receive a credit for the additional $20,000 distribution that she received in the calendar year 2009 against her required minimum distribution for the calendar year 2010?

ANSWER: No. Darlene will not receive a credit of $20,000 against her required minimum distribution for the calendar year 2010. Although Darlene received substantially more than required in 2009, she must figure her required minimum distribution for 2010 under the regular rules, following the steps in Question 3.66, but using the account balance at the end of 2009 and a revised life expectancy determined in the year 2010. The revised life expectancy depends on whether the term-certain election is made or whether the recalculation method is applicable as discussed in Questions 3.70–3.74.

QUESTION 3.70: May Darlene use the recalculation method of determining her life expectancy when figuring her minimum required distributions from Sheldon's IRA for the calendar year 2010 and subsequent years?

ANSWER: Yes. The recalculation method may be used by a surviving spouse who is receiving distributions under the designated beneficiary rules.

QUESTION 3.71: May Darlene elect the term-certain method instead of the recalculation method to figure her minimum required distributions from Sheldon's IRA?

ANSWER: Perhaps. Most IRA plan documents permit the surviving spouse to elect the term-certain method.

QUESTION 3.72: Assume that the IRA plan document permits Darlene to elect the term-certain method. When must Darlene elect the term-certain method?

ANSWER: Darlene must elect the term-certain method by no later than the time of her first required minimum distribution. Because Darlene must receive her first required minimum distribution by the end of 2009 (see answer to Question 3.61), she must also elect the term-certain method with the IRA institution by no later than December 31, 2009.

QUESTION 3.73: How does Darlene elect the term-certain option?

ANSWER: Darlene should send the IRA institution a written term-certain election.

　　The written election should be sent to the IRA institution by registered mail, return receipt requested. The general approach that should be used in making an election was previously discussed in Chapter 2.

QUESTION 3.74: Assume that Darlene dies in the calendar year 2017. Would you please compare the life-expectancy period that Darlene would use under the term-certain method with the life expectancy that would be used if she recalculated life expectancy for the calendar years 2009 through 2017?

ANSWER: The following schedule compares the two life-expectancy methods for the calendar years 2009 through 2017.

DARLENE'S AGE	CALENDAR YEAR	TERM-CERTAIN LIFE EXPECTANCY	RECALCULATION METHOD LIFE EXPECTANCY
57	2009	26.8	26.8
58	2010	25.8	25.9
59	2011	24.8	25.0
60	2012	23.8	24.2
61	2013	22.8	23.3

62	2014	21.8	22.5
63	2015	20.8	21.6
64	2016	19.8	20.8
65	2017	18.8	20.0

As you can see, life expectancy is reduced more slowly under the recalculation method. As a result, slightly smaller required minimum distributions are required using the recalculation method.

QUESTION 3.75: If Darlene uses the recalculation method and she dies in the year 2017 after receiving her required minimum distribution for that year, over what period of time may Darlene's estate receive the balance in Sheldon's IRA?

ANSWER: If the recalculation method is applicable, then Darlene's life expectancy is reduced to zero as of the calendar year 2018, the year following the year of her death. Darlene's estate must receive Sheldon's entire IRA balance during the period January 1, 2018, and December 30, 2018.

QUESTION 3.76: Assume that the term-certain method is applicable and Darlene dies in the year 2017. Over what period may Darlene's estate receive the balance of Sheldon's IRA?

ANSWER: If the term-certain method is applicable, then Darlene's estate may take advantage of the remaining period that is left in the initial 26.8-year term-certain period. As of the calendar year 2018 there are 17.8 years left in the initial term-certain period of 26.8 years. Darlene's estate or the beneficiaries of her estate may take advantage of the 17.8-year remaining term-certain period.

QUESTION 3.77: Assume that Sheldon had been born on June 15, 1933, instead of June 15, 1939 (Question 3.54), so that at his death on August 10, 2000, he is age 67. Based on these facts, when must Darlene make the election out of the five-year rule in order to receive distributions under the life-expectancy exception?

ANSWER: Sheldon would have attained age 70^1/2 on December 15, 2003, had he lived. Darlene must commence required minimum distributions under the exception to the five-year rule (Question 3.61) by no later than December 31, 2003. This is because December 31, 2003, the end of the year in which Sheldon would have reached age 70^1/2 had he lived is later than December 31, 2001, the end of the year following 2000, Sheldon's year of death.

Darlene must elect out of the five-year rule by the earlier of the commencement date, December 31, 2003, or December 31, 2005, the end of the calendar year that contains the fifth anniversary of Sheldon's death. Because December 31, 2003, is the earlier date, that is the deadline for Darlene's election out of the five-year method. In addition, the term-certain election must be made by the commencement date, December 31, 2003.

Therefore, in this case, Darlene's deadlines for electing the life-expectancy rule, and for actually commencing distributions are the same, December 31, 2003. Contrast this with the answer to Question 3.62, in which Darlene's deadline for electing out of the five-year rule is December 31, 2005, but the deadline for commencing her required minimum distributions is December 31, 2009.

CHAPTER FOUR

SELECTING A CHILD, GRANDCHILD, OR OTHER YOUNG PERSON AS YOUR DESIGNATED BENEFICIARY

As discussed in previous chapters, the timely selection of a designated beneficiary reduces the minimum annual distributions you are required to receive from your traditional IRA or from your employer's qualified plan after you have reached your required beginning date. By taking into account the beneficiary's life expectancy as well as your own, you are able to "spread out" the distribution period over a longer period. For a person to be treated as your designated beneficiary, that person generally must be selected by no later than your required beginning date, which for traditional IRAs is April 1 of the year following the year in which you reach age $70^{1}/_{2}$. For qualified plans, the date is generally April 1 of the year following the year in which you retire if later; see Question 2.4. See Question 3.18 for a special beneficiary designation rule in the case of a spousal rollover.

However, the tax law imposes a substantial limitation on your ability to extend the payment period by naming a younger beneficiary. If you name your child or grandchild as your designated beneficiary, you cannot use his or her actual age in determining your joint life expectancy. You must treat the beneficiary as being 10 years younger than you are, even if he or she is in fact much younger. This rule does not apply to a spouse.

The same rule also applies to any other designated beneficiary (other than your spouse) who is more than 10 years younger than you. Thus, if you select your teenage niece or cousin as your designated beneficiary, you must disregard his or her actual age and treat him or her as 10 years younger than you when determining your required minimum distributions.

Although you cannot avoid this 10-year differential rule when computing the required minimum distributions during your lifetime, the rule does not apply to your designated beneficiary after your death. By planning ahead, as discussed in this chapter, you can simplify the required minimum distribution calculations for your designated beneficiary.

If you are married, generally you must obtain the consent of your spouse to designate any other person as the designated beneficiary of your qualified plan account. Spousal consent currently is not required under federal law if an IRA is involved.

If Your Beneficiary Is More Than 10 Years Younger Than You

The following questions and answers will explain how to figure your required minimum distributions if as of your required beginning date your designated beneficiary is not your spouse and is more than 10 years younger than you. These special rules also apply where a surviving spouse sets up a spousal IRA rollover account and selects a nonspouse beneficiary who is more than 10 years younger than he or she; see Question 3.16.

QUESTION 4.1: Roberta Smart has an IRA at the EFG Bank. She will be age 70 on June 1, 1999, and age 70¹/₂ on December 1, 1999. Her son, Jason Smart, the designated beneficiary of her IRA, will be age 40 on August 1, 1999. What is the first year for which Roberta is required to receive a required minimum distribution from her IRA?

ANSWER: The first year for which Roberta must receive a required minimum distribution from her IRA is called the "first distribution calendar year." For Roberta, this is the calendar year 1999—the year in which she attains age 70^1/2.

QUESTION 4.2: Must Roberta receive a required minimum distribution from her IRA in the calendar year 1999?

ANSWER: No. Although the first required minimum distribution is for the year 1999, Roberta has until her required beginning date to receive it.

QUESTION 4.3: What is Roberta's required beginning date?

ANSWER: Roberta's required beginning date is April 1, 2000. The required beginning date for Roberta is April 1 of the calendar year following the calendar year in which she attains age 70^1/2. Roberta attains age 70^1/2 in the calendar year 1999. Her required beginning date is therefore April 1, 2000. This is the deadline for receiving the first required minimum distribution.

Roberta may receive the distribution for her first distribution calendar year at any time during the period commencing January 1, 1999, and ending April 1, 2000. Her projected tax position for each year should dictate when she should receive this distribution. The distribution will be taxable to Roberta in whichever year she receives it.

QUESTION 4.4: When must Roberta receive her required minimum distribution for her second distribution calendar year 2000?

ANSWER: Roberta must receive the required minimum distribution for the calendar year 2000 during the period January 1, 2000, to December 31, 2000.

If Roberta delayed receipt of the first required minimum distribution for 1999 until April 1, 2000 (April 1, 2000, is the required beginning date), she will have to report that distribution as well as the required minimum distribution for 2000 in her 2000 income tax return.

EFFECT OF THE MINIMUM DISTRIBUTION INCIDENTAL BENEFIT REQUIREMENT (MDIB): QUESTIONS 4.5–4.16

QUESTION 4.5: Assume that by her required beginning date Roberta selected her son, Jason, as the designated beneficiary of her IRA. Roberta would like to receive her required minimum distribution for her first distribution calendar year 1999 during 1999. Roberta's IRA balance as of December 31, 1998, is $100,000. Could you please determine Roberta's required minimum distribution for her first distribution calendar year 1999?

ANSWER: Roberta's required minimum distribution for 1999 is $3,816.79. This is determined as follows:

Roberta's IRA balance as of December 31, 1998 (account balance as of the end of the preceding year):	Divided by the applicable divisor for the calendar year 1999 which is 26.2 years:	Required minimum distribution for the calendar year 1999:
$100,000	÷26.2 years	$3,816.79

To avoid an IRS penalty, Roberta must receive at least $3,816.79 from her IRA by her required beginning date of April 1, 2000. She may, of course, withdraw more than that amount.

QUESTION 4.6: The joint life expectancy of Roberta and Jason is greater than 26.2 years. Why did you divide the account balance by only 26.2 years in the answer to question 4.5?

ANSWER: The IRS has a special rule that applies in calculating the IRA owner's lifetime required minimum distributions if the nonspouse designated beneficiary is more than 10 years younger than the owner. Under this special rule, the younger designated beneficiary is tentatively treated as being exactly 10 years younger than the owner, for each year, regardless of the beneficiary's actual age.

The special 10-year differential rule is called the Minimum Distribution Incidental Benefit Requirement (MDIB).

A special IRS "applicable divisor table" is used to compute the required minimum distributions that Roberta must receive under the MDIB requirement. Roberta must determine her attained age as of her birthday in the calendar year that she is age 70$^1/_2$. Roberta is age 70 on June 1, 1999, and attains age 70$^1/_2$ on December 1, 1999. Roberta therefore is age 70 in her first distribution calendar year 1999. Jason is age 40 in the calendar year 1999.

The IRS table assumes that Jason is 10 years younger than Roberta in order to determine Roberta's required minimum distributions. According to the IRS table, when Roberta is age 70, Jason is tentatively deemed to be age 60. The applicable divisor table is shown in Appendix A as "Table for Determining Applicable Divisor for MDIB."

If you wish to check the factor of 26.2, look up the joint life-expectancy table found in Table II of IRS Publication 590, which is reproduced in Appendix A of this book. A joint life expectancy of a 70-year-old and a 60-year-old is 26.2 years. The joint life expectancy can also be found in Table VI of 1.72-9 of the Income Tax Regulations.

QUESTION 4.7: Does this special rule regarding the applicable divisor table also apply to required minimum distributions from

qualified company plans and other retirement savings arrangements such as 403(b) annuity contracts and self-employed Keogh or SEP accounts?

ANSWER: Yes. This special rule applies to all retirement savings arrangements that are subject to the required minimum distribution rules, as discussed in the answer to Question 2.1.

QUESTION 4.8: Scott Matthews, a married IRA owner, selects his spouse Barbara as his designated beneficiary. Assume that Barbara is 15 years younger than Scott. Must the IRA owner use the applicable divisor table in determining his required minimum distributions during his lifetime?

ANSWER: No. The applicable divisor table is not used if the IRA owner timely selects his spouse as his designated beneficiary, even if the spousal beneficiary is more than 10 years younger than the IRA owner. The joint life expectancy of both the IRA owner and his spouse under the IRS tables is used in determining the IRA owner's required minimum distributions. See Chapter 3.

QUESTION 4.9: Assume that Scott's spouse Barbara is his designated beneficiary and that she is five years younger than Scott. May Scott use the applicable divisor table in determining his required minimum distributions during his lifetime?

ANSWER: No. The applicable divisor table can never be used if the IRA owner timely selects his spouse as his designated beneficiary. If the spouse is only five years younger than the IRA owner, she cannot be treated as if she is 10 years younger than the IRA owner by improperly using the applicable divisor table. As discussed in Chapter 3, the joint life expectancy of the IRA owner and his spouse under the IRS tables is used in determining the IRA owner's required minimum distributions whenever the spouse is the designated beneficiary.

QUESTION 4.10: Based on the facts of Question 4.5, would you please indicate the applicable divisor that Roberta must use in determining her required minimum distributions for each distribution calendar year from 1999 through 2009, assuming Jason was timely selected as her designated beneficiary?

ANSWER: The following schedule lists the applicable divisor that Roberta must use in determining her required minimum distributions for each distribution calendar year.

ROBERTA'S AGE	CALENDAR YEAR	DISTRIBUTION YEAR	APPLICABLE DIVISOR
70	1999	1	26.2
71	2000	2	25.3
72	2001	3	24.4
73	2002	4	23.5
74	2003	5	22.7
75	2004	6	21.8
76	2005	7	20.9
77	2006	8	20.1
78	2007	9	19.2
79	2008	10	18.4
80	2009	11	17.6

A complete copy of the applicable divisor table is found in IRS Publication 590, Appendix E. The table is reproduced in Appendix A of this book and is called "Table for Determining Applicable Divisor for MDIB."

QUESTION 4.11: Would you please explain why the factor of 25.3 years is used in order to determine Roberta's required minimum distribution for her second distribution calendar year—2000?

ANSWER: The IRS applicable divisor table must be used because the designated beneficiary of Roberta's IRA is Jason, and Jason is more than 10 years younger than Roberta. In the year 2000 Roberta is age 71 and Jason is tentatively deemed to be age 61. The joint life expectancy for a 71-year-old and 61-year-old under the IRS tables is 25.3 years. The applicable divisor table reflects this by providing an applicable divisor of 25.3 for a 71-year-old account owner.

QUESTION 4.12: Assume that Roberta did not select Jason as her designated beneficiary until April 30, 2000. Also assume that Roberta did not timely select any other designated beneficiary prior to that date. Would the MDIB requirement be applicable to Roberta?

ANSWER: No. The MDIB requirement is not applicable unless a person who is more than 10 years younger than the account owner and is not a spouse is selected as Roberta's designated beneficiary by no later than Roberta's required beginning date of April 1, 2000. If a designated beneficiary has not been selected by the required beginning date, then Roberta must figure her required minimum distributions using only her own life expectancy, as illustrated in the next question.

QUESTION 4.13: Assume that Roberta did not select a designated beneficiary of her IRA as of her required beginning date of April 1, 2000. How much must Roberta receive as a required minimum distribution for her first distribution calendar year 1999?

ANSWER: Roberta must use a single life expectancy from Table V of section 1.72-9 of the Income Tax Regulations. This table, called Table I in IRS Publication 590, is reproduced in Appendix A of this book. Roberta's life expectancy for her first distribution year of 1999 is based upon her attained age as of her birthday in the year she attains age 70^1/$_2$. In 1999, when she reached age 70^1/$_2$, Roberta had her 70th birthday. Looking up the life expectancy for a 70-year-old in the IRS table shows a single life expectancy of 16 years. The required minimum distribution for her first distribution calendar year 1999 is $6,250. This amount is determined as follows:

Roberta's IRA balance as of December 31, 1998 (account balance as of the end of the preceding year)	Divided by the single life expectancy of Roberta for the calendar year 1999 which is 16 years:	Required minimum distribution for the calendar year 1999:
$100,000	÷16 years	$6,250.00

QUESTION 4.14: Assume that the MDIB requirement was not part of the IRS rules. What is the true joint life expectancy of Roberta and Jason in the calendar year 1999?

ANSWER: The joint life expectancy of a 70-year-old and a 40-year-old is 42.9 years, according to the IRS joint life-expectancy tables; see Table II from IRS Publication 590, which is reproduced in Appendix A of the book.

QUESTION 4.15: If Roberta were not subject to the 10-year differential MDIB rule, she could have elected to calculate her required minimum distributions for years after the first distribution year under the term-certain method. How does the life-expectancy period she must use under the MDIB requirement differ from the amount allowed by the term-certain method?

ANSWER: The following schedule compares the term-certain method against the applicable divisor that must be used under the MDIB rule for Roberta's first six distribution years. Roberta must use the lesser of the applicable divisor or the term-certain period during her lifetime.

For example, on their birthdays in 1999—the year Roberta attains age 70^1/$_2$—Roberta and Jason are age 70 and 40, respectively. For the first distribution year 1999, Roberta must use the applicable divisor that assumes Jason is 10 years younger than she. Thus, the applicable divisor of 26.2 years is based on the joint expectancy of a 70-year-old and 60-year-old. If the MDIB rule did not apply and the term-certain method was elected, the joint life expectancy of 42.9 years based upon their actual ages of 70 and 40 would be used for 1999 and the 42.9 joint expectancy would be decreased by one for each subsequent year.

MDIB PERIOD

ROBERTA'S AGE	CALENDAR YEAR	DISTRI-BUTION YEAR	APPLICABLE DIVISOR	USED UNDER TERM-CERTAIN METHOD	USED IN ROBERTA'S LIFETIME
70	1999	1	26.2	42.9	26.2
71	2000	2	25.3	41.9	25.3
72	2001	3	24.4	40.9	24.4
73	2002	4	23.5	39.9	23.5
74	2003	5	22.7	38.9	22.7
75	2004	6	21.8	37.9	21.8

QUESTION 4.16: The applicable divisor table under the MDIB requirement decreases by less than one for each distribution calendar year. Is it proper to refer to the applicable divisor as a recalculation method?

ANSWER: No. Although the applicable divisor table operates like the recalculation method discussed in Chapter 3, it is not a recalculation method under the IRS rules. The applicable divisor table is not a method but merely a special table that is based upon a 10-year age spread between the IRA owner and a nonspouse designated beneficiary.

DISTRIBUTIONS TO NONSPOUSE BENEFICIARY AFTER IRA OWNER'S REQUIRED BEGINNING DATE

The following questions and answers will guide you through the special distribution rules that apply to a nonspouse designated beneficiary when an IRA owner who is more than 10 years older dies on or after the required beginning date. Distributions to the beneficiary are based on either a term-certain method or hybrid method. See Chapter 8 for the distribution rules that apply to nonspouse beneficiaries where the IRA owner dies before the required beginning date.

QUESTION 4.17: Does the MDIB requirement apply after the death of the IRA owner?

ANSWER: No. According to the IRS proposed regulations and IRS Publication 590, the MDIB requirement (Question 4.6) does not apply in years after the death of the IRA owner.

QUESTION 4.18: Assume that Roberta selected her son Jason as her designated beneficiary and also elected the term-certain method by her required beginning date. Also assume that Roberta dies in the calendar year 2004 after receiving her required minimum distribution for the distribution calendar year 2004. If Jason survives Roberta, when will he have to start receiving his required minimum distributions from Roberta's IRA?

ANSWER: Jason must start to receive his required minimum distributions from Roberta's IRA during the calendar year following the year of Roberta's death. The calendar year following the year of Roberta's death is the calendar year 2005.

QUESTION 4.19: What is the true joint life expectancy of Roberta and Jason in the year Roberta attained age 70$^1/_2$?

ANSWER: Roberta attained age 70$^1/_2$ in 1999. In that year she is age 70 and Jason is age 40. The joint life expectancy of a 70-year-old and 40-year-old under the IRS tables is 42.9 years. See the table in Appendix A.

QUESTION 4.20: Over what period of time may Jason receive his required minimum distributions from Roberta's IRA?

ANSWER: Jason must commence distributions from Roberta's IRA in the calendar year 2005, the year after the year of Roberta's death. Jason may use a life-expectancy period of 36.9 years in determining his required minimum distributions.

QUESTION 4.21: How did you determine the 36.9-year life-expectancy period that Jason may use after Roberta's death?

ANSWER: Roberta timely selected Jason as her designated beneficiary and timely elected the term-certain method. The term-certain period as of Roberta's required beginning date is 42.9 years (see Question 4.19). Because Roberta lived for six distribution calendar years, the remaining period that is left in the 42.9-year period is 36.9 years. That period of time is available for Jason. This is true although Roberta, while she was alive, could not use the 42.9-year period because of the MDIB rule discussed earlier in this chapter.

QUESTION 4.22: How and when should Roberta elect the term-certain method?

ANSWER: Roberta should elect in writing with the IRA institution by certified mail, return receipt requested, that she wishes to use the term-certain method and not the recalculation method. She should make the election by her required beginning date of April

1, 2000. See sample term-certain language in the answer to Question 4.26.

QUESTION 4.23: Could Roberta use the recalculation method of figuring life expectancy instead of the term-certain method?

ANSWER: Not if Jason is her designated beneficiary. The MDIB rule must be used during Roberta's lifetime.

QUESTION 4.24: Can the recalculation method ever be used for Jason?

ANSWER: No. The recalculation method may never be used for a nonspouse designated beneficiary. During Roberta's lifetime, the MDIB rule must be used to determine Roberta's required minimum distributions. If she did not elect the term-certain method, then after her death, Jason's single life expectancy as of Roberta's first distribution calendar year must be reduced by one each year under the hybrid method discussed in question 4.36.

QUESTION 4.25: If Roberta does not timely elect the term-certain method, what happens?

ANSWER: Many IRA plan documents automatically default into the recalculation method where the term-certain method is not elected by the required beginning date. However, this is academic because the MDIB rule must be used during Roberta's lifetime. After Roberta's death, Jason must use the hybrid method to figure his single life expectancy (see Questions 4.36–4.39) if Roberta did not timely elect the term-certain method.

QUESTION 4.26: Roberta is concerned that after her death Jason may be confused about the IRA distribution period that he may use. Roberta would like to make a specific term-certain election

in order to clarify the IRA distribution period for Jason. Can you suggest any language that Roberta could use in her term-certain election?

ANSWER: Roberta should file a term-certain election with the IRA institution by certified mail, return receipt requested. The election may state something like this:

> I, Roberta Smart, have timely designated my son, Jason Smart, as my designated beneficiary. I hereby elect that my required minimum distributions to me be based upon a term-certain period of 42.9 years based upon my life expectancy and my designated beneficiary's life expectancy determined in the calendar year 1999. The calendar year 1999 is the calendar year in which I attained age $70^1/_2$. However, I recognize that during my lifetime the required minimum distributions to me shall be based upon the Minimum Distribution Incidental Benefit Requirement and this requires the use of a special applicable divisor table in order to determine my required minimum distributions. However, in the calendar year following my death and for all calendar years thereafter my son, Jason, may use the original 42.9-year term-certain period reduced by one for each distribution calendar year that I was alive in order to determine the required minimum distributions that he must receive from this IRA after my death. The year of my death shall count as a full year in this computation. In addition, after my death Jason shall be permitted to accelerate distributions from time to time.

Caution: The above election is illustrative only. It is based upon the term-certain rules in effect during 1999. It should be reviewed by a professional advisor and modified to the extent necessary. It must be signed and dated by Roberta Smart, of course.

A more detailed sample term-certain election is shown in Appendix B.

QUESTION 4.27: Why should Roberta or any other IRA owner pre-pare such a detailed election as described in Question 4.26?

ANSWER: If the election is detailed, then it provides a guidepost for the IRA institution and Jason. Upon Roberta's death in the cal-endar year 2004, Jason automatically knows that he may receive his required minimum distributions from Roberta's IRA over a period that does not exceed 36.9 years. The 42.9-year period is reduced by six years.

QUESTION 4.28: If Jason survives Roberta and then dies, who receives the remaining payments from Roberta's IRA?

ANSWER: Generally, Jason's estate. However, prior to his death, Jason can select a successor beneficiary for the remainder of the payments with the consent of the IRA institution; see Question 8.43.

QUESTION 4.29: What options are available to Jason's estate?

ANSWER: Distributions should be paid to the estate over the remaining term-certain period left unused at Jason's death. Jason's executor may accelerate in whole or in part the remain-ing required minimum distributions of Roberta's IRA. In addi-tion, Jason's executor may assign the rights to the remaining required minimum distributions to Jason's heirs. Jason's heirs may then receive the remaining required minimum distributions from Roberta's IRA or accelerate the distributions from Roberta's IRA from time to time.

QUESTION 4.30: Assume that Roberta does not wish to make a detailed election with the IRA institution, but still wants to use the term-certain method so that Jason may use it in the years after her death. What should Roberta do?

ANSWER: She may write to the IRA institution and state that she wishes to use the term-certain method. This should automatically trigger the same results that were previously described in Questions 4.26 through 4.29. The only difference is that Jason and the IRA institution do not have a specific road map as to the integration of the Minimum Distribution Incidental Benefit Requirement (MDIB) and the required minimum distribution rules.

QUESTION 4.31: Assume that Roberta timely made the specific term-certain election and died during the calendar year 2004 after receiving her required minimum distribution from her IRA for the calendar year 2004. Assume that the balance in Roberta's IRA as of December 31, 2004, is $115,000. Would you please calculate Jason's required minimum distribution for the calendar year 2005?

ANSWER: Jason must commence his required minimum distributions from Roberta's IRA in the calendar year 2005. In the calendar year following Roberta's death and all years thereafter, Jason may use the balance that is left in the original term-certain period of 42.9 years after subtracting the six distribution calendar years that have elapsed for the calendar year 1999 through 2004. The year of death, 2004, is counted as an elapsed year. Therefore Jason has a remaining life-expectancy period of 36.9 years (42.9 minus 6 elapsed years) that he may use in determining his required minimum distributions from Roberta's IRA. Jason's required minimum distribution for the calendar year 2005 is $3,116.53.

This is determined as follows:

Roberta's IRA balance as of December 31, 2004:	Divided by the life expectancy available to Jason for the calendar year 2005 which is 36.9 years:	Jason's required minimum distribution for the calendar year 2005:
$115,000.00	÷36.9 years	$3,116.53

QUESTION 4.32: Assume the facts in Question 4.31. Also assume that Roberta's IRA balance as of December 31, 2005, is $118,000. Would you please calculate Jason's required minimum distribution for the calendar year 2006 under the term-certain method?

ANSWER: Jason's required minimum distribution for the calendar year 2006 under the term-certain method is $3,286.91. This is determined as follows:

Roberta's IRA balance as of December 31, 2005:	Divided by the remaining life expectancy available to Jason under the term-certain method for the calendar year 2006 which is 35.9 years:	Required minimum distribution for the calendar year 2006:
$118,000.00	÷35.9 years	$3,286.91

QUESTION 4.33: Assume the facts in Question 4.31. Would you please indicate the life expectancy under the term-certain method that Jason may use in determining his required minimum distributions from Roberta's IRA for the calendar years 2005 through 2009?

ANSWER: The following schedule indicates the life expectancy that Jason may use under the term-certain method in determining his required minimum distributions for the calendar years 2005 through 2009.

JASON'S AGE	CALENDAR YEAR	TERM-CERTAIN JOINT LIFE EXPECTANCY
46	2005	36.9
47	2006	35.9
48	2007	34.9
49	2008	33.9
50	2009	32.9

As you can see, the life expectancy that can be used by Jason drops by one for each calendar year.

QUESTION 4.34: Assume that Roberta timely selects Jason as the designated beneficiary of her IRA. Under the terms of the IRA plan, the default option is the recalculation method if the term-certain method is not elected. In determining Roberta's required minimum distributions during her lifetime, does it make a difference to her whether or not she timely elected the term-certain method or defaulted into the recalculation method?

ANSWER: No, it does not affect the amount of the required minimum distributions she must receive. Because Jason is more than 10 years younger than Roberta, the Minimum Distribution Incidental Benefit Requirement is applicable during Roberta's lifetime. Roberta must therefore use the applicable divisor table in calculating her required minimum distributions during her lifetime. The applicable divisor is based upon a 10-year age difference between Roberta and Jason for each year that Roberta is alive. The IRS requires that Roberta's required minimum distribution from her IRA be determined by dividing her IRA balance as of the appropriate December 31 date by the lesser of (1) the applicable divisor or (2) the applicable life expectancy determined under the term-certain method or the hybrid method. Naturally, the applicable divisor table that assumes a 10-year age differential is used while Roberta is alive. The applicable life expectancy would never be used while Roberta is alive because the actual age difference between Roberta and Jason is 30 years. The life-expectancy method, whether it be term-certain or the hybrid method, cannot be used because it would always result in a greater period than that determined under the applicable divisor table.

QUESTION 4.35: Assume that Roberta timely selects Jason as the designated beneficiary of her IRA and timely elects the term-certain method; she dies during the calendar year 2004 before receiving her required minimum distribution for the calendar year 2004. What should Jason do in order to avoid any possible 50-percent penalty asserted by the IRS?

ANSWER: Jason should determine the amount of the required minimum distribution that Roberta should have received using the MDIB rule (Question 4.10) for the calendar year 2004. Jason should then receive the amount calculated as Roberta's required minimum distribution for the calendar year 2004 as soon as possible. The IRS will not assert any penalty if Jason acts promptly. In addition, Jason must commence his required minimum distributions from Roberta's IRA in the calendar year 2005 and in all calendar years thereafter.

HYBRID METHOD FOR BENEFICIARY IF TERM-CERTAIN NOT TIMELY ELECTED: QUESTIONS 4.36–4.39

QUESTION 4.36: If Roberta failed to make a term-certain election and defaulted into the recalculation method with respect to her own life expectancy, how does this affect the minimum distributions that Jason must receive from her IRA in calendar years after her death?

ANSWER: Upon Roberta's death, Jason must use the hybrid method to determine his single life expectancy. This method uses the IRS single life-expectancy table for Jason as of the calendar year that Roberta attained age 70^1/$_2$ and reduces that life expectancy by one for each distribution calendar year that Roberta was alive. The reduction by one is also applicable for the calendar year in which Roberta died. Jason's life expectancy under the IRS single life expectancy table is determined under Table V of 1.72-9 of the Income Tax Regulations. This table, called Table I in IRS Publication 590, is shown in Appendix A of this book.

QUESTION 4.37: How would Jason determine his required minimum distributions under the hybrid method if Roberta died in 2004 after receiving her required minimum distribution for that year?

ANSWER: Under the hybrid method, Jason must first determine his single life expectancy in 1999, which is Roberta's first distribution calendar year (the year in which she reached age 70^1/$_2$). Under the single life-expectancy table shown in Appendix A, the life expectancy of Jason in the calendar year 1999 at age 40 is 42.5 years. Jason then subtracts from 42.5 years the six distribution calendar years 1999 through 2004 that Roberta was alive, counting 2004, the year of her death, as a full year. Therefore, for 2005, Jason has a remaining life expectancy under the hybrid method of 36.5 years that he may use in determining his required minimum distributions from Roberta's IRA. The following schedule indicates the life expectancy that Jason may use under the hybrid method in determining his required minimum distributions for the calendar years 2005 through 2009. As you can see, the life expectancy of 36.5 years used for 2005, the year following the year of Roberta's death, is reduced by one for each subsequent year:

JASON'S AGE	CALENDAR YEAR	HYBRID METHOD SINGLE LIFE EXPECTANCY
46	2005	36.5
47	2006	35.5
48	2007	34.5
49	2008	33.5
50	2009	32.5

To calculate the required minimum distribution for each year, Jason would divide the hybrid method life expectancy into the account balance of the IRA as of the end of the preceding year. If, for example, the account balance as of December 31, 2005, was $122,000, Jason would have to receive at least $3,436.62 from the IRA ($122,000 divided by 35.5) during 2006 to satisfy the required minimum distribution rules.

QUESTION 4.38: Is the difference between the hybrid method and the term-certain method significant as far as Jason is concerned?

ANSWER: No. Jason's life expectancy is practically identical under both methods. The following schedule compares the two methods for the calendar years 2005 through 2009:

JASON'S AGE	CALENDAR YEAR	TERM-CERTAIN JOINT LIFE EXPECTANCY	HYBRID METHOD SINGLE LIFE EXPECTANCY
46	2005	36.9	36.5
47	2006	35.9	35.5
48	2007	34.9	34.5
49	2008	33.9	33.5
50	2009	32.9	32.5

QUESTION 4.39: Under the hybrid method, why isn't Roberta's life expectancy considered in the calculation for the calendar year 2005 and thereafter?

ANSWER: Under the hybrid method, Roberta has a zero life expectancy in the calendar year following her year of death and all years thereafter. Because Roberta died in the calendar year 2004, she has a zero life expectancy in the calendar year 2005 and all subsequent years.

CHAPTER FIVE

USING A CUSTODIAL ACCOUNT OR TRUST FOR A DESIGNATED BENEFICIARY WHO IS A MINOR

When the beneficiary of a qualified plan or IRA is a very young child, it may be better to have the distributions paid to a custodian who will receive the distributions on behalf of the minor, rather than to the child directly.

Another alternative is to use an irrevocable trust or a revocable trust when your intended designated beneficiary is a minor.

This chapter will discuss how a custodial account or trust can be used to handle retirement death benefits for the benefit of a minor.

BENEFITS OF A CUSTODIAL ACCOUNT

The following series of questions and answers explains how a custodial account can be used to receive qualified plan or IRA benefits.

QUESTION 5.1: Is there any way for an IRA distribution to be payable for the benefit of a minor after the death of the IRA

owner while avoiding the jurisdiction of the local probate courts?

ANSWER: Yes. Either an irrevocable trust or revocable trust (discussed in this chapter starting with Question 5.55) can be created to receive the IRA distributions on behalf of the minor or, if permitted under state law, a custodian under the Uniform Gifts to Minors Act or Uniform Transfers to Minors Act can be designated to receive the IRA distributions on behalf of the minor. In the event that the IRA owner dies before his required beginning date, then the Trustee of the irrevocable trust may make the appropriate timely written election of a distribution method on behalf of the minor. A custodian generally under state law does not have the authority to make any election on behalf of the minor. However, many IRA plan documents permit an IRA owner to select a distribution method on behalf of a designated beneficiary in the event the IRA owner dies before his required beginning date. If that option is available to the IRA owner, then the IRA owner who is selecting a custodian for the benefit of a minor as a beneficiary may make a protective election of a distribution method in the event that he dies before his required beginning date. The protective election is discussed in this chapter. The rules that are triggered in the event the IRA owner dies on or after his required beginning date were previously discussed in detail in Chapter 4.

QUESTION 5.2: How do you know if a custodian can receive IRA distributions?

ANSWER: The Uniform Gifts to Minors Act or Uniform Transfers to Minors Act for the particular state will generally have specific provisions in the statute that permits the custodian to receive retirement type distributions on behalf of the minor.

CUSTODIAL ACCOUNT BASICS:
QUESTIONS 5.3–5.17

QUESTION 5.3: What type of language should one look for in order to determine whether or not the particular state permits retirement assets to be paid to a custodian?

ANSWER: Many states (e.g., Alabama, Colorado, Florida, Massachusetts, North Dakota, Rhode Island, and Virginia) use the following language in their Uniform Transfers to Minors Act:

> *A person having the right to designate the recipient of property upon the occurrence of a future event may revocably nominate a custodian to receive the property for a minor beneficiary.... The nomination may be made in a will, trust ... or in a writing designating a beneficiary of contractual rights which is registered with or delivered to the payor, issuer or other obligor of the contractual rights.*

QUESTION 5.4: If the beneficiary on behalf of the minor is a custodian under the Uniform Gifts to Minors Act or Uniform Transfers to Minors Act, may the custodian elect the distribution method for the IRA death benefits?

ANSWER: No. Custodians under the Uniform Gifts to Minors Act or Uniform Transfers to Minors Act are not granted the same powers as a Trustee and have no right to elect a method of payment of the IRA death benefits. This, of course, could be changed by state legislation.

QUESTION 5.5: Why is it better to name a custodian under the Uniform Gifts to Minors Act or Uniform Transfers to Minors Act on behalf of the minor as the beneficiary of the IRA death benefits instead of the minor directly?

ANSWER: If the minor was named the direct beneficiary of IRA benefits, the local probate court could require that a guardian for the minor's property be appointed. Naming a custodian eliminates the jurisdiction of the local probate court. In addition, the custodian under the Uniform Gifts to Minors Act or Uniform Transfers to Minors Act has a greater degree of flexibility in applying the funds for the use and benefit of the minor.

QUESTION 5.6: Who may be selected as the custodian for the minor?

ANSWER: State law determines who may be selected as the custodian. Generally, the custodian may be a member of the minor's family such as the minor's parent, grandparent, brother, sister, uncle, or aunt. Some states permit a trust company to act as custodian, while other states permit any adult person to act as custodian.

QUESTION 5.7: Should the donor ever be selected as a custodian?

ANSWER: No. According to the IRS and the federal courts, if the custodian is the donor and the custodial account is still in existence at the date of death of the donor, then the value of the property transferred to the custodial account is included in the gross estate of the donor for federal estate tax purposes.

QUESTION 5.8: If a grandparent during his lifetime made a gift of $1,000 to a custodial account for the benefit of a grandchild and named himself or herself as custodian, what should he or she do?

ANSWER: The grandparent should immediately resign as custodian and the parent of the child or another member of the family should be made the custodian.

QUESTION 5.9: Charles Smith wishes to establish a custodial account in the amount of $5,000 for the benefit of his grandchild, Michael Smith. Charles's son, George Smith, is selected as

the custodian. What should Charles do in order to establish the custodial account?

ANSWER: The grandparent, Charles Smith, should make out a check for $5,000 payable to George Smith as custodian under the Uniform Gifts to Minors Act of State X for the benefit of Michael Smith until his 18th birthday (or 21st birthday, depending on state law). George should then open an account with a broker or other financial institution in the name of George Smith as custodian under the Uniform Gifts to Minors Act of State X for the benefit of Michael Smith until his 18th birthday (or 21st birthday, depending on state law) and endorse the check over to the broker or other financial institution. If these steps are taken, then the $5,000 gift will never be included in the estate of the grandparent, Charles Smith, under any set of circumstances. In addition, the custodial account will not be included in the estate of George Smith as custodian because George Smith's funds were not used to establish the custodial account.

QUESTION 5.10: If a grandparent lives in New York State and his or her grandchild lives in Florida, where should the custodial account be established?

ANSWER: The custodial arrangement is governed by state law. Many states allow the custodian to be appointed pursuant to the law of the state where the transferor resides, the state where the minor resides, or the state where the custodian resides. If the grandchild lives in Florida, then it is probably best that the custodian laws of the State of Florida be used because the custodian would probably reside in Florida as well.

QUESTION 5.11: May the custodian use the funds in the custodial account to support a minor?

ANSWER: No. Several state courts have held that the custodian may not legally use the custodial account in order to satisfy the support obligations of the parents. Thus, even if the Uniform Gifts to Minors Act statute seems to allow the custodian to use the custodial account for the support and maintenance of the minor, the custodian should not do so unless the parents do not have the ability to satisfy their support obligations to the minor. If the minor must be supported and the parents refuse to support the minor, then the custodian should bring this to the attention of the state court and request permission to use the custodial funds for the support of the minor. The court may authorize such use or force the parents to prove that they have no assets. The custodial funds are assets of the child and may not be used to avoid the support obligation of the parents.

QUESTION 5.12: Why is there an issue as to whether the custodian may use the custodial account for the support of the minor?

ANSWER: Several states have language in their custodian statutes that state the following:

> *The custodian shall pay over to the minor for expenditure by him, or expend for the minor's benefit, so much or all of the custodial property as the custodian deems advisable for the support, maintenance, education and benefit of the minor in the manner, at the time and to the extent that the custodian in his discretion deems suitable and proper, with or without court order, with or without regard to the duty of himself or any other person to support the minor or his ability to do so ....*

The above language causes the problem and the litigation because the custodian thinks that the custodial funds can be used to take care of the support of the minor without considering the issue of the parental obligation of support.

The state courts have held that the custodian may not use the custodial account for a support obligation of the parent. It makes no difference as to who may be the custodian. In one case the minor child successfully sued the custodian who happened to be the minor's mother.

QUESTION 5.13: How have some states avoided the confusing language described in the above question?

ANSWER: A number of states have revised their custodian statutes to eliminate the inference that the custodial funds may be used for support of the minor. These states have custodian statutes that state the following:

> *A custodian may deliver or pay to the minor or expend for the minor's benefit so much of the custodial property as the custodian considers advisable for the use and benefit of the minor, without court order and without regard to (1) the duty or ability of the custodian personally or of any other person to support the minor, or (2) any other income or property of the minor which may be applicable or available for that purpose. A delivery, payment, or expenditure ... is in addition to, not in substitution for, and does not affect any obligation of a person to support the minor.*

The language of the last sentence should deter the custodian from using the custodial funds in order to satisfy the parental obligation to support the minor. Obviously the funds may have to be used to support the minor if the parents do not have the resources to support the minor.

QUESTION 5.14: Does the IRS always tax the income earned on the custodial account to the minor?

ANSWER: No. If the custodian uses the custodial funds to discharge the legal obligation of a parent to support or maintain a minor, then according to the IRS the parent is taxed on the income earned on the custodial property to the extent that the property is so used. The IRS will attempt to tax the parent on the income used to support the minor even if the parent is not the custodian.

QUESTION 5.15: Is there a defense that can be used by the parent in order to avoid being taxed on custodial account income used to support the child?

ANSWER: Yes. The defense is that the custodian in the absence of a court order may not use the custodial funds to eliminate the parental obligation to support the minor. Therefore, the custodian is obligated to return the funds to the custodial account and therefore the parent should not be required to pay taxes on the erroneous application of the funds by the custodian. This defense is based upon case law and the custodian statutes that are applicable in many states. Many state statutes provide that an expenditure by a custodian for the use and benefit of a minor does not affect any obligation of a person to support the minor.

QUESTION 5.16: A custodian may expend funds for the use and benefit of the minor. What type of expenditures may the custodian make on behalf of the minor?

ANSWER: The custodian may pay a minor's legally enforceable obligations such as tax liabilities or tort claims. If the parents are not affluent and cannot afford to send the child to a private college, then it is possible that the custodian may legally use the custodial funds to pay for college tuition.

QUESTION 5.17: What is considered to be a parent's support obligation to a child?

ANSWER: A parent's support obligation to a child is the duty to provide the child with necessaries. Expenditures for a child's business use is not considered a necessary. Whether an expenditure is a necessary depends on the station in life of the parent and his or her ability to pay for the expenditure. Whether or not college tuition payments are a necessary is based upon state law. A state court might find that a wealthy parent who promised his or her son or daughter a college education is legally obligated to pay for the college tuition and expenses but that a parent who earns a modest living does not have this obligation.

OWNER'S PROTECTIVE ELECTION OF LIFE-EXPECTANCY DISTRIBUTION METHOD FOR MINOR BENEFICIARY: QUESTIONS 5.18–5.24

QUESTION 5.18: Jack Phillips, who is age 67 on March 1, 1999, has several IRAs. He is fond of his grandson, Craig Phillips, age 4, and would like upon his death to have one of his IRAs used for the benefit of Craig. Jack is not in the best of health. Craig's father, Thomas Phillips, earns a reasonable salary. Thomas files a joint return with his wife, Mary, and they will be in the 31-percent federal income tax bracket for many years to come. Jack selects an IRA containing approximately $20,000 to be used for the benefit of his grandson, Craig. He would like to select a custodian for the benefit of Craig as the beneficiary of his IRAs. How should the IRA beneficiary form read?

ANSWER: The beneficiary form of Jack Phillips's IRA should read something like this:

Thomas Phillips, custodian for Craig Phillips under the State X Uniform Gifts to Minors Act until the 18th birthday of Craig Phillips and then to Craig Phillips directly after he attains his 18th birthday.

The title should be based upon the state law where the IRA is located. In addition, some states allow you to use age 18 or age 21. If you feel that age 21 is a better age and the state law permits it, then use age 21. The social security number of Craig Phillips is used on the custodial account for income tax purposes.

QUESTION 5.19: If Jack Phillips selects his son, Thomas, as custodian for his grandson, Craig, to be the beneficiary of his IRA, is Thomas or Craig the designated beneficiary for tax purposes?

ANSWER: Obviously, Craig Phillips is the designated beneficiary. Thomas Phillips will merely hold the funds in the custodian account for the benefit of Craig Phillips. Under state law the true owner of the custodial account is the minor. The IRS in

Revenue Ruling 59-357 discussed the Uniform Gifts to Minors Act and the Model Gifts of Securities to Minors Act and concluded that the minor is the true owner of the assets in the custodial account. Revenue Ruling 59-357 states in part the following:

Uniform laws have been adopted in many states to facilitate gifts to minors. Generally, these laws eliminate the usual requirement that a guardian be appointed or a trust set up when a minor is to be the donee of a gift.... The Uniform Gifts to Minors Act provides ... that a bank, trust company, or any adult may act as custodian. When a gift is made pursuant to the model or uniform act the property vests absolutely in the minor.

QUESTION 5.20: If Jack dies before his required beginning date, what distribution options are available to Thomas, as custodian for Craig?

ANSWER: Jack's required beginning date is April 1 of the calendar year following the calendar year in which he attains age $70^{1}/_{2}$. If Jack dies before that date, then either a five-year distribution period or a life-expectancy distribution period applies. The plan document may specify which option applies, or the plan may permit the designated beneficiary to elect which method applies. However, Thomas, as custodian, lacks the legal authority to elect a distribution method. If the IRA prototype document allows Jack as the IRA owner to make a distribution method election, he should do so.

If the IRA owner dies before his required beginning date, then under the five-year rule the entire account must be distributed by no later than December 31 of the fifth year following the year of the account owner's death.

Under the life-expectancy rule, payments from the account may be made over the life expectancy of the designated beneficiary. In this case, Craig's life expectancy would be used. The first required minimum distribution to the custodian would be due no later than December 31 of the year following the year of Jack's death.

QUESTION 5.21: May Thomas Phillips, as the custodian for Craig Phillips, make a protective election out of the five-year rule?

ANSWER: No. Thomas Phillips as custodian may not legally elect out of the five-year rule under current state law. Jack Phillips must make the protective election out of the five-year rule if the life-expectancy rule is desired. This is important because it is possible that Jack Phillips may die before his required beginning date.

QUESTION 5.22: Why is the election out of the five-year rule generally the better approach?

ANSWER: The life-expectancy method has greater flexibility and takes advantage of the longer payout period that is available to Craig based upon his life expectancy. The life-expectancy method also takes advantage of Craig's lower income tax bracket. As shown in Question 5.23, it is possible that under the kiddie tax rules for children under age 14, Craig could incur a substantial federal income tax liability if the five-year rule were applicable. That problem can be avoided if Craig's grandfather, Jack, makes a protective election out of the five-year rule so that distributions after his death would be based on Craig's life expectancy.

QUESTION 5.23: If Jack wants to make a protective election what should he do?

ANSWER: Jack should examine the IRA plan document in order to determine whether it permits him to make an election out of the five-year rule. If the IRA plan document permits him to make an election, then Jack Phillips should make a protective election out of the five-year rule with the IRA institution. The protective election should be signed and dated by Jack and sent to the IRA institution by certified mail, return receipt requested.

QUESTION 5.24: How could Jack specifically write a protective election with the IRA institution in order to elect out of the five-year rule and into the life-expectancy rule?

ANSWER: Assuming that the IRA plan document permits an election out of the five-year rule, the election should state the following:

In the event that I, Jack Phillips, should die prior to my required beginning date of April 1, 2003, and I am survived by my grandson, Craig Phillips, then I elect that the required minimum distributions of my IRA maintained with the ABC institution, Account No. 10006, be paid based upon the life expectancy of my designated beneficiary, Craig Phillips, and that while Craig Phillips is under the age of 18 that the required minimum distributions be paid to Thomas Phillips as custodian for Craig Phillips under the State X Uniform Gifts to Minors Act or similar act until the 18th birthday of Craig Phillips and thereafter directly to Craig Phillips after he attains his 18th birthday. Upon Craig Phillips reaching age 18, he may accelerate distributions from this IRA at any time or transfer this IRA directly in whole or in part to any other institution provided that the IRA is still maintained in my name. Craig Phillips may accelerate distributions from any transferee IRA at any time after reaching his 18th birthday. The custodian shall notify the ABC institution each year as to the amount of the required minimum distribution that shall be paid to the custodian each calendar year. The ABC institution shall have no liability in determining the amount of the required minimum distribution that shall be paid to the custodian. The life expectancy of Craig in the event that I die prior to my required beginning date shall be based upon Craig's life expectancy under the appropriate IRS table and shall be based upon his life expectancy as determined in the calendar year after my death. The first required minimum distribution must be paid to the custodian by no later than December 31 of the calendar year following the year of my death. Subsequent distributions must be paid by December 31 of each calendar year thereafter.

QUESTION 5.25: Assume that Jack Phillips dies in December 1999 at age 67. Craig Phillips is age 6 in 1999. What are the tax

ramifications if Jack did not make the protective election out of the five-year rule and the five-year rule is applicable?

ANSWER: If Jack Phillips dies at age 67 in 1999, then under the five-year rule the entire IRA would have to be paid to the custodian by no later than December 31, 2004. Craig is age 11 in 2004. The custodian would not be permitted to do any effective long-term tax planning and the entire account would be subject to income taxes in the calendar year 2004. The custodian would have no legal right under state law to demand partial payments from the IRA during the five-year period. Because Craig is under age 14 at the end of the calendar year 2004, a substantial portion of the IRA would be taxed at his parents' 31-percent federal income tax bracket under the so-called kiddie tax rules. Assume that in 2004 the decedent's IRA is worth $32,000 when it is distributed to the custodian. Also assume that the kiddie tax threshold for minors under age 14 in 2004 is $2,000 and that unearned income over $2,000 is taxed at Craig's parents' rate under the kiddie tax. Federal income tax liability on the $32,000 distribution would be computed as follows:

	Income Tax Bracket
1st $1,000 of income:	0 percent
2nd $1,000 of income:	15 percent
Next $30,000 of income at parents' tax bracket because Craig is under age 14 in calendar year 2004:	31 percent

The estimated federal income tax liability to Craig for the calendar year 2004 is as follows:

1st $1,000:	$-0-
2nd $1,000 at 15 percent:	$150.00

Next $30,000 at 31 percent:	$9,300.00
Total federal income tax liability:	$9,450.00

QUESTION 5.26: If Craig was age 9 instead of age 6 in 1999 and the five-year rule was applicable, then what would Craig's income tax liability be in the calendar year 2004?

ANSWER: The federal income tax liability would be significantly different because Craig is age 14 in the calendar year 2004 and the kiddie tax is not applicable. Assume the following federal income tax brackets are applicable to a minor age 14 or over in 2004:

	Income Tax Bracket
1st $1,000 of income:	0 percent
Next $29,000 of income:	15 percent
Next $2,000 of income:	28 percent

The estimated federal income tax liability to Craig for the calendar year 2004 is as follows:

1st $1,000:	$-0-
Next $29,000 at 15 percent:	$4,350.00
Next $2,000 at 28 percent:	$560.00
Total federal income tax liability:	$4,910.00

CASE STUDY

Questions 5.27–5.54 illustrate the tax consequences of IRA distributions payable to a custodian on behalf of a minor if the protective election of the life-expectancy method has been made.

QUESTION 5.27: Assume that Craig was age 6 in 1999. Also assume that Jack dies in 1999 at age 67 and his IRA as of December 31, 1999, was valued at $22,000. Why would Craig's federal income tax liability be reduced if Jack Phillips had filed a protective written election in which he elected out of the five-year rule?

ANSWER: If Jack Phillips had elected out of the five-year rule and died in 1999 at age 67, then the required minimum distributions would be based upon the life expectancy of Craig Phillips in 2000, which is the calendar year following Jack's year of death. In 2000 Craig is age 7. According to the IRS life-expectancy tables, Craig's life expectancy in 2000 is 74.7 years. The required minimum distribution for 2000 is based upon the decedent's IRA balance as of December 31, 1999. If Jack's IRA as of December 31, 1999, is worth $22,000, then a required minimum distribution of $294.51 must be made to the custodian on behalf of Craig in the calendar year 2000. This is calculated as follows:

Jack's IRA balance as of December 31, 1999:	Divided by Craig's life expectancy in 2000:	Required minimum distribution for calendar year 2000:
$22,000.00	÷74.7 years	$294.51

The life-expectancy method permits Craig to take advantage of the standard deduction and minimize his federal income tax liability. Craig's income tax liability depends on the amount of his other income.

QUESTION 5.28: Assume that Craig has no other income for the calendar year 2000. Is there any federal income tax liability that Craig is subject to for the calendar year 2000?

ANSWER: No. Craig is entitled to a standard deduction of more than $294.51 and, therefore, will incur no federal income tax liability for the calendar year 2000.

QUESTION 5.29: If Jack dies in 1999 and his IRA has a balance of $23,000 as of December 31, 2000, what is the required minimum distribution that must be paid to the custodian on behalf of Craig for the calendar year 2001 based upon the life-expectancy method discussed in Question 5.27?

ANSWER: The custodian must receive a required minimum distribution of $312.08 for the calendar year 2001. The required minimum distribution for 2001 is based upon the decedent's account balance as of December 31, 2000, divided by Craig's remaining life expectancy of 73.7 years. Craig's remaining life expectancy is based upon his initial life expectancy determined in 2000 of 74.7 reduced by one for each year including 2000. This is calculated as follows:

Jack's IRA balance as of December 31, 2000:	Divided by Craig's remaining life expectancy in 2001:	Required minimum distribution for calendar year 2001:
$23,000.00	÷73.7 years	$312.08

QUESTION 5.30: Assume that the required minimum distributions were paid to the custodian for each calendar year including the calendar year in which Craig attained age 18. Why is this an effective income tax–planning arrangement?

ANSWER: The custodian would receive a substantial amount of tax-free income for a 12-year period. For the calendar years 2000 through 2011 (when Craig attains age 18), the custodian should receive amounts below Craig's standard deduction. If we assume the required minimum distributions, plus the interest income earned on such amounts by the custodian averaged $500 per year over the 12-year period, then in essence Craig will receive approximately $6,000 in tax-free income. This is an excellent way of building up a nest egg for Craig's future.

QUESTION 5.31: What must the custodian, Thomas Phillips, do when Craig attains age 18 in 2011?

ANSWER: Thomas Phillips must turn over the balance in the custodial account to Craig Phillips in 2011 because the custodial account was only to last until Craig's 18th birthday.

QUESTION 5.32: If Jack Phillips is unhappy about the ability of Craig to accelerate distributions at age 18, what should he do?

ANSWER: He could set up a trust to receive the IRA funds on behalf of Craig. The trust for the benefit of Craig can be structured in such a manner so that Craig does not have access to a substantial portion of Jack Phillips's IRA until his 25th birthday, 30th birthday, or a later age.

QUESTION 5.33: Has Jack Phillips maximized the benefits to Craig under federal income tax law by having the required minimum distributions payable to the custodian?

ANSWER: Probably not. If we assume that Craig's federal standard deduction will generally be in excess of the required minimum distributions and his other income during the calendar years 2000 through 2011 when Craig attains age 18, then Jack Phillips has not maximized the federal income tax benefits that are available to Craig.

QUESTION 5.34: Assume that Craig's standard deduction for the calendar year 2000 is $750. Is Jack guilty of poor tax planning?

ANSWER: Yes. If we assume that Craig's standard deduction for the calendar year 2000 is $750, then in effect Craig could have received gross income of up to $750 instead of $294.51 (the required minimum distribution for 2000) without incurring any federal income tax liability.

QUESTION 5.35: How could Jack Phillips take advantage of Craig's federal standard deduction in making the protective election?

ANSWER: Jack Phillips, together with his professional advisor, should estimate the amount of the federal standard deduction that will be available to Craig and integrate that estimate into the protective election. Craig's projected other income and state income taxes should be considered as well where applicable.

For example, assume that Jack Phillips and his professional advisor do not know what the federal standard deduction will be for Craig in the future. They estimate that it will be in the range of $750 to $1,000 over the next 15 years. Jack Phillips may use certain language in the protective election that may reduce Craig's overall income tax liability during the period of his minority. The protective election described in the answer to Question 5.24 could state "that the greater of the required minimum distribution or $1,000 shall be paid annually to Thomas Phillips, as custodian...."

QUESTION 5.36: What is the advantage of using the protective election language suggested in the answer to Question 5.35?

ANSWER: By Jack Phillips stating in the protective election "that the greater of the required minimum distribution or $1,000 shall be paid annually to Thomas Phillips, as custodian," he and his professional advisor have accomplished effective tax planning by maximizing use of Craig's standard deduction. If the average standard deduction over the 12-year period is $800, then in effect Craig will receive $9,600 in tax-free income.

QUESTION 5.37: Assume that Jack Phillips dies in 1999 and Thomas Phillips, as custodian for Craig, receives $1,000 in 2000 from Jack's IRA. Craig is age 7 in 2000. If Craig has no other income, and his standard deduction in 2000 is $700, what is Craig's federal income tax liability for 2000?

ANSWER: Craig's federal income tax liability in 2000 is $37.50. This is computed as follows:

Craig's gross income:	$1,000.00
Less: Standard deduction:	$750.00
Taxable income:	$250.00
Tax rate on 1st $750 of taxable income:	15 percent
Federal income tax:	$37.50

Craig's effective federal income tax rate is 3.75 percent ($37.50/1,000). The income that is received by Thomas Phillips, as custodian, is taxed to Craig at Craig's income tax rates.

QUESTION 5.38: Assume the same facts as in Question 5.37, and that in 2001, Thomas Phillips, as custodian for Craig, receives $70 of interest income in addition to the $1,000 from Jack's IRA. What is Craig's federal income tax liability in 2001 if we assume that Craig's federal standard deduction in 2001 is $750?

ANSWER: Craig's federal income tax liability in 2001 would be $48.00. This is computed as follows:

Craig's gross income:	$1,070.00
Less: Standard deduction:	$750.00
Taxable income:	$320.00
Tax rate on 1st $750 of taxable income:	15 percent
Federal income tax:	$48.00

Craig's effective federal income tax rate is 4.49 percent ($48.00/$1,070).

QUESTION 5.39: Assume that Jack Phillips made a timely protective election to avoid the five-year rule. Thomas Phillips, as custodian for Craig, receives $1,000 annually from the Jack Phillips, deceased, IRA for each calendar year beginning with 2000 (the year following the year of Jack's death). Craig attains his 7th birthday in 2000. Assume further that Jack's IRA earns a 7-percent interest rate and that the $1,000 distribution to Thomas Phillips, as custodian, is made at the end of each calendar year. How much is left in Jack's IRA as of the end of calendar year 2011, the year in which Craig attains age 18?

ANSWER: $31,659.76. The details of this computation are as follows:

CRAIG'S AGE	YEAR	EARNINGS	ACTUAL DISTRIBUTION	IRA BALANCE
	1999			$ 22,000.00
7	2000	$1,540.00	$1,000.00	22,540.00
8	2001	1,577.80	1,000.00	23,117.80
9	2002	1,618.25	1,000.00	23,736.05
10	2003	1,661.52	1,000.00	24,397.57
11	2004	1,707.83	1,000.00	25,105.40
12	2005	1,757.38	1,000.00	25,862.78
13	2006	1,810.39	1,000.00	26,673.17
14	2007	1,867.12	1,000.00	27,540.29
15	2008	1,927.82	1,000.00	28,468.11
16	2009	1,992.77	1,000.00	29,460.88
17	2010	2,062.26	1,000.00	30,523.14 ➤

| 18 | 2011 | 2,136.62 | 1,000.00 | 31,659.76 |

$21,659.76 $12,000.00

QUESTION 5.40: Assume that Thomas Phillips, as custodian, earns a total of $5,500 on the annual distributions of $1,000 that he receives during the 12-year period. How much has Thomas Phillips, as custodian for Craig, accumulated by the end of the calendar year 2011?

ANSWER: Thomas Phillips, as custodian for Craig Phillips, has accumulated approximately $17,500. This is computed as follows:

Distributions received from Jack Phillips's IRA during the period 2000 to 2011:	$12,000.00
Earnings by the custodian during the 12-year period:	$5,500.00
Total:	$17,500.00*

Federal income tax will be due on the distributions of $12,000 paid to the custodian, plus the $5,500 of earnings realized by the custodian. Assume that the taxes are paid by Craig's parents, and are estimated to be approximately $1,200. If the custodian had paid these taxes through the custodian account, then the earnings by the custodian would be reduced, and so would the taxes on the earnings.

QUESTION 5.41: At the end of calendar year 2011, to how much money does Craig have access?

ANSWER: Craig will receive approximately $17,500 from the custodian, plus he has the ability to draw $31,659.76 from the Jack Phillips, deceased, IRA. If Craig draws down the $31,659.76 from the Jack Phillips, deceased, IRA in one calendar year, then he will pay federal and state income taxes on that amount.

Craig, therefore, has access to $49,159.76 ($17,500 + $31,659.76). The $17,500 is after tax monies and the $31,659.76 is before tax monies. If we assume that the $31,659.76 after deductions and his exemption is subject to an overall tax liability of approximately $5,000, then Craig will have access to a net amount of approximately $44,000.

QUESTION 5.42: Assume that only the required minimum distributions are paid to Craig's custodian before Craig attains age 18 and thereafter to Craig based upon his life expectancy under the IRS tables. Further assume that the IRA earns 7 percent during the payout period. How much will Craig receive from the IRA over his life expectancy?

ANSWER: As of 2000, the year following Jack's death, Craig's life expectancy, at age 7, is 74 years (74.7 rounded down to 74 for illustrative purposes). Craig will receive required minimum distributions of $731,908.09 based upon a 74-year life expectancy and assumed interest of 7 percent on $22,000, the balance of Jack's IRA as of December 31, 1999. This assumes that Craig does not accelerate distributions from the IRA during the payout period. The compounding effect of the interest is the key in this calculation. The following schedule illustrates the details of this calculation.

Initial amount: $22,000.00; Earnings: 7 percent

DISTRIBUTIONS OVER 74 YEARS

YEAR	EARNINGS	REQUIRED MINIMUM DISTRIBUTION	BALANCE
			$22,000.00
1	$1,540.00	$297.30	23,242.70
2	1,626.99	318.39	24,551.30 ➤

3	1,718.59	340.99	25,928.90
4	1,815.02	365.20	27,378.72
5	1,916.51	391.12	28,904.11
6	2,023.29	418.90	30,508.50
7	2,135.60	448.65	32,195.45
8	2,253.68	480.53	33,968.60
9	2,377.80	514.68	35,831.72
10	2,508.22	551.26	37,788.68
11	2,645.21	590.45	39,843.44
12	2,789.04	632.44	42,000.04
13	2,940.00	677.42	44,262.62
14	3,098.38	725.62	46,635.38
15	3,264.48	777.26	49,122.60
16	3,438.58	832.59	51,728.59
17	3,621.00	891.87	54,457.72
18	3,812.04	955.40	57,314.36
19	4,012.01	1,023.47	60,302.90
20	4,221.20	1,096.42	63,427.68
21	4,439.94	1,174.59	66,693.03
22	4,668.51	1,258.36	70,103.18 →

YEAR	EARNINGS	REQUIRED MINIMUM DISTRIBUTION	BALANCE
23	4,907.22	1,348.14	73,662.26
24	5,156.36	1,444.36	77,374.26
25	5,416.20	1,547.49	81,242.97
26	5,687.01	1,658.02	85,271.96
27	5,969.04	1,776.50	89,464.50
28	6,262.52	1,903.50	93,823.52
29	6,567.65	2,039.64	98,351.53
30	6,884.61	2,185.59	103,050.55
31	7,213.54	2,342.06	107,922.03
32	7,554.54	2,509.81	112,966.76
33	7,907.67	2,689.68	118,184.75
34	8,272.93	2,882.55	123,575.13
35	8,650.26	3,089.38	129,136.01
36	9,039.52	3,311.18	134,864.35
38	9,852.91	3,804.21	146,804.49
39	10,276.31	4,077.90	153,002.90
40	10,710.20	4,371.51	159,341.59
41	11,153.91	4,686.52	165,808.98
42	11,606.63	5,024.51	172,391.10
43	12,067.38	5,387.22	179,071.26 →

44	12,534.99	5,776.49	185,829.76
45	13,008.08	6,194.33	192,643.51
46	13,485.05	6,642.88	199,485.68
47	13,964.00	7,124.49	206,325.19
48	14,442.76	7,641.67	213,126.28
49	14,918.84	8,197.16	219,847.96
50	15,389.36	8,793.92	226,443.40
51	15,851.04	9,435.14	232,859.30
52	16,300.15	10,124.32	239,035.13
53	16,732.46	10,865.23	244,902.36
54	17,143.17	11,662.02	250,383.51
55	17,526.85	12,519.18	255,391.18
56	17,877.38	13,441.64	259,826.92
57	18,187.88	14,434.83	263,579.97
58	18,450.60	15,504.70	266,525.87
59	18,656.81	16,657.87	268,524.81
60	18,796.74	17,901.65	269,419.90
61	18,859.39	19,244.28	269,035.01
62	18,832.45	20,695.00	267,172.46
63	18,702.07	22,264.37	263,610.16	➤

YEAR	EARNINGS	REQUIRED MINIMUM DISTRIBUTION	BALANCE
64	18,452.71	23,964.56	258,098.31
65	18,066.88	25,809.83	250,355.36
66	17,524.88	27,817.26	240,062.98
67	16,804.41	30,007.87	226,859.52
68	15,880.17	32,408.50	210,331.19
69	14,723.18	35,055.20	189,999.17
70	13,299.94	37,999.83	165,299.28
71	11,570.95	41,324.82	135,545.41
72	9,488.18	45,181.80	99,851.79
73	6,989.63	49,925.90	56,915.52
74	3,984.09	60,899.61	0.00
	$709,908.09	$731,908.09	

QUESTION 5.43: Jack Phillips has selected his grandson, Craig, as the designated beneficiary of his IRA in order to provide for Craig's future. He has selected his son, Thomas Phillips, as the custodian for Craig until Craig's 18th birthday. In wording his protective election out of the five-year rule, Jack has focused on saving Craig federal income taxes. Has he saved Craig state income taxes as well?

ANSWER: Probably. Most states have a state income tax. By mandating a distribution that is the greater of the required minimum distribution or $1,000 to be paid annually, Jack Phillips may have saved Craig state income taxes as well.

QUESTION 5.44: Why should Jack Phillips be concerned about Craig's potential state income taxes?

ANSWER: Most states have a state income tax. State income tax rates generally are incremental in nature and may be significant if no effective tax planning is done.

QUESTION 5.45: Will state law allow an individual such as Craig, who may be claimed as a dependent on another's tax return, to claim an exemption deduction for himself on his own state income tax return?

ANSWER: Maybe. It depends on the state income tax laws of the particular state. A number of states allow a single individual who may be claimed as a dependent the exemption deduction, but many states do not. For example, in Alabama, Arizona, Connecticut, Georgia, Louisiana, Massachusetts, and Mississippi, a single individual is entitled to an exemption deduction that is well in excess of $1,000 per year, even if that individual may be claimed as a dependent. States that do not allow an exemption deduction to a single individual who may be claimed as a dependent include Colorado, Delaware, Georgia, Hawaii, Idaho, Illinois, and Kansas. New York State does not allow any taxpayer (adult or minor) to claim a personal exemption, but it does allow an exemption deduction for dependents claimed by the taxpayer.

QUESTION 5.46: Do states allow a standard deduction for a single individual who may be claimed as a dependent on another tax return?

ANSWER: Maybe. Many states allow an individual who is single a significant standard deduction. Thus, a single individual may obtain a standard deduction that is well in excess of $1,000, even though that single person is also being claimed as another's dependent. This applies in such states as California, Georgia,

Hawaii, Kansas, Louisiana, Mississippi, and North Carolina. However, a number of states limit the standard deduction in instances where a single individual can be claimed as a dependent of another. These states include Colorado, Idaho, Maine, Minnesota, Missouri, New Mexico, New York, and Oregon.

QUESTION 5.47: What type of state income tax structure do states use?

ANSWER: State income-tax rates vary from state to state. A few states like Florida, Nevada, South Dakota, and Texas have no state income tax. A number of states have a flat tax rate. Most states have incremental income tax rates.

QUESTION 5.48: Is Craig exposed to any significant state income tax liability based upon the annual distributions that Thomas Phillips, as custodian, received (including earnings)?

ANSWER: Probably not. The typical state income tax law allows its taxpayers either a significant standard deduction or an exemption deduction, or possibly both deductions in determining the taxable income of its taxpayers. Basically, these deductions should eliminate between $1,500 and $3,000 of state gross income in many states.

QUESTION 5.49: Assume that Craig, now age 19, needs the balance from his grandfather's IRA for a business that he plans to open within the next two years. If Craig is interested in minimizing his income tax liability after his 18th birthday, what course of action should he take?

ANSWER: Craig should take the distributions from Jack's IRA during the next two years in amounts that will take advantage of the federal standard deduction, the 15-percent federal income tax rate, and the lowest state income tax rate.

QUESTION 5.50: How much of an income tax savings was accomplished by Jack Phillips's selection of Craig (through his custodian Thomas) as the designated beneficiary of his IRA as opposed to selecting his son, Thomas, directly as the designated beneficiary?

ANSWER: The income tax savings are significant. Let us assume that Thomas Phillips is in the 31-percent federal income tax bracket and that Thomas lives in State X where he is in the 6-percent state income tax bracket. Because the 6-percent state income tax is deductible on his federal income tax return, Thomas Phillips has an effective overall tax rate of approximately 35 percent.

Assume that Craig receives 12 annual distributions of $1,000 each from Jack's IRA. Approximately $9,600 of these distributions are tax free because of Craig's annual standard deduction. Craig receives approximately $5,500 of earnings on the distributions. He will pay approximately $1,200 in federal income tax on the taxable portion of his IRA distributions and the earnings on the distributions. No state income tax is applicable because of the state exemption deduction and/or the state standard deduction.

Had Thomas Phillips received the $12,000 directly he would have paid approximately $4,200 in federal and state income tax on the distributions. This is based upon the assumption that Thomas has an effective tax bracket of 35 percent (federal and state) that is applied to the 12 annual distributions of $1,000. In addition, Thomas Phillips would receive approximately $3,000 of earnings, and not the $5,500 of earnings that Craig received. The reason for the lower earnings is that Thomas Phillips will pay more taxes than Craig and, therefore, have less money working for him. The $3,000 of earnings is taxable to Thomas Phillips at 35 percent, or $1,050. The total tax liability on the $12,000 of distributions and $3,000 of earnings at 35 percent is $5,250. Thus, Thomas Phillips will pay approximately $4,050 more in federal and state income tax on the first $12,000 of IRA distributions than will Craig. This is computed as follows:

Approximate taxes paid by Thomas Phillips on the $12,000 of IRA distributions:	$4,200
Approximate taxes paid by Thomas Phillips on the earnings of $3,000:	$1,050
Total approximate taxes paid by Thomas Phillips:	$5,250
Approximate taxes paid by Craig on the $12,000 of IRA distributions and on the earnings of $5,500:	$1,200
Additional taxes paid by Thomas Phillips:	$4,050

QUESTION 5.51: Assume that Craig decides to take the balance of Jack's IRA of $31,659.76 plus earnings thereon (see answer to Question 5.39) in two equal installments of approximately $17,600. Assume that Craig's overall effective federal and state income tax rate is 18 percent. What is Craig's tax liability on these two distributions of $17,600?

ANSWER: Craig's tax liability is $3,168 for each year or a total of $6,336 for both years. Each $17,600 IRA distribution is subject to an 18-percent effective tax rate.

QUESTION 5.52: Assume in Question 5.51 that Thomas Phillips was the designated beneficiary and received these two equal distributions of $17,600. Thomas has an overall tax rate of 35 percent. What is the tax liability of Thomas on these two distributions of $17,600?

ANSWER: Thomas would have a tax liability of $6,160 for each year or a total of $12,320 for both years. The $17,600 distribution for each year is subject to a 35-percent effective tax rate.

QUESTION 5.53: Based upon your answers to Questions 5.40, 5.50, 5.51, and 5.52, how much of an income tax savings is there if Craig Phillips (through his custodian) is selected as the designated beneficiary of the IRA instead of Thomas directly?

ANSWER: The income tax savings is $10,034.

If Thomas Phillips was directly selected as the designated beneficiary, then Thomas would have a tax liability of $17,150. This is computed as follows:

Answer to Question 5.50	$5,250
Answer to Question 5.52	12,320
Tax liability of Thomas Phillips	$17,570

If Craig was selected as the designated beneficiary, then Craig and his parents would have a tax liability of $7,536. This is computed as follows:

Answer to Question 5.40:	$1,200
Answer to Question 5.51:	6,336
Tax liability of Craig and his parents:	$7,536

If Craig is the designated beneficiary instead of Thomas, then the tax savings is $10,034. This is computed as follows:

Tax liability of Thomas Phillips:	$17,570
Tax liability of Craig Phillips and his parents:	7,536
Difference:	$10,034

QUESTION 5.54: Could the tax savings be greater than $10,034?

ANSWER: Yes. If the remaining balance of $31,659.76 in Jack's IRA were paid to Craig over a period that exceeded the two-year period described above, then the tax-deferred growth would result in a greater overall tax savings.

BENEFITS OF TRUSTS

The following questions and answers will guide you in determining how an irrevocable trust or a revocable trust can be used as an effective tool in retirement-distribution planning for the family unit.

QUESTION 5.55: When should a trust be used as the beneficiary of an IRA?

ANSWER: A trust should be considered when the designated beneficiary is a minor.

If there are several minors involved and the intended beneficiaries of your IRAs are minors, then it may be best for ease of administration that a separate trust be set up for each minor's benefit.

Although that may seem to create more paperwork, it makes it easier to control the benefits that flow to the particular designated beneficiary. The IRS rules permit the use of trusts in determining the period over which payments can be made to the individual who benefits from the trust.

QUESTION 5.56: Why bother with a trust if a custodian under the Uniform Gifts to Minors Act can be used as the beneficiary on behalf of the minor?

ANSWER: Depending on state law, the custodian can only receive the IRA proceeds until the beneficiary reaches either age 18 or 21. If there are significant sums of money involved, then those ages may not be appropriate because the funds must be turned over to the beneficiary at that point in time.

QUESTION 5.57: If a trust for the benefit of the grandchild is to receive the IRA distributions, over how long a period may the trust last?

ANSWER: The trust may last as long as the life expectancy of the grandchild based upon the IRS life-expectancy rules.

QUESTION 5.58: Donald Johnson, age 66 in 1999, has a considerable amount of assets as well as $300,000 in several IRAs. He has two grandchildren, Robert, age 2, and Keith, age 6. Donald would like to make both grandchildren the designated beneficiaries of one of his IRAs that contains $200,000. Should he do so?

ANSWER: No. Because both grandchildren are minors and may be minors at the time of Donald's death, the probate court will become involved if he names the grandchildren directly as the designated beneficiaries of his IRA.

QUESTION 5.59: Assuming that Donald's grandchildren were age 18 and 24, should he name both grandchildren as the designated beneficiaries of one IRA?

ANSWER: In the absence of a letter ruling to the contrary, no. If both grandchildren are the designated beneficiaries of one IRA, then the younger grandchild is deemed to be the older grandchild's age for purposes of the IRS life-expectancy payout rules. This age difference of six years can make a big difference in terms of the ultimate payout. The younger beneficiary is placed at a disadvantage by being deemed the age of the older beneficiary.

QUESTION 5.60: Is there a better approach that Donald could use to provide benefits to adult grandchildren?

ANSWER: Yes. It is best that two IRAs of $100,000 each be established. Each adult grandchild should be the designated beneficiary of a separate IRA. This will result in some additional paperwork, but in the long run it will permit greater tax-planning opportunities on behalf of the younger designated beneficiary.

QUESTION 5.61: If Donald established an irrevocable trust for the benefit of Robert and an irrevocable trust for the benefit of Keith and named each irrevocable trust as the beneficiary of a separate IRA that contained $100,000, can Donald change the terms of the irrevocable trust?

ANSWER: No. The terms of an irrevocable trust cannot be changed.

QUESTION 5.62: Does that mean that he cannot change his beneficiary designation?

ANSWER: No. An irrevocable trust is not an irrevocable beneficiary. Donald can always change the beneficiary or designated beneficiary of his IRA as long as he is alive and competent to do so.

QUESTION 5.63: Can you illustrate the distinction between an irrevocable beneficiary and an irrevocable trust in the context of an IRA beneficiary?

ANSWER: Yes. Assume that Donald establishes IRA No. 1 in the amount of $100,000 and selects the irrevocable trust for the benefit of Robert as the beneficiary of the death benefits of IRA No. 1. Donald later realizes that his son, Mark, is not doing well and will need the IRA death benefits. Donald can change the designated beneficiary of IRA No. 1 to Mark instead of the irrevocable trust for the benefit of Robert. Donald can always change his beneficiary or designated beneficiary during his lifetime.

QUESTION 5.64: Is a trust a beneficiary or a designated beneficiary?

ANSWER: A trust is technically a beneficiary and not a designated beneficiary.

QUESTION 5.65: If Robert is the beneficiary of an irrevocable or revocable trust created by his grandfather Donald, is Robert considered to be a designated beneficiary for purposes of the IRS distribution rules?

ANSWER: According to the IRS, if certain requirements are met, Robert is deemed to be a designated beneficiary even though he takes his distributions through a trust. The rules that must be followed are:

a. The trust is a valid trust under state law, or would be but for the fact that there is no corpus.

b. The trust is irrevocable or will by its terms become irrevocable upon the death of the IRA owner.

c. The beneficiary of the trust is identifiable.

d. A copy of the trust is filed with the plan administrator while the taxpayer is alive. In addition, the taxpayer must agree that any amendments to the trust will be filed with the plan administrator within a reasonable period of time. Also, by the end of the ninth month beginning after the death of the taxpayer, the trust, including any amendments, must once again be filed with the plan administrator. This post-death act is done by the trustee. Alternatively, certain certification rules may be used. Naturally, the trust must be specifically referred to in the beneficiary forms that are on file with the IRA institution.

QUESTION 5.66: Under the first test in Question 5.65, what do the words "but for the fact that there is no corpus" mean?

ANSWER: The language means that there need not be any assets in the trust before the IRA owner's date of death.

QUESTION 5.67: Are there any other reasons why Donald should consider selecting a trust for the benefit of a grandchild as the beneficiary of his IRA?

ANSWER: Yes. If the ultimate beneficiary of the trust cannot handle funds, then the trustee of the trust will protect the grandchild from making poor investment decisions and from dissipating the IRA assets over a short period of time. In addition, the trustee will protect the grandchild from the influence of third parties. The assets of the IRA will also be protected from the creditors of the grandchild. If the grandchild were the direct beneficiary of the IRA, then the IRA would be more vulnerable to creditors of the grandchild. Further, the trustee may consider the income tax liability of the grandchild in determining whether to accelerate distributions to the grandchild.

An irrevocable trust or revocable trust for a child may be established for the same reasons as those described above.

QUESTION 5.68: Is there an advantage of selecting a revocable trust as the beneficiary of retirement type assets?

ANSWER: Yes. It is possible to change any portion of a revocable trust by an amendment. The terms of an irrevocable trust cannot be changed.

QUESTION 5.69: Who should be the trustee of the trust for the benefit of a grandchild?

ANSWER: The trustee can be an institutional trustee or it can be a member of the family. If the trust for the benefit of a grandchild is established by a grandfather, then he can name a series of trustees such as the grandmother as the first trustee, then a parent or parents of the grandchild, then an aunt or uncle or accountant or attorney as successor trustee.

QUESTION 5.70: How should the trustee be compensated?

ANSWER: Because the trustee controls the IRA investments after the IRA owner's death and will have to maintain trust accounting records and file fiduciary income tax returns, then he should be compensated based upon the statutory fees under state law or fees as stated in the trust document. These fee arrangements should be spelled out in the trust document. Often, the trust document will provide that no trustee commissions shall be paid to the grandparents, the parents of the child, or any other relatives who serve as trustee. The trust should provide that if a nonrelative serves as trustee that such trustee shall receive the greater of the statutory fees under state law or the fees as stated in the trust document.

QUESTION 5.71: What other provisions should be provided in the trust document?

ANSWER: Because the trustee of the trust controls the IRA investments, he or she should be guided in terms of the characteristics of the investments that should be made. This may include the percentage of IRA assets that should be invested in fixed-income instruments and equity investments and whether or not an investment advisor should be used for investing in equities. This is important, because the trustee could be vulnerable to a lawsuit by the beneficiary of the trust if poor investment decisions are made.

QUESTION 5.72: May the trust provide that the minor be made a trustee when he or she gets older?

ANSWER: Yes. The trust document should provide that at a certain age the ultimate beneficiary shall become the trustee. For example, if the trust is for the benefit of a minor and the IRA life expectancy for the minor is 70.7 years, then the trust should provide that at some age the beneficiary of the trust should become the trustee. The trust could state, for example, that at age 35, the beneficiary of the trust shall become the trustee.

QUESTION 5.73: May the trust provide for acceleration rights of distribution from the IRA?

ANSWER: Yes. The trust may provide that the trustee can accelerate additional distributions from the IRA based upon a certain standard or for any reason. In addition, the trust must receive the required minimum distributions from the IRA each year.

QUESTION 5.74: Must the trustee pay out the distributions that it receives each year from the IRA to the beneficiary of the trust?

ANSWER: It depends on the terms of the trust. If the trust instrument states that it must pay out all the distributions it receives annually to the beneficiary, then the trustee must follow the provisions of the trust document. In the absence of an IRS letter ruling to the contrary, the trust provisions should provide that all required minimum distributions and any other distributions that are received by the trustee from the IRA shall be paid out to the identifiable beneficiary of the trust.

QUESTION 5.75: If the beneficiary of the trust is a minor, what provision should be made in the trust agreement in order to avoid the jurisdiction of the probate court?

ANSWER: The trust instrument may state that if the beneficiary of the trust is a minor that the distribution may be withheld until the minor's 18th birthday or 21st birthday or that it may be paid to a custodian under the Uniform Gifts to Minors Act or Uniform Transfers to Minors Act for the benefit of the minor during his minority. The trust instrument should state that the distribution shall be paid to the person entitled to receive the distribution under state law on behalf of the minor including but not limited to a custodian under the Uniform Transfers to Minors Act or similar act.

QUESTION 5.76: Is there an estate tax savings to the estate of the deceased IRA owner if the IRA proceeds are payable to a trust for the benefit of a child instead of directly to the child?

ANSWER: No. The IRA is included in the gross estate of the deceased IRA owner. It makes no difference if the trust is the beneficiary of the IRA or if the IRA is payable directly to the child.

QUESTION 5.77: Is there an estate tax liquidity problem that may be solved if the trust receives the distributions before paying it to the child?

ANSWER: Yes. Many taxpayers have estates that lack liquidity. If the IRA is subject to a significant estate tax liability, then the trustee of the trust should be required to remit its share of the estate tax liability to the executor of the estate or directly to the IRS and state tax department. This must be done unless the identifiable beneficiary of the IRA makes arrangements to satisfy the estate tax liability in a manner that is satisfactory to the executor and the trustee.

QUESTION 5.78: If the estate lacks liquidity, can the IRA be paid directly to the estate instead of having the IRA paid to the trust and then having the trustee of the trust remit its share of estate taxes back to the estate?

ANSWER: Yes. The IRA can be paid to the estate of the deceased IRA owner if the estate is selected as the beneficiary of the IRA. This approach should be used only if you suspect that the child will not pay his share of the estate taxes from other assets that he owns.

QUESTION 5.79: If the estate lacks liquidity is there an alternative approach to either selecting the trust or the estate as the beneficiary of the IRA?

ANSWER: Yes. Multiple IRAs can be created. One IRA can name the estate as the beneficiary and the other IRA can name the child or a trust for the child as the beneficiary.

QUESTION 5.80: If you have confidence in your child, can you name the child as the direct beneficiary of your IRA even if your estate lacks liquidity?

ANSWER: Yes. However, the executor may have a problem if the child for whatever reason refuses to pay his or her share of the estate taxes that are attributable to the IRA.

QUESTION 5.81: If you have several children each of whom is a designated beneficiary of a separate IRA and your estate is not liquid, what approach should be used?

ANSWER: If you think the children may refuse to use assets of their own to pay the estate taxes, you may have no choice but to establish a separate trust for the benefit of each child so that the trustee of each trust may pay such child's share of the estate tax liability.

CHAPTER SIX

IF YOUR BENEFICIARY IS OLDER OR IS NO MORE THAN TEN YEARS YOUNGER THAN YOU

We discussed in Chapter 4 the distribution rules that apply if you select a nonspouse designated beneficiary who is more than 10 years younger than you. If you select a nonspouse designated beneficiary who is no more than 10 years younger than you or is *older* than you, there are different rules for calculating your required minimum distributions from your IRA when you reach your required beginning date (Chapter 2).

If your designated beneficiary is not your spouse, and is no more than 10 years younger than you or is older than you, then the amount of your required minimum distribution each year after your required beginning date depends on whether the term-certain method or a special hybrid method is used. The method used by you as the account owner after your required beginning date will also affect the distribution rules for your designated beneficiary after your death. Rules for designated beneficiaries of owners who die before their required beginning date are in Chapter 8.

These rules apply to traditional IRAs, qualified plans, and 403(b) annuity contracts.

TAKING INTO ACCOUNT DESIGNATED BENEFICIARY'S LIFE EXPECTANCY

The following questions and answers discuss how the choice of a nonspouse designated beneficiary affects the life-expectancy period the account owner may use in determining his required minimum distributions.

QUESTION 6.1: Paul Wilson wants to select his brother Bernard as the designated beneficiary of his IRA. May Paul take advantage of the life expectancy of Bernard in determining his required minimum distributions?

ANSWER: Yes. Paul may consider Bernard's life expectancy in determining his required minimum distributions provided that Bernard is selected as the designated beneficiary by Paul's required beginning date. Paul's required beginning date is April 1 of the calendar year following the calendar year in which he attains age $70^1/2$.

QUESTION 6.2: In order to determine the joint life expectancy of Paul and Bernard, as of what year is the joint life expectancy determined?

ANSWER: The calendar year in which the IRA owner attains age $70^1/2$ is the year that the joint life expectancy is determined. We need to review how old Paul and Bernard are as of their birthdays in the year Paul attains age $70^1/2$. Assume that Paul's 70th birthday is May 5, 1999; he is age $70^1/2$ on November 5, 1999. Thus, for Paul, we use age 70. After that we determine Bernard's age on his birthday in the calendar year 1999. Assume that on his birthday in 1999 Bernard is age 62. Therefore, the joint life expectancy of Paul and Bernard under the IRS table is based upon combined ages of 70 and 62.

QUESTION 6.3: Based on their ages in 1999, what is the combined life expectancy of Paul and Bernard in order to determine Paul's required minimum distributions for his first distribution calendar year?

ANSWER: Paul's first distribution calendar year is 1999, the first year for which he is required to receive a required minimum distribution under the IRS rules. The combined life expectancy of Paul and Bernard as of Paul's first distribution calendar year based upon age 70 and 62 is 24.9 years. If Paul timely selects his brother, Bernard, as the designated beneficiary of his IRA by no later than his required beginning date, which is April 1, 2000, then he may use his brother's life expectancy in determining his required minimum distributions from his IRA. The joint life expectancy of Paul and Bernard is shown in Table II of IRS Publication 590, which is included in Appendix A of this book. The same IRS table is referred to as Table VI in Section 1.72-9 of the Income Tax Regulations.

QUESTION 6.4: Assume that Paul initially selected his estate as the beneficiary of his IRA as of his required beginning date. He then made Bernard the designated beneficiary of his IRA after his required beginning date. Must Paul use the single life-expectancy table in determining his required minimum distributions from his IRA?

ANSWER: Yes. Because Paul had selected his estate as the beneficiary of his IRA as of his required beginning date, then he must use the single life-expectancy table in calculating the required minimum distributions from his IRA. The subsequent selection of his brother, Bernard, as the designated beneficiary of his IRA after his required beginning date comes too late in the game.

QUESTION 6.5: May Paul change the beneficiary to a designated beneficiary of his IRA after his required beginning date?

ANSWER: Yes. One can always change a beneficiary or designated beneficiary of an IRA at any time. However, for purposes of figuring required minimum distributions, the IRS life-expectancy rules that are described in this book depend on who is the designated beneficiary of the IRA owner as of the IRA owner's required beginning date.

QUESTION 6.6: Assume that as of December 31, 1999, Paul had selected his estate as the beneficiary of his IRA. Paul selects his brother, Bernard, as the designated beneficiary of his IRA by his required beginning date of April 1, 2000. May Paul take advantage of the IRS joint life-expectancy tables in calculating his required minimum distribution for the calendar year 1999?

ANSWER: Yes. The IRS rules state that an IRA owner may select his designated beneficiary by no later than his required beginning date, which here is April 1, 2000. Paul can anticipate the fact that he will select Bernard as his designated beneficiary by no later than his required beginning date of April 1, 2000. Therefore, Paul may calculate his required minimum distribution for the calendar year 1999 based upon an IRS joint life-expectancy period of 24.9 years. If Bernard should die before April 1, 2000, then Paul may select another designated beneficiary by that date or leave his estate as his beneficiary. If Paul should leave his estate as his beneficiary as of his required beginning date, then he must receive his required minimum distribution for the calendar year 1999 by no later than April 1, 2000, based upon a single life expectancy of 16 years, the single life expectancy of a 70-year-old under IRS Table I from Publication 590, shown in Appendix A of this book.

QUESTION 6.7: Assume that Paul's IRA balance as of December 31, 1998, is $96,000. During the calendar year 1999 Paul selected his estate as his beneficiary, but he anticipates selecting his

brother, Bernard, as his designated beneficiary by no later than April 1, 2000, Paul's required beginning date. How much must Paul receive from his IRA for the calendar year 1999 to avoid an IRS penalty, based upon his anticipated selection of his brother Bernard as his designated beneficiary?

ANSWER: $3,855.42. Paul's first distribution calendar year is 1999. In order to determine his required minimum distribution for the first distribution calendar year 1999, Paul must use the value of his IRA balance as of the end of the prior year, which is divided by the appropriate life expectancy that is applicable to the first distribution calendar year 1999. The account balance as of December 31, 1998, of $96,000 is divided by 24.9 years, the joint life expectancy of Paul and Bernard as of 1999; see Question 6.3. Use of the 24.9-year period assumes that Paul selects Bernard as his designated beneficiary by April 1, 2000, Paul's required beginning date. Dividing $96,000 by 24.9 years results in a required minimum distribution for 1999 of $3,855.42.

ELECTING TERM-CERTAIN METHOD:
QUESTIONS 6.8–6.18

QUESTION 6.8: Assume that Paul timely selects his brother, Bernard, as the designated beneficiary of his IRA. Also assume that the IRA plan document permits Paul to elect the term-certain method by no later than his required beginning date. Should Paul elect the term-certain method and how would he do so if he wanted to?

ANSWER: Paul should elect the term-certain method. Otherwise, he would have to use a more complicated "hybrid" method. Distributions to Paul's beneficiary, Bernard, would have to be paid over a shorter period under the hybrid method. The hybrid method is discussed starting at Question 6.35.

Paul should timely elect in writing to use the term-certain method. He should send off a certified letter, return receipt requested, to his IRA institution so that it is received by the institution no later than his required beginning date. Paul should elect the maximum term-certain period of 24.9 years, because he may always accelerate distributions from time to time. However, if he wishes he may elect a term-certain period of 24 years for convenience purposes. The maximum term-certain period of 24.9 years is the joint life expectancy of Paul and Bernard as of the year Paul attains age $70^{1}/_{2}$; see Question 6.3.

QUESTION 6.9: Assume that Paul timely selected Bernard as the designated beneficiary of his IRA. Also assume that Paul timely elects the term-certain method without specifying the term-certain period. Would the term-certain period be deemed to be 24.9 years?

ANSWER: Probably. The IRS has not issued any guidelines on the mechanics of making the election. As a result, the IRS letter rulings have been liberal in nature and reasonable in their interpretation of the distribution rules where possible. Therefore, the 24.9-year term-certain period would probably be deemed to have been automatically elected.

QUESTION 6.10: Assume that Paul timely selected Bernard as the designated beneficiary of his IRA. Also assume that Paul timely elected a 20-year term-certain period by his required beginning date. Could he later change his mind after his required beginning date and switch to 24.9 years as the term-certain period?

ANSWER: In the absence of a letter ruling to the contrary, no. However, the IRS has stated its position in the case of annuity distributions from a defined benefit plan as follows:

Once payments have commenced over a period certain, the period certain may not be lengthened even if the period certain is shorter than the maximum permitted.

QUESTION 6.11: Based upon the answer to Question 6.10, what should Paul do if he wishes to maximize the term-certain period?

ANSWER: Paul should timely elect the maximum term-certain period by his required beginning date in order to play it safe. He can round down the maximum period if he wishes. If he merely elects the term-certain method without specifying a term-certain period, then the IRS will probably have no alternative but to permit him to automatically use the maximum term-certain period. Paul should not elect a term-certain period of 20 years and then hope to expand it at a later date. There is currently no authority to allow a subsequent expansion of the distribution period from 20 years to 24.9 years after the required beginning date.

QUESTION 6.12: Assume that Paul selected his brother Bernard as the designated beneficiary of his IRA by his required beginning date. If Paul timely elects to receive his required minimum distributions over a term-certain period of 24.9 years, what life-expectancy period would he use during his first seven distribution calendar years in determining his required minimum distributions?

ANSWER: The following schedule indicates the life-expectancy period that Paul would use under the term-certain method. As you can see, the term-certain period decreases by one with each distribution calendar year.

PAUL'S AGE	DISTRIBUTION YEAR	CALENDAR YEAR	TERM-CERTAIN PERIOD
70	1	1999	24.9
71	2	2000	23.9
72	3	2001	22.9

PAUL'S AGE	DISTRIBUTION YEAR	CALENDAR YEAR	TERM-CERTAIN PERIOD
73	4	2002	21.9
74	5	2003	20.9
75	6	2004	19.9
76	7	2005	18.9

QUESTION 6.13: Assume that Paul timely selected his brother Bernard as the designated beneficiary of his IRA by no later than his required beginning date of April 1, 2000. Also assume that Paul timely elected with the IRA institution to receive his required minimum distributions from the IRA over a term-certain period of 24.9 years. May Paul accelerate distributions from his IRA from time to time?

ANSWER: Yes. Nothing prevents Paul from accelerating his distributions from his IRA from time to time. The law only provides that Paul must receive annual required *minimum* distributions from his IRA in order to avoid the 50-percent penalty that is applicable to a shortfall in a required minimum distribution. Paul can always withdraw more than the minimum amount required to avoid a penalty.

QUESTION 6.14: Assume that Bernard dies on March 1, 2000. Paul then selects his estate as the beneficiary of his IRA. He withdrew $3,855.42 from his IRA during his first distribution calendar year 1999. What should Paul do in order to avoid any penalty with respect to his required minimum distribution for his first distribution calendar year 1999?

ANSWER: Paul has until April 1, 2000, to take his required minimum distribution for his first distribution calendar year 1999. Paul's required distribution for the calendar year 1999 would be

$6,000, equal to his $96,000 account balance as of December 31, 1998, divided by 16 years. This 16-year period is based upon the single life expectancy of Paul. Because Paul received $3,855.42 during his first distribution calendar year 1999, he must receive an additional $2,144.58 by no later than April 1, 2000, in order to avoid any 50-percent penalty. The difference between $6,000 and $3,855.42 is $2,144.58, which is the balance that is necessary in order to satisfy the required minimum distribution for the first distribution calendar year 1999.

DISTRIBUTIONS TO A NONSPOUSE DESIGNATED BENEFICIARY UNDER TERM-CERTAIN METHOD FOLLOWING REQUIRED BEGINNING DATE

The following questions and answers consider the manner in which a nonspouse designated beneficiary must receive required minimum distributions following the account owner's death, assuming the owner had timely elected the term-certain method as described in the answer to Question 6.8.

QUESTION 6.15: Assume that Paul timely selected (see the answer to Question 6.8) Bernard as his designated beneficiary and elected a term-certain period of 24.9 years over which to receive his required minimum distributions from his IRA. Also assume that Paul died in 2005 at age 76. The year 2005 is Paul's seventh distribution calendar year (see answer to question 6.12). He received his required minimum distribution for his seventh distribution calendar year 2005 before the date of his death. Assume that Bernard survived Paul and is still the designated beneficiary of Paul's IRA. When must Bernard commence his required minimum distributions from Paul's IRA?

ANSWER: Bernard must commence his required minimum distributions from Paul's IRA in 2006, the calendar year following

Paul's year of death. This is necessary in order for Bernard to satisfy the required minimum distribution rules that are now applicable to Bernard upon Paul's death.

QUESTION 6.16: Based upon the facts in Question 6.15, over how many years may Bernard receive required minimum distributions from Paul's IRA?

ANSWER: Bernard may receive required minimum distributions from Paul's IRA over a 17.9 year term-certain period. This is based upon the fact that Paul elected a 24.9-year term-certain period over which to receive required minimum distributions from his IRA and seven years have elapsed in the 24.9-year term-certain period, counting the year of Paul's death as a full elapsed year. The balance of the term-certain period that Bernard may use is 17.9 years.

QUESTION 6.17: Assume the facts in Question 6.15. Also assume that Paul's IRA balance as of December 31, 2005, is $85,000. How much must Bernard receive from Paul's IRA during the calendar year 2006 in order to satisfy the IRS required minimum-distribution rules?

ANSWER: $4,748.60. Bernard calculates his required minimum distribution from Paul's IRA by dividing Paul's IRA balance as of December 31, 2005, of $85,000 by the 17.9 years that remains in the initial term-certain period of 24.9 years. The result is $4,748.60.

QUESTION 6.18: Under the facts in Question 6.15, Bernard may receive required minimum distributions over a term-certain period of 17.9 years following Paul's death, but may Bernard accelerate distributions from Paul's IRA from time to time?

ANSWER: Yes. Nothing prevents Bernard from accelerating distributions from Paul's IRA from time to time. The law only requires that Bernard receive required *minimum* distributions annually from Paul's IRA in order to avoid the 50-percent penalty that is applicable to a shortfall in a required minimum distribution. Bernard is free to withdraw more than the required minimum amount.

QUESTION 6.19: Assume that Bernard survives Paul. Bernard is not sophisticated in financial matters and has Paul's IRA retitled into his own name. Will there be a tax problem as a result of the change in the name of Paul's IRA into Bernard's name?

ANSWER: Yes. The IRA institution will issue a Form 1099-R to Bernard, and he will have instant taxable income on Paul's entire IRA balance. It is as if the entire balance had been distributed to Bernard. Bernard is not permitted to roll over Paul's IRA.

QUESTION 6.20: What should Bernard do in order to prevent the tax problem discussed in Question 6.19?

ANSWER: Paul's IRA must be maintained in Paul's name. Bernard would then receive required minimum annual distributions as Paul's designated beneficiary as described in Questions 6.15–6.18. Paul's IRA should indicate that Paul is deceased and indicate the date of Paul's death. In addition, Bernard's social security number should be used on Paul's IRA account for tax purposes.

QUESTION 6.21: Assume that Paul elected a term-certain period of 24.9 years over which to receive his IRA distributions. Also assume that Paul died in 2005 at age 76. The year 2005 is Paul's seventh distribution calendar year. However, Paul died before he received his required minimum distribution for his seventh distribution calendar year. Bernard survived Paul and is still the designated beneficiary of Paul's IRA. What action should Bernard take after Paul's death?

ANSWER: As soon as Bernard ascertains that Paul did not receive his required minimum distribution for year 2005, Bernard should withdraw that amount from Paul's IRA within a reasonable period of time. By law Bernard is entitled to the distribution because he is Paul's designated beneficiary. The distribution for the year 2005 would be based on a term-certain period of 18.9 years, because six years had elapsed in the 24.9-year term-certain period elected by Paul. The required minimum distribution for 2005 that Bernard should withdraw is the IRA balance as of December 31, 2004, divided by 18.9.

This withdrawal by Bernard for the year of Paul's death is necessary in order to avoid any possible penalty by the IRS. The law permits Paul to receive the required minimum distribution for the year 2005 by December 31, 2005. If Paul dies before that date, the IRS will not assert any penalty for the failure of Paul to receive his required minimum distribution for the calendar year 2005. However, Bernard should receive Paul's required minimum distribution for the calendar year 2005 within a reasonable period of time in order to avoid any possible penalty.

In addition, Bernard must commence his required minimum distributions from Paul's IRA starting in the calendar year 2006 and for each calendar year thereafter for the remaining 17.9-year term-certain period. Bernard may accelerate distributions from Paul's IRA from time to time.

DISTRIBUTIONS FOLLOWING THE DEATH OF THE OWNER'S DESIGNATED BENEFICIARY: QUESTIONS 6.22–6.30

QUESTION 6.22: Assume that Bernard died after receiving required minimum distributions from Paul's IRA over a five-year period. Who would receive required minimum distributions from Paul's IRA after the death of Bernard?

ANSWER: Bernard's estate. In the absence of any direction by Bernard, the required minimum distributions of Paul's IRA would be paid to Bernard's estate. This is a matter of state law and not IRS rules. The required minimum distributions are governed by IRS rules. However, property rights are governed by state law.

QUESTION 6.23: Over what period of time would Bernard's estate receive required minimum distributions from Paul's IRA?

ANSWER: Bernard's estate would receive required minimum distributions from Paul's IRA over a 12.9-year period. This is based upon the fact that there are only 12.9 years left in the initial 24.9-year term-certain period. This is computed as follows:

Initial term-certain period elected by Paul:	24.9 years
Less: Years used by Paul:	(7.0) years
Less: Years used by Bernard:	(5.0) years
Balance of term-certain period:	12.9 years

QUESTION 6.24: May Bernard's estate accelerate distributions from Paul's IRA from time to time?

ANSWER: Yes. Nothing prevents Bernard's estate from accelerating distributions from Paul's IRA from time to time. The estate may choose to receive more than the required minimum annual distributions.

QUESTION 6.25: Assume that Bernard's executor does not wish to keep Bernard's estate open for 12.9 years (Question 6.23) in order to receive required minimum distributions from Paul's IRA. What options are available to Bernard's executor?

ANSWER: Bernard's executor may either accelerate the distributions from Paul's IRA to Bernard's estate or assign the rights to the future payments from Paul's IRA to the beneficiaries of Bernard's estate.

QUESTION 6.26: Which option is better?

ANSWER: It is generally better to assign the future payments to the beneficiaries of Bernard's estate if the amounts are significant.

QUESTION 6.27: Before assigning the future payments from Paul's IRA to the beneficiaries of Bernard's estate, what action should Bernard's executor take?

ANSWER: He should discuss the assignment approach with the IRA institution and beneficiaries to make certain that they understand it. In addition, the IRA institution should agree in writing that it will honor the assignment of the IRA payments to the heirs of Bernard's estate.

QUESTION 6.28: Assume that the heirs of Bernard's estate are assigned the remaining future installment payments from Paul's IRA. May the beneficiaries accelerate the payments from Paul's IRA from time to time?

ANSWER: Yes. However, if some of the beneficiaries of Bernard's estate wish to accelerate payments from Paul's IRA from time to time while others do not, then a problem may arise in accounting for the distributions from Paul's IRA. In that case it is best that a number of IRAs then be established and maintained in Paul's name. Each beneficiary of Bernard's estate will then control an IRA that has been allocated to him or her.

QUESTION 6.29: Is there any other reason for establishing a separate IRA that is maintained in Paul's name for each beneficiary of Bernard's estate?

ANSWER: Yes. It is possible that each beneficiary may have a different investment philosophy in investing Paul's IRA funds. By separating IRAs a potential conflict in investment philosophy is avoided.

QUESTION 6.30: Can you think of any other reason for splitting up IRAs so that each beneficiary controls his or her allocated share of Paul's IRA?

ANSWER: The IRA institution may only be able to use the Social Security number of one beneficiary for purposes of reporting annual distributions on Form 1099-R. By having separate IRAs in Paul's name, each beneficiary will receive a separate Form 1099-R.

IF IRA OWNER CHANGES BENEFICIARY AFTER REQUIRED BEGINNING DATE

QUESTION 6.31: Assume that Paul had timely elected the term-certain method in determining his required minimum distributions from his IRA. Also assume that Paul dropped Bernard and selected his own estate as the designated beneficiary of his IRA in the calendar year 2002. What life expectancy would Paul use in determining his required minimum distributions from his IRA for the first seven distribution calendar years under the term-certain method?

ANSWER: The following schedule indicates the period of time that Paul may use in determining his required minimum distributions from his IRA under the term-certain method as a result of dropping Bernard and selecting his own estate as his beneficiary in the calendar year 2002.

PAUL'S AGE	DISTRIBUTION YEAR	CALENDAR YEAR	TERM-CERTAIN METHOD
70	1	1999	24.9
71	2	2000	23.9
72	3	2001	22.9
73	4	2002	21.9
74	5	2003	12.0
75	6	2004	11.0
76	7	2005	10.0

QUESTION 6.32: Why must Paul use a shorter life expectancy under the term-certain method for the calendar year 2003 and thereafter?

ANSWER: The IRS has special rules that are triggered if the IRA owner changes a designated beneficiary while the designated beneficiary is still alive. Paul may no longer use Bernard's life expectancy as of 2003, the calendar year following the calendar year 2002 in which Bernard was dropped as a designated beneficiary and Paul's estate was selected as the beneficiary of his IRA. Paul had timely elected the term-certain method in determining his required minimum distributions from his IRA. He must continue to use the term-certain method even though he may not take advantage of Bernard's life expectancy as of the calendar year 2003 and thereafter. Paul must revert to a single life expectancy as of the calendar year 2003 based upon a term-certain period. The estate has no life expectancy. Paul must determine his single life expectancy as of his birthday in the calendar year that he attained age 70½. Paul attained age 70 and age 70½ in 1999 (Question 6.2). Therefore, Paul's single life expectancy as of 1999 is based on age 70. The single life expectancy for a person who is 70 years old is 16 years, as shown in Table I of IRS Publication 590. This table is included in Appendix A of this book. For each subsequent year, the 16-year period is reduced by one year. As of the calendar year 2003, the remaining term-certain period available to Paul is 12 years. For each year after 2003, the 12-year period is reduced by one year.

QUESTION 6.33: Assume that the term-certain method was applicable and that Bernard was dropped as Paul's designated beneficiary, and Paul's estate selected in the calendar year 2002. Also assume that Paul died in the calendar year 2005 after receiving his required minimum distribution from his IRA for the calendar year 2005. Over what period of time may Paul's estate receive required minimum distributions from Paul's IRA?

ANSWER: Because Paul timely elected the term-certain method, his estate may continue to receive distributions from his IRA over the balance of the 16-year term-certain period based upon Paul's single life expectancy as of 1999 (Question 6.32). In the calendar year 2005 Paul's term-certain period is 10 years (Question 6.31). Therefore, Paul's estate may receive required minimum distributions from Paul's IRA over the remaining nine-year period commencing in the calendar year 2006.

QUESTION 6.34: Assume that Paul timely selected Bernard as the designated beneficiary of his IRA. In the calendar year 2002, Paul dropped Bernard as his designated beneficiary and immediately substituted his other brother, Michael, as his designated beneficiary. Michael is two years younger than Bernard. May Paul take advantage of Michael's life expectancy in determining his required minimum distributions from his IRA?

ANSWER: No. A special rule applies if a younger designated beneficiary replaces an older designated beneficiary after an IRA owner's required beginning date. The life expectancy of the older designated beneficiary is used even though the older designated beneficiary is no longer the designated beneficiary of the

IRA owner. Thus, Michael is deemed to be the same age as Bernard and Michael's younger age is ignored.

Hybrid Method of Figuring Required Minimum Distributions if Term-Certain Method Not Elected

If the IRA owner does not elect the term-certain method (Question 6.8) of calculating required minimum distributions by the required beginning date, then a more complicated "hybrid" method must be used. This hybrid method is explained in the answers to Questions 6.35–6.51.

QUESTION 6.35: Assume that Paul selected Bernard as the designated beneficiary of his IRA as of his required beginning date but failed to elect the term-certain method of distribution. How does Paul's failure to elect the term-certain method of distribution affect the required minimum distributions that Paul must receive?

ANSWER: The distribution rules become much more complex. The law states that the IRA owner may recalculate his or her life expectancy each year, but the nonspouse designated beneficiary's life expectancy may not be recalculated.

QUESTION 6.36: What does recalculation of life expectancy mean?

ANSWER: Recalculation of life expectancy means that when the owner looks up life expectancy in the IRS tables, the owner's age on his or her birthday in each year is used. For example, in his first distribution calendar year of 1999, Paul is age 70 (see Question 6.2). If the recalculation method applies, then for the second distribution calendar year of 2000, Paul's age is 71 when applying the IRS life-expectancy tables. For each subsequent year, Paul's age continues to increase by one year and the life expectancy for that age (from the IRS life-expectancy table) is used.

QUESTION 6.37: How do we know if the IRA owner Paul must recalculate his life expectancy each year?

ANSWER: The IRA plan document must be consulted in order to determine whether or not the term-certain method could have been timely elected by Paul. The IRA plan document may specify whether or not the life expectancy of Paul must be recalculated in the event that Paul fails to make a timely election of a distribution method. If the IRA plan document is silent concerning distribution methods, then under the IRS rules Paul must automatically default into the recalculation method as far as his own life expectancy is concerned. The recalculation method is not applicable to a nonspouse designated beneficiary.

CASE STUDY
Questions 6.38–6.51 illustrate how an IRA owner figures required minimum distributions under the hybrid method, and how distributions to a designated beneficiary are figured under the hybrid method.

QUESTION 6.38: Assume that Paul defaults into the recalculation method in calculating his required minimum distributions. Also assume that Bernard has been timely selected as the designated beneficiary of Paul's IRA. What is the method that is used in determining Paul's required minimum distributions each year?

ANSWER: It is neither the term-certain method nor the recalculation method. It is a hybrid method for determining Paul's required minimum distributions from his IRA. The hybrid method recalculates Paul's life expectancy each year but uses a term-certain method with respect to Bernard's life expectancy. Remember that Bernard is 8 years younger than Paul (Question 6.2).

QUESTION 6.39: Would you please indicate the applicable life expectancy that would be used by Paul in determining his required minimum distributions from his IRA for the first seven calendar years if he defaulted into the hybrid method?

ANSWER: The following schedule reflects the life expectancy that Paul would use under the hybrid method.

PAUL'S AGE	DISTRIBUTION YEAR	CALENDAR YEAR	HYBRID METHOD
70	1	1999	24.9
71	2	2000	23.4
72	3	2001	22.5
73	4	2002	21.6
74	5	2003	20.8
75	6	2004	19.3
76	7	2005	18.5

QUESTION 6.40: How did you arrive at the life expectancy that was determined under the hybrid method as described in your answer to Question 6.39?

ANSWER: Unless the owner has timely elected the term-certain method, the special IRS hybrid method rules apply if an individual has a nonspouse designated beneficiary who is older or no more than 10 years younger than the IRA owner. Bernard is a nonspouse designated beneficiary of Paul's IRA and is eight years younger than Paul. Because Paul failed to timely elect the term-certain method with the IRA institution and defaulted into the hybrid method, the IRS special rules must be followed.

For the first distribution calendar year, the computation of joint life expectancy under the hybrid method is the same as under the term-certain method. However, for subsequent years, the hybrid method of figuring joint life expectancy is more complicated. In the second distribution calendar year and for each subsequent year, Paul's recalculated age is his attained age on his birthday in that year. To determine Bernard's age for purposes of the joint life-expectancy computation, his single life expectancy as of Paul's first distribution calendar year is reduced by one for each elapsed year and then a revised age for Bernard is determined by looking up in the IRS single life-expectancy table the age that corresponds to his reduced life expectancy. If the reduced life expectancy falls between two life expectancies listed in the IRS table, the shorter of the two life expectancies (the older age) applies and that older age is Bernard's revised age for years following the first distribution calendar year. Given the complications of figuring the revised age of the designated beneficiary, it may be advisable to obtain the assistance of a tax professional if the hybrid method applies.

QUESTION 6.41: Assume that Paul timely selected his brother Bernard as the designated beneficiary of his IRA. Can you please compare the applicable life expectancy that would be used by Paul in determining his required minimum distributions from his IRA for the first seven distribution calendar years under the hybrid method and under the term-certain method?

ANSWER: The following schedule reflects the comparison of the hybrid method and the term-certain method. Although the applicable life expectancy under the two methods is practically the same, the hybrid computation is much more complicated, as discussed in the answer to Question 6.40.

PAUL'S AGE	DISTRIBUTION YEAR	CALENDAR YEAR	HYBRID METHOD	TERM-CERTAIN METHOD
70	1	1999	24.9	24.9
71	2	2000	23.4	23.9
72	3	2001	22.5	22.9
73	4	2002	21.6	21.9
74	5	2003	20.8	20.9
75	6	2004	19.3	19.9
76	7	2005	18.5	18.9

QUESTION 6.42: Assume that Paul timely selected Bernard as the designated beneficiary of his IRA. For the years 1999 through 2005, Paul receives required minimum distributions using the hybrid method. During the calendar year 2005, Paul dies after receiving his required minimum distribution for the calendar year 2005. Assume that Bernard survives Paul. Over what period of time may Bernard receive his required minimum distributions under the hybrid method after the death of Paul?

ANSWER: The IRS has special rules that apply in order to determine the period of time that Bernard may receive his required minimum distributions under the hybrid method. Bernard must initially determine his single life expectancy under the IRS life-expectancy tables in the calendar year that Paul attained age 70^1/2. In the year that Paul attained age 70^1/2, Bernard was age 62. The single life expectancy of an individual age 62 under Table V of 1.72-9 of the Income Tax Regulations is 22.5 years. This table is shown in Appendix A as Table I from IRS Publication 590. That 22.5-year period is used in calculating the life expectancy that can be used by Bernard after the year of death of Paul. Because Paul lived for seven distribution calendar years (counting the year of death as a full year) then seven years are subtracted from the 22.5-year period in order to determine the remaining period that can be used by Bernard in determining his required minimum distributions from Paul's IRA. Thus, Bernard may receive his required minimum distributions from Paul's IRA over 15.5 years starting in the calendar year 2006.

QUESTION 6.43: Assume that Paul dies in the calendar year 2005 and that Bernard, his designated IRA beneficiary, survives him. Paul received his required minimum distribution for 2005 before he died. Would you please compare the remaining period that Bernard could use in determining his required minimum distributions under the hybrid method versus the term-certain method over a 12-year period commencing in 2006?

ANSWER: The following schedule indicates the difference in the remaining period that can be used by Bernard under the hybrid method versus the term-certain method. The hybrid method applies unless Paul elected the term-certain method by his required beginning date of April 1, 2000. Bernard must commence his required minimum distributions from Paul's IRA in 2006, the calendar year following the year of Paul's death.

BERNARD'S AGE	DISTRIBUTION YEAR	CALENDAR YEAR	HYBRID METHOD	TERM-CERTAIN METHOD
69	1	2006	15.5	17.9
70	2	2007	14.5	16.9
71	3	2008	13.5	15.9
72	4	2009	12.5	14.9
73	5	2010	11.5	13.9
74	6	2011	10.5	12.9
75	7	2012	9.5	11.9

BERNARD'S AGE	DISTRIBUTION YEAR	CALENDAR YEAR	HYBRID METHOD	TERM-CERTAIN METHOD
76	8	2013	8.5	10.9
77	9	2014	7.5	9.9
78	10	2015	6.5	8.9
79	11	2016	5.5	7.9
80	12	2017	4.5	6.9

QUESTION 6.44: Assume that Bernard dies in the calendar year 2017 after receiving his required minimum distribution for the year 2017. Over what period of time may Bernard's estate receive required minimum distributions from Paul's IRA?

ANSWER: That depends upon whether the hybrid method or the term-certain method of distribution was used in determining Paul's required minimum distributions. Under the hybrid method Bernard's estate could receive required minimum distributions from Paul's IRA over a 3.5-year period starting in 2018. If the term-certain was applicable, then Bernard's estate could receive required minimum distributions from Paul's IRA over a 5.9-year period starting in 2018. The difference between the two methods is 2.4 years.

QUESTION 6.45: Assume that Paul had timely selected Bernard as the designated beneficiary of his IRA. Paul failed to timely elect the term-certain method and therefore defaulted into the hybrid method. Further assume that Bernard, his designated beneficiary, dies in Paul's third distribution calendar year 2001. Would you please tell me what period of time Paul may use in determining his required minimum distributions from his IRA under the hybrid method for the calendar years 1999 through 2005?

ANSWER: The following schedule indicates the period of time that Paul may use in determining his required minimum distributions from his IRA under the hybrid method even though Bernard died in the calendar year 2001.

PAUL'S AGE	DISTRIBUTION YEAR	CALENDAR YEAR	HYBRID METHOD
70	1	1999	24.9
71	2	2000	23.4
72	3	2001	22.5
73	4	2002	21.6
74	5	2003	20.8
75	6	2004	19.3
76	7	2005	18.5

QUESTION 6.46: Your answer to Question 6.45 is the same as your answer to Question 6.39. Can you explain why your answer to each question is the same?

ANSWER: Yes. According to the IRS, if Bernard is the designated beneficiary of Paul's IRA as of Paul's required beginning date, then Bernard's remaining life expectancy is fixed and can be used by Paul after Bernard dies.

QUESTION 6.47: May Paul change the beneficiary of his IRA to his estate after Bernard dies and still take advantage of Bernard's life expectancy in determining his required minimum distributions?

ANSWER: Yes. The calculation that is made for Paul's required minimum distributions after Bernard's death is made as if Bernard were still alive. Once again, Bernard's remaining life expectancy is fixed and his death will not result in a change in the payout period.

QUESTION 6.48: Assume that Bernard did not die but that Paul eliminated Bernard as his designated beneficiary and selected his own estate as the beneficiary of his IRA in the calendar year 2002. Would your answer to Question 6.47 change?

ANSWER: Yes. If Paul drops Bernard and selects his own estate as his designated beneficiary while Bernard is alive in the calendar year 2002, then Paul loses the benefit of Bernard's life expectancy in the calendar year 2003 and for all calendar years thereafter.

QUESTION 6.49: Assume that Paul dropped Bernard and selected his own estate as the beneficiary of his IRA in the calendar year 2002. Further assume that the hybrid method was applicable. Could you please indicate the life expectancy that would be used by Paul in determining his required minimum distributions from his IRA for the first seven distribution calendar years under the hybrid method?

ANSWER: The following schedule indicates the period of time that Paul may use in determining his required minimum distributions from his IRA under the hybrid method as a result of dropping Bernard and selecting his own estate as his designated beneficiary in the calendar year 2002.

PAUL'S AGE	DISTRIBUTION YEAR	CALENDAR YEAR	HYBRID METHOD
70	1	1999	24.9
71	2	2000	23.4
72	3	2001	22.5

→

73	4	2002	21.6
74	5	2003	13.2
75	6	2004	12.5
76	7	2005	11.9

QUESTION 6.50: Based upon the facts in Question 6.49, why is there such a dramatic drop in the life-expectancy table that Paul may use under the hybrid method for the calendar year 2003 and calendar years thereafter?

ANSWER: Because Bernard was dropped as the designated beneficiary during 2002, Paul may not use Bernard's remaining life expectancy in the calendar year 2003 or later calendar years. Because Paul is under the hybrid method he must use the recalculation method based upon his single life expectancy. The single life-expectancy table from IRS Publication 590, shown in Appendix A, provides the single life expectancy that Paul must use for the calendar year 2003 and calendar years thereafter. The table from IRS Publication 590 is based upon Table V of Section 1.72-9 of the Income Tax Regulations. The table provides a life expectancy of 13.2 years for a 74-year-old person. Each year his life expectancy is recalculated based on the table and used in determining his required minimum distributions from his IRA.

QUESTION 6.51: Assume the facts in Question 6.49 but then Paul dies in 2005. When must Paul's estate receive Paul's IRA?

ANSWER: Paul's life expectancy under the recalculation method is reduced to zero in the calendar year following his year of death. Because Paul died during the calendar year 2005, Paul's estate must receive his entire IRA balance during the period between January 1, 2006, and December 30, 2006.

CHAPTER SEVEN

THE ESTATE AS BENEFICIARY OF IRA OR QUALIFIED PLAN

Most IRA owners and plan participants designate specific beneficiaries for their qualified employer retirement plans and IRA's. Generally, it is preferable to timely select a designated beneficiary because the selection of a designated beneficiary will allow a longer life-expectancy period for the payout of plan or IRA benefits. These life-expectancy rules have been discussed in the previous chapters that relate to specific types of beneficiaries. However, in the event that the IRA owner or plan participant does not select anyone to benefit from his retirement benefits, then the estate becomes the beneficiary. This chapter will review the lifetime required minimum distribution rules for IRA owners and plan participants who select their estates as their beneficiaries, as well as the distribution rules for the estate following the death of the IRA owner or plan participant.

DISADVANTAGE OF SELECTING YOUR ESTATE AS BENEFICIARY

QUESTION 7.1: Why is it beneficial to timely select a designated beneficiary of my retirement plan assets?

ANSWER: The timely selection of the designated beneficiary is important because the life expectancy of the designated beneficiary is considered in determining the calculation of the required minimum distributions that must be paid to you on and after your required beginning date; see Questions 2.2 and 2.3. In addition, the life expectancy of a designated beneficiary is considered in determining the calculation of the required minimum distributions that must be paid to the designated beneficiary after your death.

QUESTION 7.2: Is an estate considered to be a designated beneficiary?

ANSWER: No. An estate is considered a beneficiary but not a designated beneficiary. Only an individual may be a designated beneficiary. The estate does not have a life expectancy that you may use in calculating your required minimum distribution.

Because the estate does not have a life expectancy, the required minimum distributions that you must receive starting at your required beginning date will be payable over your single life expectancy; see Questions 7.3–7.8. Rules for distributions to an estate following the death of an IRA owner or plan participant are discussed in Questions 7.9–7.34.

RECALCULATION METHOD AND TERM-CERTAIN METHOD

Questions 7.3–7.24 explain how to figure the amount of required minimum distributions under the recalculation and term-certain methods if an estate is the beneficiary and how the choice of methods also affects distributions to your estate if you die on or after your required beginning date.

QUESTION 7.3: Assume that Marshall Jones attains age 70 and also 70¹/₂ in the calendar year 1999. He is single and has selected his

estate as the beneficiary of his IRA. He fails to timely elect the term-certain method by his required beginning date of April 1, 2000. The IRA plan document states that the recalculation method is applicable if the IRA owner fails to timely elect not to use the recalculation method. Assume that Marshall lives until 2019. Can you please indicate what the life expectancy is for Marshall for each distribution calendar year under the recalculation method?

ANSWER: If the recalculation method applies, the following schedule reflects the life-expectancy period that Marshall would use to compute his required minimum distributions until his death in 2019 at age 90. The schedule would be different under the term-certain method as discussed in Question 7.5.

Recalculation Method

MARSHALL'S AGE	DISTRIBUTION YEAR	CALENDAR YEAR	LIFE EXPECTANCY
70	1	1999	16.0
71	2	2000	15.3
72	3	2001	14.6
73	4	2002	13.9
74	5	2003	13.2
75	6	2004	12.5
76	7	2005	11.9
77	8	2006	11.2
78	9	2007	10.6 →

79	10	2008	10.0
80	11	2009	9.5
81	12	2010	8.9
82	13	2011	8.4
83	14	2012	7.9
84	15	2013	7.4
85	16	2014	6.9
86	17	2015	6.5
87	18	2016	6.1
88	19	2017	5.7
89	20	2018	5.3
90	21	2019	5.0
91	22	2020	0.0

QUESTION 7.4: How did you arrive at the life expectancy of Marshall under the recalculation method for each of the distribution calendar years described in Question 7.3?

ANSWER: Marshall must use the single life-expectancy table under Table V of section 1.72-9 of the Income Tax Regulations. The single life expectancy of Marshall may also be found in Table I of IRS Publication 590, which is included in Appendix A of this book. The table shows a 16-year life expectancy for a 70-year-old person.

Marshall must use his single life expectancy because under the law the estate as his beneficiary has no life expectancy.

QUESTION 7.5: How does the single life-expectancy table work if the recalculation method is used for Marshall and how does this compare to the term-certain method?

ANSWER: If the recalculation method is used, then the life-expectancy table must be consulted each year. Using his attained age as of his birthday in each year, Marshall's life expectancy from the IRS table changes each year by less than one. Under the recalculation method, Marshall's life expectancy is reduced to zero in the year following the year of his death.

Under the term-certain method, Marshall's life expectancy is reduced by one for each distribution calendar year that follows Marshall's first distribution calendar year. Thus, Marshall's term-certain period of 16 years for the first distribution year of 1999 would be reduced to 15 years for 2000, to 14 years for 2001, and so on until it is reduced to zero in the year 2015. In addition, the term-certain method survives Marshall's death should he die before the end of the term-certain period; see Question 7.16.

QUESTION 7.6: In Marshall's first distribution calendar year, is the required minimum distribution under the recalculation method less than under the term-certain method?

ANSWER: No. Marshall's life expectancy is 16 years in his first distribution calendar year under both the term-certain method and recalculation method. The required minimum distribution under both methods is identical for the first distribution calendar year. There is no difference between the methods until the second distribution year.

QUESTION 7.7: How much must Marshall receive as his required minimum distribution for his first distribution calendar year 1999?

ANSWER: Marshall must divide his single life expectancy of 16 years (Question 7.4) into his IRA balance as of December 31, 1998, the end of the year preceding the first distribution calendar year 1999. The first distribution calendar year is 1999 because that is the year during which Marshall attains age 70$^{1}/_{2}$. Assuming that the account balance as of December 31, 1998, is $96,000, Marshall's required minimum distribution for the first distribution calendar year 1999 is $6,000. This is the minimum amount Marshall must receive to avoid an IRS penalty (Question 7.11). He may of course receive more than that minimum.

QUESTION 7.8: Assume that Marshall received his $6,000 required minimum distribution for his first distribution calendar year 1999 on October 31, 1999. Further assume that his account balance in his IRA as of December 31, 1999 is $96,700. How much must Marshall receive during the second distribution calendar year 2000 under the recalculation method in order to satisfy the required minimum distribution rules for the calendar year 2000?

ANSWER: $6,320.26. The calendar year 2000 is Marshall's second distribution calendar year. He must receive his required minimum distribution for his second distribution calendar year by December 31, 2000. In order to determine his required minimum distribution for the calendar year 2000, the value of his account balance as of December 31, 1999, must be divided by the appropriate life expectancy that is applicable to the calendar year 2000. The account balance of $96,700 is divided by 15.3 years, which is the life expectancy of Marshall under the recalculation method as of the second distribution calendar year 2000 as shown in the answer to Question 7.3. The result is a required minimum distribution of $6,320.26.

DISTRIBUTIONS TO ESTATE IF IRA OWNER DIES AFTER REQUIRED BEGINNING DATE: QUESTIONS 7.9–7.24

QUESTION 7.9: Assume that Marshall has selected his estate as the beneficiary of his IRA. Marshall failed to elect the term-certain

method by his required beginning date. The IRA plan document states that unless he elects out of the recalculation method by his required beginning date, he defaults into the recalculation method. Further assume that Marshall dies September 1, 2004, after receiving his required minimum distribution for the calendar year 2004. The calendar year 2004 is his sixth distribution calendar year (Question 7.3). Assume that as of December 31, 2004, the account balance in Marshall's IRA is $100,000. What happens to Marshall's IRA in the calendar year 2005 under the recalculation method?

ANSWER: The IRS requires that the IRA be liquidated and paid out in its entirety to Marshall's estate by no later than December 30, 2005. This payout would include any earnings on the $100,000 account balance in Marshall's IRA as well. Any losses would, of course, reduce the balance.

QUESTION 7.10: Why does the entire account balance have to be paid to Marshall's estate before the last day of the year following the year of Marshall's death?

ANSWER: Under the IRS rules, if Marshall is using the recalculation method, his life expectancy is reduced to zero in the calendar year following the calendar year of his death. Marshall's expectancy is reduced to zero as of 2005. The IRA institution must distribute Marshall's entire remaining interest in the account prior to the last day of 2005, the calendar year following the year of his death.

Marshall's estate must receive the entire balance in Marshall's IRA during the period between January 1, 2005, and December 30, 2005.

QUESTION 7.11: Assume that Marshall's estate receives all but $20,000 of Marshall's IRA during the period between January 1, 2005, and December 30, 2005. The remaining $20,000 is received by the estate in the calendar year 2006. May the IRS assess a penalty against Marshall's estate?

ANSWER: Yes. Marshall's estate received an insufficient distribution from Marshall's IRA during the calendar year 2005. The short-fall is $20,000. The IRS may assess a penalty of 50 percent of the shortfall of $20,000 against the estate for the calendar year 2005. Thus, Marshall's estate may be subject to a penalty of $10,000 for the calendar year 2005.

QUESTION 7.12: May the IRS waive the $10,000 penalty described in Question 7.11?

ANSWER: Yes. The IRS may waive the penalty if the shortfall was due to reasonable error and reasonable steps are being taken to remedy the shortfall.

QUESTION 7.13: Should Marshall's estate select a calendar year for estate income tax purposes?

ANSWER: No. If Marshall's estate uses a calendar year, then the entire balance in Marshall's IRA would be received in one tax-able year of the estate.

QUESTION 7.14: Assume that Marshall died on September 1, 2004. What fiscal year could Marshall's estate elect?

ANSWER: The executor of Marshall's estate could elect a fiscal year for the estate such as September 1, 2004, through August 31, 2005.

QUESTION 7.15: If Marshall's executor elected the fiscal year September 1, 2004, through August 31, 2005, may that election result in an overall income tax savings to the estate and/or the heirs of the estate?

ANSWER: Yes. Marshall's life expectancy is reduced to zero under the recalculation method as of 2005, the year after the year

(2004) of his death. Therefore, Marshall's estate must receive Marshall's entire interest in his IRA between the period January 1, 2005, through December 30, 2005. If Marshall's estate has a fiscal year, then the IRA distribution from Marshall's IRA may be received in two fiscal years of the estate. A portion of Marshall's IRA may be received during the estate's fiscal year September 1, 2004, through August 31, 2005, and a portion of Marshall's IRA may be received during the estate's fiscal year September 1, 2005 through August 31, 2006. Remember that the entire interest of Marshall's IRA must be paid to Marshall's estate during the period January 1, 2005, through December 30, 2005. Allocating income over two fiscal years is generally worthwhile because it gives the executor and heirs an additional opportunity for tax planning. Income-tax splitting and deferral of income tax liability is important in view of the high income tax rates that are currently applicable to estates and beneficiaries.

QUESTION 7.16: Assume that Marshall selected his estate as the beneficiary of his IRA. Prior to his required beginning date he timely elected to receive his required minimum distributions from his IRA over a 16-year term-certain period. Assume that Marshall died on September 1, 2004, after receiving his required minimum distribution from his IRA for his sixth distribution calendar year 2004. Must Marshall's estate receive the entire interest from Marshall's IRA during the period January 1, 2005, through December 30, 2005?

ANSWER: No. Marshall's estate may receive the required minimum distributions from Marshall's IRA over the remaining 10 years that is left in the original 16-year term-certain period.

If an IRA owner timely elects a term-certain period and dies on or after his or her required beginning date, then the term-certain period may continue after the IRA owner's death. Because Marshall timely elected a 16-year term-certain period and died in his sixth distribution calendar year, his estate may receive required minimum distributions for the remaining 10-year period that is left in the initial 16-year term-certain period. In this situation, it does not matter that the estate is the beneficiary.

QUESTION 7.17: Based upon the answer to Question 7.16, must Marshall's estate receive the required minimum distributions from Marshall's IRA over the remaining 10-year period?

ANSWER: No. Although the estate may not receive required minimum distributions over a period that exceeds the 10-year term-certain period, the executor may accelerate distributions from Marshall's IRA from time to time. The IRS asserts a 50-percent penalty when the recipient receives an insufficient distribution. No penalties apply if a distribution is greater than the required minimum distribution.

QUESTION 7.18: Assume that the executor of Marshall's estate does not wish to keep the estate open for 10 years. What action can the executor take other than accelerating distributions from Marshall's IRA?

ANSWER: The executor may assign the remaining unpaid installments from Marshall's IRA to the beneficiaries of Marshall's estate. In that case, the beneficiaries may continue to receive the installments from Marshall's IRA over the balance of the term-certain period or accelerate distributions from time to time. However, before the installments are assigned to the beneficiaries of Marshall's estate, the IRA institution should be consulted. If the IRA institution refuses to go along with the assignment, then it may be necessary to obtain a letter ruling from the IRS in order to convince the IRA institution that the transaction is not in violation of any IRA rules.

QUESTION 7.19: Assume that Marshall's date of death is September 1, 2004. Upon Marshall's death, how should his IRA read to indicate that his estate is his beneficiary?

ANSWER: The IRA must be maintained in Marshall's name. It should read "Marshall Jones, deceased IRA (date of death: September 1, 2004), Estate of Marshall Jones, beneficiary ID No. 18-1000000." The failure to use the exact words described above should not prove fatal as long as the IRA is maintained in Marshall's name.

QUESTION 7.20: Assume that Marshall's IRA is erroneously changed after Marshall's death to read "Estate of Marshall Jones" and there is no reference in the account name to Marshall's IRA. What is the tax consequence of the change in the name of the account?

ANSWER: The estate has a serious tax problem. The IRS will attempt to tax the entire account as a distribution of the IRA to the estate. The IRA must be maintained in Marshall's name in order to avoid a taxable event to the estate. If this situation should come up, then the estate should ask the financial institution to explain the error to the IRS. In the event that this explanation is not acceptable to the IRS, then the estate will have to litigate the tax issue with the IRS.

QUESTION 7.21: What is the advantage of Marshall's electing the 16-year term-certain period described above?

ANSWER: In the event that Marshall dies during the 16-year term-certain period, then his estate can continue to use the balance of the term-certain period in order to receive the required minimum distributions from Marshall's IRA. This is especially beneficial if Marshall should die during the first half of the term-certain period.

QUESTION 7.22: What is the advantage of Marshall using the recalculation method of receiving required minimum distributions from his IRA?

ANSWER: If Marshall uses the recalculation method and lives beyond 2014 when he attains age 85, he will still be able to continue to receive required minimum distributions from his IRA; see the recalculation table accompanying Question 7.3. This assumes that Marshall has not withdrawn all of his money from his IRA at an earlier point in time. Under the term-certain method, the entire account would have to be distributed by the end of 2014.

QUESTION 7.23: Assume that Marshall selected his estate as the beneficiary of his IRA. What is the disadvantage of Marshall's using the recalculation method of receiving required minimum distributions from his IRA?

ANSWER: If Marshall uses the recalculation method and he should die at a point in time when he has a substantial amount of assets in his IRA, then the entire interest in his IRA must be paid out between January 1 and December 30 of the calendar year following the calendar year of his death. This will result in an acceleration of income and the loss of the tax-deferred growth of his IRA.

QUESTION 7.24: Which approach should Marshall select: the term-certain method or the recalculation method?

ANSWER: There is no easy answer. If Marshall is conservative and wishes to protect the heirs of his estate, then he should use the term-certain method. If he is a gambler and wishes to bet on a long life and is not concerned with the potential income acceleration problem that is attendant with the recalculation method, then he should use the recalculation method. Marshall should be told about the pros and cons of each method and should make the ultimate decision.

ACCOUNT OWNER DIES BEFORE THE REQUIRED BEGINNING DATE

Questions 7.25–7.34 discuss the special distribution rules that apply to your estate, as your beneficiary, if you die before your required beginning date.

QUESTION 7.25: Assume that John Rogers, an employee of XYZ Corporation, is a participant in the corporation's qualified retirement plan. John, who is unmarried, dies at age 69 on July 1, 1999, leaving his qualified plan death benefits payable to his estate. What are the IRS distribution rules that are applicable to the qualified plan death benefits?

ANSWER: For an employee who is not a 5-percent owner, the required beginning date for receiving required minimum distributions is generally April 1 of the calendar year following the calendar year in which the employee retires; see Question 2.4. There are special rules if someone dies before the April 1 required beginning date. John died at age 69 before his required beginning date. The distribution rules that are applicable depend on who is going to receive the qualified plan death benefits. In this case the death benefits are payable to an estate. If John dies before his required beginning date and the estate is the beneficiary, then the estate must receive the qualified plan death benefits based upon a five-year rule. Thus, if John died at age 69 on July 1, 1999, then according to the Internal Revenue Code the estate must receive the entire distribution within five years from his date of death. This would bring the deadline for distribution of the death benefits to June 30, 2004. However, the IRS has administratively extended the date to December 31 of the calendar year that contains the fifth anniversary of the plan participant's date of death. Thus, the estate could receive the qualified plan death benefits by no later than December 31, 2004.

The IRS has issued several private letter rulings that indicate that if the estate is a conduit for payments to the surviving spouse of the plan participant, then the five-year rule may not be applicable. Because John was not married, this "conduit" exception has no application here.

QUESTION 7.26: May partial distributions be made to John's estate during the period between July 1, 1999, and December 31, 2004?

ANSWER: Yes. The IRS rules set the outer limits for the timing of the payments of the qualified death benefits to the estate if the plan participant dies before his required beginning date. However, for tax-planning purposes, partial distributions of the qualified plan death benefits may be made to the estate during the following periods:

July 1, 1999, to December 31, 1999

January 1, 2000, to December 31, 2000

January 1, 2001, to December 31, 2001

January 1, 2002, to December 31, 2002

January 1, 2003, to December 31, 2003

January 1, 2004, to December 31, 2004

Another tax planning option would be for the estate to elect a fiscal year; see Question 7.28.

QUESTION 7.27: Why would the estate want to receive partial distributions rather than withdrawing the full amount immediately?

ANSWER: The longer the funds stay in the qualified plan, the greater the tax-deferred growth. In addition, significant tax planning can take place if a longer period of deferral is available.

QUESTION 7.28: I was informed that estates were placed in a high income tax bracket by the 1993 tax act. Therefore, what is the value of deferring income only to have it paid to the estate and taxed at a high income tax bracket?

ANSWER: Through proper tax planning you can avoid the high income tax bracket that is applicable to an estate under the 1993 tax act. The 1993 tax act quickly moves estate taxable income into the 36 percent bracket. For example, under the 1999 tax rate schedules, the 36 percent bracket applies to an estate with taxable income in excess of $6,200, and the 39.6 percent bracket applies if estate taxable income exceeds $8,450.

The $6,200 and $8,450 amounts are adjusted annually for inflation.

These high income tax rates can be avoided. One of several approaches that can be used is to elect a fiscal year for the estate and to make timely distributions to the beneficiaries. In this way the taxable income is shifted to the beneficiaries whose individual income tax brackets are generally not as high as the estate income tax brackets.

QUESTION 7.29: What happens if the final distribution of the qualified plan death benefits in the amount of $100,000 is not made to John's estate until after December 31, 2004?

ANSWER: The IRS can penalize both the plan and the estate.

QUESTION 7.30: What type of tax liability can the IRS assess against the plan?

ANSWER: The IRS can penalize the plan for violating the required minimum distribution rules. The amount of penalty is negotiable and is based upon the degree of negligence of the plan administrator.

QUESTION 7.31: What type of penalty can be assessed against the estate?

ANSWER: The penalty against the estate can be significant. The Internal Revenue Code provides for a penalty of 50 percent of the shortfall in the distribution, which in this case amounts to $50,000 (50 percent of $100,000). However, the IRS states that the penalty may be waived if the shortfall is due to a reasonable error and reasonable steps are taken to correct the shortfall.

QUESTION 7.32: Several years before his death, John was told that he could select his son, Ralph, as the designated beneficiary of

his qualified plan benefits instead of his estate. Would there have been an advantage if he had selected his son as the designated beneficiary?

ANSWER: Yes. If John had selected his son Ralph as the designated beneficiary of his retirement assets, then Ralph would have had distribution options that are not available to John's estate. These options for the son are discussed in Chapter 8.

QUESTION 7.33: Why is there a difference in the distribution rules when an individual is selected as the designated beneficiary?

ANSWER: The IRS rules are quite liberal when it comes to paying death benefits to a designated beneficiary instead of an estate.

QUESTION 7.34: Is an estate considered to be a designated beneficiary?

ANSWER: No. An estate is considered to be a beneficiary, not a designated beneficiary. Only an individual may be a designated beneficiary. In addition, an individual who receives retirement distributions under a trust is considered to be a designated beneficiary as well. As explained in Chapter 8, when the account owner dies before the required beginning date, then death benefits to a nonspouse designated beneficiary are paid under the five-year rule, or, if the appropriate timely election is made, over the designated beneficiary's single life expectancy. Death benefits to an estate must be paid under the five-year rule as explained in the answer to Question 7.25 if death takes place before the required beginning date.

CHAPTER EIGHT

DISTRIBUTION OPTIONS FOR YOUR NONSPOUSE DESIGNATED BENEFICIARIES

The IRS retirement distribution rules affect not only your lifetime payments from traditional IRAs and qualified employer plans but also the timing and amount of distributions that will be made to your designated beneficiaries after your death. Different rules will apply to your designated beneficiaries depending on your age when you die, and, in many cases, upon who is the designated beneficiary.

If you have reached your required beginning date (Question 2.3 and 2.4), and have begun to take required minimum distributions from your account, then after your death, your designated beneficiary will have to follow the same method you were using in order to calculate the amount that he or she must receive as required minimum distributions. The specific application of these designated beneficiary rules is discussed throughout this book in the relevant chapters. For example, the distribution rules for spousal beneficiaries are in Chapter 3, the rules for designated beneficiaries more than 10 years younger are in Chapter 4, and the rules for other adult beneficiaries are in Chapter 6. The distribution rules for estates are discussed in Chapter 7.

In this chapter we will cover the special distribution rules that apply to *nonspouse* designated beneficiaries where a traditional IRA owner or participant in a qualified employer plan dies *before his or her required beginning date,* which generally is April 1 of the calendar year following the calendar year in which he or she would have reached age $70^{1}/2$. For participants of qualified employer plans other than 5-percent owners who continue to work for the employer beyond the year in which they reach age $70^{1}/2$, the required beginning date may be extended until April 1 of the calendar year following the year of retirement, as discussed in Question 2.4.

The distribution rules for surviving spouse beneficiaries are discussed in Chapter 3, which covers deaths before and on or after the required beginning date.

Chapter 7 has the rules for distributions to an estate, regardless of whether the account owner's death is before, on, or after the required beginning date.

DESIGNATED BENEFICIARY BASICS

Questions 8.1–8.8 provide an introduction to the distribution rules for designated beneficiaries.

QUESTION 8.1: Will the designated beneficiaries of my corporate retirement plans be subject to the same payout schedule rules as the beneficiaries of my IRAs?

ANSWER: Yes. Beneficiaries of the following types of retirement plans are subject to the same distribution requirements:

a. Individual retirement plans such as an Individual Retirement Account or an Individual Retirement Annuity;

b. Annuity contracts under IRC Sec. 403(b);

c. Qualified plans of a corporation or self-employed employer, such as a pension plan, profit-sharing plan, or stock-bonus plan;

d. Qualified annuity plans under IRC Sec. 403(a);

e. Simplified employee pensions; and

f. Any SIMPLE retirement account.

QUESTION 8.2: What distribution options will my designated beneficiaries have after my death?

ANSWER: Different distribution options apply depending on whether or not the date of death is before your required beginning date. The required beginning date is April 1 of the calendar year following the year in which you attain age $70^1/2$. Exceptions for certain employees were previously discussed in Chapter 2, Question 2.4.

If the date of death is *on or after* the required beginning date, then your designated beneficiary's options generally depend on whether your required minimum distributions were being determined under the term-certain method, recalculation method, or hybrid method. These rules were discussed in the previous chapters of this book.

If the date of death is *before* the required beginning date, then under the IRS rules your designated beneficiary may be able to choose between receiving distributions from your account under the five-year rule or the life-expectancy rule, as explained in this chapter. However, the terms of your plan must be followed. If your plan document is not as liberal as the IRS rules, then the IRS requires the more restrictive plan rules to be followed.

Special averaging may be available to a beneficiary or a designated beneficiary for a lump-sum distribution from a qualified employer plan if the employee died at or after age $59^1/2$. Chapter 3 outlined the averaging rules for a spousal beneficiary

(Questions 3.41–3.44) but averaging may also be allowed to a nonspousal beneficiary.

QUESTION 8.3: If under the IRS rules my designated beneficiary can receive distributions over his or her life expectancy, which happens to be 40 years, but the plan limits the distribution period to 20 years, does my designated beneficiary lose 20 years of tax-deferred growth?

ANSWER: Yes. The IRS requires the plan document provisions to be followed. The plan document provisions may be stricter than the IRS distribution payment rules. The administrator of your plan may not wish to be burdened with the responsibility of paying out distributions to a designated beneficiary over a 40-year period, even though that period does not exceed the designated beneficiary's life expectancy. Many company plans that have been approved by the IRS limit the payout period to 20 years or less.

QUESTION 8.4: Can the plan document provide that distributions be made over a greater period than the IRS permits?

ANSWER: No. It would be illegal for the plan document to provide for distributions to be made over a greater period than that permitted under the IRS rules, which follow the guidelines spelled out by Congress in the Internal Revenue Code.

QUESTION 8.5: Assume that my son has been properly designated as my designated beneficiary under a corporate qualified plan. Is there anything I can do to take advantage of the longer payment rules that are available to my son as my designated beneficiary if my current plan has a restricted payout period that is not as good as the maximum IRS payout period?

ANSWER: Ask your employer to consider amending the plan to provide for increased payout flexibility in the event of your death.

If your employer states that it is too difficult or that it would be an administrative nightmare to create a sophisticated distribution payout arrangement, then you have a problem. In this case, your employer's plan is preventing your son from taking advantage of the extended payout period that the IRS would otherwise allow to your son as your designated beneficiary.

QUESTION 8.6: Assume that the employer refuses to amend the plan to increase the period over which distributions can be paid. Is there any other solution to resolve this problem?

ANSWER: Yes. First you should point out to the president of the company that many employees are affected by the payout option and that perhaps the employer should amend the plan to allow any employee who has attained retirement age in the plan to receive a within-service plan distribution although continuing to work for the employer. Such a within-service plan distribution would permit the individual plan participant to transfer the value of his or her benefits in the plan directly to an IRA that has liberal payout options. Naturally, the necessary paperwork and spousal consents, where required, would have to be obtained. This amendment would be valuable to the key employees of the corporation as well as to the rank and file employees and should not be unduly burdensome to the plan administrator.

QUESTION 8.7: Is there any other approach that can be used?

ANSWER: Yes. If the employer is still not interested in amending the plan to provide for a liberalization of the payout terms or for an in-service plan distribution, then if the stakes are high enough you might consider separating from service. Many plans provide for a lump-sum distribution upon separation from service. If you are contemplating retirement or leaving the company, then examine the plan document in order to determine whether you are entitled to a lump-sum distribution upon termination of employment.

QUESTION 8.8: What happens if the plan document distribution rules are based upon an old plan document that does not conform with the current IRS rules?

ANSWER: The plan document must conform with the IRS distribution rules. The IRS rules override any distribution options in the plan that are inconsistent with current law.

THE FIVE-YEAR RULE AND LIFE-EXPECTANCY RULE FOR NONSPOUSE BENEFICIARIES

Questions 8.9–8.42 discuss the basic five-year distribution rule and the life-expectancy exception rule that may be available to nonspouse designated beneficiaries of plan participants on IRA owners who die before the required beginning date. The rules for a surviving spouse beneficiary are in Chapter 3.

QUESTION 8.9: John Smyth is the sole owner of a corporation and has accumulated $1,000,000 in his qualified profit-sharing plan. John is the only participant in the qualified plan and has no intention of hiring any new employees, other than his son, Richard. Richard is his only child and his sole beneficiary. John's wife passed away during 1998. John dies on July 1, 1999, at the age of 69. Richard is age 40 on his birthday in 1999. What distribution options are available to Richard?

ANSWER: If John dies at the age of 69, before his required beginning date, then Richard, as John's designated beneficiary, may have a choice of options under the terms of the plan document as to when he must commence distributions from the plan. These options may include the following:

   a. The entire distribution must be received by Richard by December 31 of the fifth year following the year of John's date of death; or

b. Payments may be paid over Richard's life or over a period not extending beyond Richard's life expectancy.

QUESTION 8.10: Are the two options described above always available to Richard?

ANSWER: No. The plan document may provide that only one option applies, or the plan may permit Richard as the designated beneficiary to elect which rule applies. In addition, if the plan document is silent, or if no election is made by Richard, then the five-year rule is automatically applicable. This automatic five-year rule applies only where the designated beneficiary is someone other than a surviving spouse.

QUESTION 8.11: If the plan document permits the designated beneficiary to make the election as to which method to use, how is the election made?

ANSWER: The IRS does not indicate the mechanics of making the election. However, if the designated beneficiary is not a surviving spouse, then the election into the life-expectancy rule must be made by no later than December 31 of the year following the year of the plan participant's date of death. In addition, payments must commence by that December 31 date as well. The election must be irrevocable.

QUESTION 8.12: How is the election described above made by Richard if he wishes to avoid the five-year rule?

ANSWER: The IRS rules do not describe the form of the election or where to file the election. Obviously, the election should be in writing in order to prove to the IRS that it was timely made. If the election is not timely made, then the five-year rule becomes operative. Richard should make a timely written election with the plan administrator by no later than December 31 of the year following the year in which his father died and must commence required minimum distributions by that date as well. The election must be irrevocable.

Richard should make a timely written election with the plan administrator of the qualified profit-sharing plan electing to receive the required minimum distributions from the qualified plan over a period of years that does not exceed his life expectancy as determined under the IRS life-expectancy tables. Once again it is possible that the plan does not permit the payments to be made over a period that is tied to Richard's life expectancy. The plan may have an arbitrary cutoff period of perhaps 20 years or less.

QUESTION 8.13: Specifically, if John dies on July 1, 1999, before his required beginning date, what should Richard do in order to elect out of the five-year rule?

ANSWER: Richard should do the following:

a. He should indicate in writing by no later than December 31, 2000, that he wishes to elect out of the five-year rule. The deadline of December 31, 2000, is the end of the year following the year (1999) in which his father died.

b. He should elect in writing that he wishes to receive his required minimum distributions from the profit-sharing plan based upon a term-certain period that does not exceed his life expectancy. It is best that the term-certain period be indicated in the written election form filed with the plan administrator. However, failure to indicate the term-certain period should not prove fatal.

c. The election should specify that the term-certain period is based upon the life expectancy of Richard. The life expectancy of Richard is based upon IRS life-expectancy tables. The life expectancy that is used is the IRS life expectancy of Richard as determined in the calendar year 2000, the year following the year of John's death. Because Richard reaches age 40 in 1999, the year of his father's death, his attained age in 2000 is 41.

The life expectancy at age 41 is 41.5 years, as shown in Table I of Appendix A of this book.

d. The written election should be sent to the plan administrator of the qualified profit-sharing plan by no later than December 31, 2000. This written election should be sent by certified mail, return receipt requested, to prove the timeliness of the election.

e. The written election should state that this election to receive required minimum distributions over a term-certain period that does not exceed his life expectancy is irrevocable with respect to Richard and all subsequent beneficiaries. This term-certain period is currently 41.5 years but is subject to being increased to the extent permitted by law and IRS rules. This, of course, assumes that the qualified profit-sharing plan does not limit the distribution period to a lesser period of perhaps 20 years.

f. The written election should state that Richard may accelerate payments to the extent permitted by the plan document from time to time during the term-certain period that he has elected.

g. The written election may cover additional contingencies. For example, it could specify what happens to the remaining payments if Richard dies during the payout period.

h. In order for the exception to the five-year rule to be operative, the first required minimum distribution to Richard must be received from the qualified profit-sharing plan by no later than December 31, 2000.

QUESTION 8.14: Assume that John's account balance at his date of death on July 1, 1999, is $1,000,000. The plan year of the qualified profit-sharing plan is a calendar year. On December 31, 1999, his account balance is $1,050,000. Also assume that under the terms of the plan, Richard may receive the $1,050,000 of death benefits from the qualified profit-sharing plan over a 20-year term-certain period in equal annual installments. This is accomplished by the plan trustees purchasing a 20-year term-certain annuity contract with an insurance company. Assume that the annual installments are based upon a 7-percent interest assumption. How much money will Richard receive over a 20-year term-certain period based upon equal annual installment payments?

ANSWER: Richard will receive equal annual payments of $99,112.57 for a period of 20 years for a total distribution of $1,982,251.40.

QUESTION 8.15: Assume that Richard may receive the $1,050,000 of death benefits from the qualified profit-sharing plan over a 20-year period based upon the required minimum distribution rules instead of under an annuity contract as in Question 8.14. Assume that the required minimum distributions are based upon a 7-percent interest assumption. How much money will Richard receive over the 20-year period based upon the required minimum distribution rules?

ANSWER: Richard will receive total required minimum distributions over the 20-year period of $2,361,224.28. The following schedule illustrates the computation of the required minimum distribution over a 20-year period.

Initial amount: $1,050,000.00; Earnings: 7 percent

DISTRIBUTIONS OVER 20 YEARS

YEAR	EARNINGS AT 7 PERCENT	REQUIRED MINIMUM DISTRIBUTIONS	BALANCE
			$1,050,000.00
1	$73,500.00	$52,500.00	1,071,000.00
2	74,970.00	56,368.42	1,089,601.58
3	76,272.11	60,533.42	1,105,340.27 ➤

YEAR	EARNINGS AT 7 PERCENT	REQUIRED MINIMUM DISTRIBUTIONS	BALANCE
4	77,373.82	65,020.02	1,117,694.07
5	78,238.58	69,855.88	1,126,076.77
6	78,825.37	75,071.78	1,129,830.36
7	79,088.13	80,702.17	1,128,216.32
8	78,975.14	86,785.87	1,120,405.59
9	78,428.39	93,367.13	1,105,466.85
10	77,382.68	100,496.99	1,082,352.54
11	75,764.68	108,235.25	1,049,881.97
12	73,491.74	116,653.55	1,006,720.16
13	70,470.41	125,840.02	951,350.55
14	66,594.54	135,907.22	882,037.87
15	61,742.65	147,006.31	796,774.21
16	55,774.19	159,354.84	693,193.56
17	48,523.55	173,298.39	568,418.72
18	39,789.31	189,472.91	418,735.12
19	29,311.46	209,367.56	238,679.02
20	16,707.53	255,386.55	0.00
	$1,311,224.28	$2,361,224.28	

QUESTION 8.16: Assume that under the terms of John's plan Richard may receive the $1,050,000 of death benefits from the

qualified profit sharing plan over a 41-year (41.5-year life expectancy rounded down to 41 years for illustrative purposes) term-certain period in equal annual installments. This is accomplished by the plan trustees purchasing a 41-year term-certain annuity contract with an insurance company. Assume that the annual installments are based upon a 7-percent interest assumption. How much money will Richard receive over a 41-year period based upon equal annual installment payments?

ANSWER: Richard will receive equal annual payments of $78,392.61 for a period of 41 years for a total distribution of $3,214,097.01.

CASE STUDY
Questions 8.17–8.42 illustrate how Richard, as beneficiary of John's profit-sharing plan, may receive distributions over his life expectancy.

QUESTION 8.17: Assume that Richard may receive the $1,050,000 of death benefits from the qualified profit-sharing plan over a 41-year period (41.5 years rounded down to 41 years for illustrative purposes) based upon the required minimum-distribution rules instead of under an annuity contract as in Question 8.16. Assume that the required minimum-distribution calculations are based upon a 7-percent interest assumption. How much money will Richard receive over the 41-year period under the required minimum-distribution rules?

ANSWER: Richard will receive total required minimum distributions over the 41-year period of $6,180,876.46. The following schedule illustrates the computation of the required minimum distribution over a 41-year period.

Initial amount: $1,050,000.00; Earnings: 7 percent

DISTRIBUTIONS OVER 41 YEARS

YEAR	EARNINGS AT 7 PERCENT	REQUIRED MINIMUM DISTRIBUTIONS	BALANCE
			$1,050,000.00
1	$73,500.00	$25,609.76	1,097,890.24
2	76,852.32	27,447.26	1,147,295.30
3	80,310.67	29,417.83	1,198,188.14
4	83,873.17	31,531.27	1,250,530.04
5	87,537.10	33,798.11	1,304,269.03
6	91,298.83	36,229.70	1,359,338.16
7	95,153.67	38,838.23	1,415,653.60
8	99,095.75	41,636.87	1,473,112.48
9	103,117.87	44,639.77	1,531,590.58
10	107,211.34	47,862.21	1,590,939.71
11	111,365.78	51,320.64	1,650,984.85
12	115,568.94	55,032.83	1,711,520.96
13	119,806.47	59,017.96	1,772,309.47
14	124,061.66	63,296.77	1,833,074.36
15	128,315.21	67,891.64	1,893,497.93
16	132,544.86	72,826.84	1,953,215.95
17	136,725.12	78,128.64	2,011,812.43
18	140,826.87	83,825.52	2,068,813.78 →

19	144,816.96	89,948.43	2,123,682.31
20	148,657.76	96,531.01	2,175,809.06
21	152,306.63	103,609.96	2,224,505.73
22	155,715.40	111,225.29	2,268,995.84
23	158,829.71	119,420.83	2,308,404.72
24	161,588.33	128,244.71	2,341,748.34
25	163,922.38	137,749.90	2,367,920.82
26	165,754.46	147,995.05	2,385,680.23
27	166,997.62	159,045.35	2,393,632.50
28	167,554.28	170,973.75	2,390,213.03
29	167,314.91	183,862.54	2,373,665.40
30	166,156.58	197,805.45	2,342,016.53
31	163,941.16	212,910.59	2,293,047.10
32	160,513.30	229,304.71	2,224,255.69
33	155,697.90	247,139.52	2,132,814.07
34	149,296.98	266,601.76	2,015,509.29
35	141,085.65	287,929.90	1,868,665.04
36	130,806.55	311,444.17	1,688,027.42
37	118,161.92	337,605.48	1,468,583.86
38	102,800.87	367,145.96	1,204,238.77	➤

YEAR	EARNINGS AT 7 PERCENT	REQUIRED MINIMUM DISTRIBUTIONS	BALANCE
39	84,296.71	401,412.92	887,122.56
40	62,098.58	443,561.28	505,659.86
41	35,396.19	541,056.05	0.00
	$5,130,876.46	$6,180,876.46	

QUESTION 8.18: Under the facts of Question 8.17, how is Richard's required minimum distribution for 2000 determined?

ANSWER: The account balance as of the end of the plan year in which John died is used in the calculation together with Richard's life expectancy. Richard's life expectancy is determined in the calendar year 2000 and is based upon the IRS single life-expectancy tables. John died on July 1, 1999. The plan year is a calendar year and therefore the decedent's account balance as of December 31, 1999, must be used. The account balance as of December 31, 1999, is $1,050,000. The IRS life expectancy of Richard in 2000, the year following John's date of death, is 41.5 years. The account balance of $1,050,000 is divided by 41.5 years in order to determine Richard's required minimum distribution for the calendar year 2000. Richard's required minimum distribution for 2000 is therefore $25,301.20 ($1,050,000÷41.5 years). The schedule in the answer to Question 8.17 shows a slightly higher total than this because a 41-year period (rather than 41.5) was used in the schedule for illustrative purposes.

QUESTION 8.19: May Richard receive an amount in excess of $25,301.20 from the qualified plan during the calendar year 2000?

ANSWER: Yes. $25,301.20 is the required minimum distribution that Richard must receive from the qualified profit-sharing plan in order to satisfy the law and avoid an IRS penalty. He can receive an amount in excess of $25,301.20 without any penalty. This assumes that the plan permits the acceleration of distributions from time to time.

QUESTION 8.20: Because Richard must continue to receive required minimum distributions in subsequent years as well, how much must he receive during the calendar year 2001?

ANSWER: Richard must receive a required minimum distribution for the calendar year 2001, which is equal to the decedent's account balance as of December 31, 2000, divided by the remaining years that are left in Richard's life expectancy.

QUESTION 8.21: If we assume that the account balance as of December 31, 1999, is $1,075,000, then how much must Richard receive as a required minimum distribution in 2000?

ANSWER: Richard must receive a required minimum distribution of $26,543.21 from the qualified plan for the calendar year 2001. This is calculated by dividing the decedent's account balance of $1,075,000 as of December 31, 2000, by 40.5 years.

QUESTION 8.22: Why is 40.5 years used in calculating the required minimum distribution for Richard for the calendar year 2001?

ANSWER: Richard's life expectancy is required to be reduced by one for each calendar year after 2000. The first year for which Richard had to receive a required minimum distribution is the calendar year 2000.

QUESTION 8.23: How would Richard's required minimum distribution from the qualified plan be calculated for the calendar year 2002?

ANSWER: The decedent's account balance as of December 31, 2001, would be divided by 39.5 years. The required minimum distribution to Richard (assuming a reasonable rate of return) should increase each year.

QUESTION 8.24: Must Richard continue to receive his required minimum distributions from the qualified plan for the balance of the 41.5-year period?

ANSWER: No. If he decides to take out the entire balance in the qualified plan in a given year, then his required minimum distribution in subsequent years would be zero. Given the large account balance, Richard would incur a substantial tax liability in withdrawing the balance in one year or even over several years, and should take this into account in consultation with his tax advisor. This assumes that the qualified plan permits the acceleration of distributions from time to time.

QUESTION 8.25: Assume that Richard is required to receive a required minimum distribution of $40,000 in a given year, but only receives $30,000 for that calendar year. What penalty may the IRS assess against Richard?

ANSWER: The IRS may assess a 50-percent penalty on the shortfall distribution. On a shortfall of $10,000, the penalty is $5,000. However, the penalty of $5,000 may be abated if Richard can explain the reason for the discrepancy to the IRS.

QUESTION 8.26: If Richard wishes to withdraw $50,000 from the qualified plan in a given year when he is only required to withdraw $40,000, may he receive a credit for this extra $10,000 against a subsequent year's required minimum distribution?

ANSWER: No. The IRS does not permit a credit to be taken if a designated beneficiary receives a distribution in excess of his required minimum distribution. The extra money Richard took will have an indirect effect on his required minimum distributions in subsequent years. This is because the decedent's account balance has been reduced by the extra $10,000 with-drawal and the reduced account balance is used in order to determine the required minimum distribution for subsequent calendar years.

QUESTION 8.27: Because Richard is under the age of 59¹/₂ at the time he starts to receive the required minimum distributions from the qualified plan, is he subject to the 10 percent-penalty on early distributions?

ANSWER: No. The law provides that certain distributions are not subject to the 10-percent early-distribution penalty. One of the exceptions to the 10-percent penalty is payments that are made to a designated beneficiary or a beneficiary upon the death of the plan participant. Richard can receive without penalty death benefits from the qualified plan and it does not matter whether he as the designated beneficiary is over or under age 59¹/₂ at the date of the plan participant's death.

QUESTION 8.28: Assume that John had selected his estate as his beneficiary instead of Richard. If John died at age 55, would the estate be subject to the 10-percent early-distribution penalty?

ANSWER: No. Distributions of death benefits from a qualified plan are not subject to the 10-percent additional tax on early distri-butions. It does not matter whether the decedent at the date of his death was under or over age 59¹/₂. Furthermore, it makes no difference whether a designated beneficiary (Richard) or a bene-ficiary (estate) receives the death benefits from a qualified plan. The estate has no life expectancy and as beneficiary would have to receive the entire account balance under the five-year rule.

QUESTION 8.29: Richard would like to know whether he can roll over the qualified plan death benefits into an Individual Retirement Account (IRA). Can he make such a rollover?

ANSWER: No. If the designated beneficiary is not a surviving spouse, then he or she cannot roll over the plan death benefits into an IRA.

QUESTION 8.30: Will there be any problems for the profit-sharing plan if Richard withdraws the plan death benefits over a period that does not exceed his 41.5-year life expectancy?

ANSWER: Perhaps. The IRS has indicated that the qualified plan must be an active plan and not a wasting trust. Richard must therefore continue the profit-sharing plan and make employer contributions to the plan from time to time in order to have an active plan.

QUESTION 8.31: Should Richard take over his father's corporation and keep the plan active?

ANSWER: Perhaps. Richard may not be interested in maintaining his father's corporation. Richard may have no interest in his father's business or in maintaining the corporation for a 41.5-year period.

QUESTION 8.32: What may the IRS do if Richard refuses to keep his father's corporation active?

ANSWER: The IRS has indicated that the tax-exempt status of a trust that is maintained by the plan may be revoked if the plan is not an active plan.

QUESTION 8.33: What is the effect of an IRS revocation of the trust's tax-exempt status?

ANSWER: If the trust's tax-exempt status is revoked, then all the earnings in the trust become taxable to the trust each year.

QUESTION 8.34: Assume that Richard receives a $30,000 distribution of plan death benefits in 2001. What happens if the plan assets earn ordinary income of $50,000 in 2001 and the IRS on audit retroactively revokes the plan's tax-exempt status for that year?

ANSWER: The IRS will assess an income tax liability against the trust. The income tax liability is computed as follows:

Income from trust:	$50,000
Less: Distribution to Richard:	(30,000)
Less: Trust exemption:	(100)
Taxable income:	$19,900

The income tax liability for 2000 can only be approximated, using the following 1999 tax rates (the latest available) as a guide. The actual rate brackets for 2000 will be different because of inflation adjustments. In 1999, the rates for a trust were as follows:

15 percent on first $1,750 of taxable income

28 percent on taxable income between $1,750 and $4,050

31 percent on taxable income between $4,050 and $6,200

36 percent on taxable income between $6,200 and $8,450

39.6 percent on taxable income in excess of $8,450

Based on the above rate schedule, the income tax liability on $19,900 would be $6,917.20. As a result of inflation adjustments to the above 1999 brackets, the actual liability for 2001 should be somewhat lower. The IRS will assess interest and penalties as well.

QUESTION 8.35: If the IRS revokes the tax-exempt status of the plan's trust what course of action is available to the employer?

ANSWER: The employer may appeal the IRS determination and try to resolve the dispute within the IRS or litigate the issue in the United States Tax Court or another federal court with jurisdiction in tax cases.

QUESTION 8.36: Is there any option that is available to the plan trustees?

ANSWER: Yes. The plan trustees may invest the plan assets in tax-exempt investments and therefore avoid having a trust income tax liability in the future.

QUESTION 8.37: Is there anything that Richard may do in order to avoid the trust income tax liability in the future?

ANSWER: Yes. He may withdraw all of the trust earnings each year so that the trust will have no taxable income in the future.

QUESTION 8.38: What can John do while he is alive in order to protect Richard from a dispute with the IRS?

ANSWER: John can arrange for the termination of the qualified profit-sharing plan and the transfer of his interest in the qualified profit-sharing plan directly to a brand new IRA. He can then select Richard as the designated beneficiary of his IRA. If this is done, then all of the options and elections that were available to Richard as the designated beneficiary of a plan participant are available to Richard as the designated beneficiary of John's IRA. All the potential problems of maintaining a qualified plan for the 41.5-year period can then be avoided.

QUESTION 8.39: If John dies on July 1, 1999, at age 69 and the qualified profit-sharing assets have previously been transferred to an IRA, then what must Richard do in order to be able to receive distributions over his life expectancy?

ANSWER: Assuming that the terms of the IRA require an election to avoid the five-year method, Richard should make such an election, in writing, with the IRA institution by no later than December 31 of the calendar year following the year in which John died. Richard must commence his required minimum distributions by that date as well. The written election is irrevocable. It should be sent certified mail, return receipt requested, to the IRA institution. The written election should contain the same information that was previously described in the answer to Question 8.13, when Richard made the election as the designated beneficiary of John's profit-sharing plan. The same required minimum distribution rules that applied to Richard on the extended payout period of 41.5 years from the qualified plan apply to the required minimum distributions from the IRA except that IRA distribution options have greater flexibility than qualified plan payout options.

QUESTION 8.40: What other reason is there to have John transfer his qualified plan assets directly to an IRA before his death?

ANSWER: Qualified plans are required to file annual reports with the Internal Revenue Service. This requirement is not applicable to IRAs. In addition, the Internal Revenue Code is frequently amended and employers are burdened with the responsibility and cost of amending plans to conform with the changes in the law and regulations. In addition, qualified plans are subject to audit by the IRS. If Richard is not interested in taking over John's corporation then the plan should be terminated, if possible, prior to John's death. The plan assets should then be immediately transferred to a new IRA in John's name. If Richard is interested in taking over John's business but is not interested in maintaining the plan for an extended period of time, then the plan should be terminated prior to John's death and the plan assets should be transferred to John's new IRA.

QUESTION 8.41: Can John transfer his qualified plan assets to an IRA without the necessity of terminating the plan?

ANSWER: Yes. A plan can be amended to provide that a participant may receive a distribution from the plan on or after reaching retirement age regardless of whether the participant separates from service with the employer. If the plan has the above provision and John has attained his retirement age as stated in the plan document, then he can receive his then-existing account balance and transfer it directly to his new IRA. At least the bulk of his account balance will be in a new IRA. This does not prevent John from having further employer contributions made to the profit-sharing plan on his behalf. To prevent withholding, John should make a "direct rollover" from the plan to the IRA, instead of actually receiving payment from the plan and then making the rollover; see Question 1.26.

QUESTION 8.42: If John transferred his qualified plan assets directly to an IRA, would Richard have greater investment control over the assets than if they had remained in the corporate plan?

ANSWER: Perhaps. Richard could maintain control of the investments made by the IRA. He could not, however, control the investments made by the plan trustees of the corporate plan unless he was also a plan trustee. Assume that Richard is not a plan trustee and that he is receiving a 41.5-year payout from the qualified corporate plan. He will be unable during the 41.5-year payout period to prevent the trustees from making unwise investments or from committing improper transactions. To the extent that the plan permits, Richard may wish to accelerate distributions from the qualified plan in order to avoid the anxiety over what might happen to the corporate plan assets over the 41.5-year payout period.

BENEFICIARY'S DEATH DURING PAYOUT PERIOD

The following questions and answers illustrate the distribution rules that apply following the death of a designated beneficiary who has begun to receive required minimum distributions.

QUESTION 8.43: Could Richard during his lifetime direct the plan administrator or IRA custodian to pay upon his death the remaining unpaid installments directly to certain beneficiaries without the necessity of going through his estate?

ANSWER: Probably yes. There is nothing in the tax law that prohibits Richard from designating beneficiaries of the remaining unpaid installments of the qualified plan death benefits or the IRA death benefits that are attributable to John. The right to designate the successor beneficiary of Richard's rights in the event of his death after John is a matter of state law. Richard should generally be able to select a successor beneficiary of the unpaid installments. If he does not have that right, or he does but fails to select a successor beneficiary, the remaining qualified plan or IRA installments would be payable to his estate.

QUESTION 8.44: Are there any advantages in having the unpaid installments of the qualified plan death benefits or IRA death benefits to which Richard is entitled payable to his estate upon his death?

ANSWER: Yes. The estate can use a fiscal year instead of a calendar year and this can result in certain tax-deferral techniques. In addition, if there is an estate tax liquidity problem, then the executor generally may accelerate distributions in order to have assets available to pay the estate taxes and other administration expenses. The qualified-plan provisions would have to be consulted in order to determine whether the executor may accelerate distributions from time to time. IRA death benefits generally may be accelerated at will.

QUESTION 8.45: Are there any other advantages in having the estate of Richard as the beneficiary of any unpaid installments of John's qualified plan death benefits or IRA death benefits?

ANSWER: Yes. If the ultimate beneficiaries of Richard's estate are not prudent investors or are relatively young and inexperienced or would tend to make unwise decisions that would cause the assets to be dissipated, then it is best that the executor have control over the option to accelerate the death benefit distributions for a period of time.

QUESTION 8.46: If Richard dies during the 41.5-year payout period while receiving payments from John's IRA and the remaining installments are paid to his estate, must his estate be kept open for the balance of Richard's 41.5-year payout period?

ANSWER: No. Richard's estate can continue to receive the remaining installment payments or may accelerate the payments from time to time if the IRA payment option provisions do not prohibit such acceleration. The estate steps into Richard's payment options. Under state law, the estate generally may assign the remaining installments to the beneficiaries of Richard's estate.

QUESTION 8.47: If the executor of Richard's estate assigns the remaining installments to the beneficiaries of Richard's estate, what options are available to the beneficiaries?

ANSWER: The beneficiaries could continue to receive the remaining installments over the installment period, or they may accelerate the distributions from time to time if the payment option provisions do not prohibit such acceleration.

QUESTION 8.48: If Richard's estate has two beneficiaries, how should the installments be assigned?

ANSWER: The executor should assign to each beneficiary a 50-percent interest in the rights to the installment payments from the qualified plan or IRA. The plan administrator or IRA institution should be notified as to the assignment of these installment rights.

QUESTION 8.49: Why is it best for Richard's estate to assign the installment rights to the beneficiaries of Richard's estate?

ANSWER: It relieves the executor of Richard's estate from the problem of leaving the estate open for many years. The executor may wish to have an informal or formal discharge from fiduciary liability and would not be able to obtain this discharge for many years if he continues to receive installments over a long period of time. In addition, the executor will have to file tax returns and maintain a set of books for the period that the estate is maintained. This may be costly and burdensome.

QUESTION 8.50: Is there any other reason that the executor should assign the installment rights to the beneficiaries of the estate?

ANSWER: Yes. If the executor assigns the rights to the future installments of the retirement assets proportionately to each beneficiary of the estate, then each beneficiary can decide whether or not to accelerate his or her respective rights to the future installments from time to time. In essence, one beneficiary can accelerate distributions if the need arises, while the other beneficiary may take the required minimum distributions. Obviously, more effective tax planning can then be done for each beneficiary if they are treated separately. A beneficiary may be in a low income tax bracket and may decide to accelerate distributions in order to increase current cash flow. Another beneficiary may be in a high income tax bracket and decide to take only the required minimum distribution in order to save on income taxes.

DIRECT TRANSFER OPTION FOR IRA BENEFICIARY

The following questions and answers illustrate the distribution options of an IRA beneficiary following the death of the account owner before the required beginning date, with a special focus on the direct transfer rules.

QUESTION 8.51: Dr. Jerome Bordon attains age 66 on March 25, 1999. He has selected his daughter, Joyce, who is age 43 in 1999 as the designated beneficiary of his IRA with the XYZ mutual fund. The IRA currently has a value of approximately $100,000. If Dr. Bordon dies on June 1, 2000, what distribution options are available for Joyce?

ANSWER: Because Dr. Bordon died at age 67 prior to his required beginning date, the terms of his IRA plan document may permit Joyce to choose between the five-year rule or the life-expectancy exception to the five-year rule. Had he lived, Dr. Bordon's required beginning date would have been April 1, 2004, the calendar year following the calendar year (2003) in which he would have attained age $70^1/2$.

QUESTION 8.52: May Joyce be required to use the five-year rule?

ANSWER: Perhaps. If the IRA document mandates the five-year rule, then Joyce may not elect out of the five-year rule. If the IRA document permits Joyce to elect out of the five-year rule, then she should make a timely written election to follow the life-expectancy distribution rules and timely implement the election. If she fails to act timely, then she will default into the five-year rule. Under the five-year rule, Joyce would have to receive the entire balance of the IRA no later than December 31, 2005. This deadline is the end of the fifth year following the year of Dr. Bordon's death (2000).

QUESTION 8.53: If the terms of Dr. Bordon's plan permit Joyce as the designated beneficiary to avoid the five-year distribution rule, how does she make the election?

ANSWER: To elect out of the five-year rule, Joyce should send the IRA institution a written election by no later than December 31, 2001 (the end of the year following the year of her father's death). The form of the written election was previously discussed in the answer to question 8.13. This is also the deadline for Joyce to begin the required minimum distributions from the IRA. In the written election, Joyce should state that she wishes to receive her required minimum distributions from her father's IRA over her 37.7-year life expectancy. On her birthday in the calendar year 2001, she attains age 45, and under the IRS single life-expectancy table shown in Appendix A of this book, the life expectancy of a 45-year-old is 37.7 years. Her life expectancy as of the calendar year 2001 is used because 2001 is the year following the year of her father's death.

QUESTION 8.54: Upon Dr. Bordon's death in 2000, may Joyce roll over Dr. Bordon's account into her own IRA?

ANSWER: No. Joyce may not roll over her father's IRA. In the case of individuals dying after December 31, 1983, the surviving spouse is the only designated beneficiary who may roll over the IRA death benefits into his or her own IRA.

QUESTION 8.55: What would happen if Joyce in 2001 rolled over Dr. Bordon's IRA into her own IRA?

ANSWER: The IRS would tax Joyce on the entire proceeds of Dr. Bordon's IRA, because the rollover was improper. In addition, the IRS will assess excess IRA contribution penalties against Joyce as well.

QUESTION 8.56: Upon Dr. Bordon's death, should the IRA be maintained in Dr. Bordon's name?

ANSWER: Yes. In order for the tax-deferred growth of the IRA to continue after Dr. Bordon's death, the IRA must be maintained in his name.

QUESTION 8.57: What approach should be used in order to maintain the tax-deferred growth of Dr. Bordon's IRA after his death?

ANSWER: The account title of the IRA should be changed to read "Jerome Bordon, deceased, Individual Retirement Account (date of death, June 1, 2000) for the benefit of Joyce Bordon, designated beneficiary." The IRA should use the Social Security number of Joyce Bordon after Jerome Bordon's death. The account title could be shortened to read "Jerome Bordon, deceased, IRA (DOD June 1, 2000) FBO Joyce Bordon, SS #100-00-0000."

MECHANICS OF MAKING A DIRECT TRANSFER: QUESTIONS 8.58–8.67

QUESTION 8.58: If Joyce would like to transfer the IRA maintained in the decedent's name to another IRA institution, may she do so?

ANSWER: Yes. The IRS has taken a practical approach and permits a direct transfer to be made by a beneficiary from one IRA institution to another as long as the IRA is maintained in the name of the deceased IRA owner.

For example, Joyce may direct that the assets be transferred from IRA No. 1 to IRA No. 2. The IRS allows the direct transfer and permits the tax-deferred status of the IRA to be continued as long as the IRA is maintained in the name of the deceased IRA owner. Joyce, as the designated beneficiary,

controls the IRA under state law and can control the investments that are made in the decedent's IRA.

**QUESTION 8.59: Must Joyce pay income taxes on the direct trans-
fer of assets from the Jerome Bordon, deceased IRA No. 1 to
the Jerome Bordon, deceased IRA No. 2?**

ANSWER: No. The direct transfer of assets from one IRA custodian
to another IRA custodian does not result in a taxable event to
Joyce as long as the IRA is maintained in the decedent's name.

**QUESTION 8.60: Is Joyce considered to have rolled over the dece-
dent's IRA assets when the assets are transferred from IRA No.
1 to IRA No. 2 as described in the previous question?**

ANSWER: No. The IRS does not consider the transfer of IRA assets
directly from IRA No. 1 to IRA No. 2 to be a rollover transaction. For the transfer to be considered a direct transfer and not a
rollover, the transfer of funds must be directly from one IRA
custodian to another IRA custodian. Joyce should not receive a
check payable to her from IRA No. 1 and then transfer it to
IRA No. 2. That would be an improper rollover transaction.
Only a surviving spouse beneficiary can make a rollover.

**QUESTION 8.61: Could Joyce transfer a portion of IRA No. 1 to IRA
No. 2 and a portion to IRA No. 3?**

ANSWER: Yes. The IRS has taken a liberal point of view and it
places no limitations on the number of IRAs that can be maintained for the deceased IRA owner.

**QUESTION 8.62: Is there a limitation on the number of IRA transfers
that Joyce can make with respect to the decedent's IRA in a
given period?**

ANSWER: No. There is no limitation on the number of direct IRA transfers that Joyce can make in a given period with respect to the decedent's IRA.

QUESTION 8.63: If Joyce divides her father's IRA into IRA No. 1, IRA No. 2, and IRA No. 3, must she receive her required minimum distributions from each IRA on a proportionate basis?

ANSWER: No. The IRS has taken a practical approach and permits the required minimum distributions that Joyce must receive for a given calendar year to be taken from one or more of the IRAs. Thus, if the total of the required minimum distributions from all three IRAs is $3,500 for the calendar year 2004, Joyce may receive distributions from any one of the IRAs, or any combination of the IRAs as she prefers, as long as at least $3,500 is received in the year 2004.

QUESTION 8.64: If Joyce wishes to make a direct transfer of her father's IRA to another IRA institution, what should she first look into?

ANSWER: Joyce should make certain that the other IRA institution permits the life-expectancy exception to the five-year rule to be operative. She should not transfer the decedent's IRA assets to an IRA institution that only has a five-year rule. In addition, if the exception to the five-year rule is permissible, she should file a copy of the timely written election that she previously made with the initial IRA custodian with the new institution. In fact, she should always check the IRA institution's plan document before she directs a transfer to that IRA institution. She should speak with a responsible official at the new institution before the transfer to make sure that the new institution will make payments to her based upon the life-expectancy exception to the five-year rule. In addition, she should make sure that the new institution opens the new IRA in the name of the decedent.

QUESTION 8.65: Are the same IRS distribution rules applicable to IRA institutions that are called trustees instead of custodians?

ANSWER: Yes. Direct transfers from an IRA custodian or an IRA trustee to an IRA custodian or an IRA trustee are nontaxable transfers. Thus, a direct transfer from an IRA custodian to an IRA trustee is a nontaxable transaction.

QUESTION 8.66: What should Joyce do in order to make sure that direct transfers of the decedent's IRAs are handled properly?

ANSWER: Joyce should give written instructions to the decedent's IRA institution that the IRA assets should be directly transferred to the receiving IRA institution. The appropriate application should be completed for the receiving IRA institution indicating that the IRA is in the decedent's name.

Joyce should speak to the transferring IRA institution to make sure that the institution does not make the check out to Joyce. If the transferring IRA institution does in fact make out the check to Joyce, it should not be negotiated but rather returned to the transferring IRA institution immediately. The check should be voided.

In addition, Joyce should advise the receiving IRA institution that under no circumstance should the decedent's IRA be titled in Joyce's name as an IRA owner. It is best to speak to a responsible official in each institution's IRA retirement department who is familiar with these rules and to follow up the point in writing with the responsible official in each IRA institution. It is imperative that the IRA be maintained in the decedent's name in order to avoid an immediate taxable event to Joyce. An error in handling this issue can wipe out decades of tax-deferred growth. Joyce should not deal with clerical staff personnel who are unfamiliar with these important issues.

QUESTION 8.67: Is there anything else Joyce should do in planning a direct transfer?

ANSWER: Joyce should make sure that the new IRA institution is willing to pay out the decedent's IRA distributions under the life-expectancy method. On occasion, a financial institution maintaining an IRA has indicated a preference towards not paying out the decedent's IRA death benefits over an extended period of time even though an election under the life-expectancy method was made. If that is the case, then the designated beneficiary should immediately arrange for a direct transfer of the decedent's IRA assets to another IRA institution which will allow the extended payout schedule.

Multiple IRA Beneficiaries

Special considerations may apply if you are planning to name more than one beneficiary for your IRA, as discussed in Questions 8.68–8.76.

QUESTION 8.68: Stuart Felding has his 67th birthday on May 12, 1999. He has a rollover IRA that at the end of 1999 has a balance of approximately $700,000 with the XYZ brokerage firm. His wife, Janice, is age 65 in 1999, and their only child, Gary, is age 42 in 1999. Stuart has designated both his wife and his son as the designated beneficiaries of his IRA. Each designated beneficiary has a 50-percent interest in Stuart's IRA with the XYZ brokerage firm. If Stuart dies in 2000 at age 68, when must Gary commence his required minimum distributions from Stuart's IRA?

ANSWER: Stuart died before his required beginning date (April 1 of the year following the year he would have reached age 70^1/2). If the terms of Stuart's IRA permit Gary to elect the life-expectancy rule instead of the five-year rule, and Gary wants to make the life-expectancy election, then he must make the election in writing and commence his required minimum distributions from his 50-percent interest in his father's IRA by no later than December 31, 2001. This deadline is the end of the year following the year of Stuart's death (2000).

If the terms of Stuart's IRA made the five-year rule mandatory, or if the five-year rule applied as the IRA's default option
upon Gary's failure to timely elect the life-expectancy rule, then
Gary would be required to receive his entire 50-percent share of
Stuart's IRA by December 31, 2005, the end of the fifth year
following Stuart's death in 2000.

QUESTION 8.69: Under the facts of Question 8.68, what options are available to Janice?

ANSWER: As surviving spouse, Janice may use the designated beneficiary rule or the spousal IRA rollover rules. These rules were
previously discussed in detail in Chapter 3.

QUESTION 8.70: Assuming Gary elects the life-expectancy rule, what is Gary's life expectancy for purposes of calculating his required minimum distributions from Stuart's IRA?

ANSWER: The IRS has issued a letter ruling to the author that
would permit a beneficiary in Gary's position to use his own life
expectancy when the IRA owner dies before his or her required
beginning date (Letter Ruling 199931048). In the absence of
such an IRS ruling, Gary is deemed to be his mother's age.
Generally, if more than one individual is selected as a designated
beneficiary, then the designated beneficiary with the shortest life
expectancy is used in order to determine the period over which
the required minimum distributions must be made. In the
absence of an IRS letter ruling to the contrary, Gary would use
Janice's life expectancy as determined in 2001. At age 67 in
2001, Janice's life expectancy is 18.4 years, as shown in the IRS
single life-expectancy table in Appendix A. Gary must, therefore, make the appropriate timely written election with the IRA
institution to receive his required minimum distributions based
upon a life expectancy of 18.4 years. Again, this assumes that
the IRA plan document permits election of the life-expectancy
rule and does not mandate the five-year rule.

DIVIDING IRA INTO SEPARATE BENEFICIARY ACCOUNTS: QUESTIONS 8.71–8.76

QUESTION 8.71: Is there an exception to the rule described above about Gary being deemed to be Janice's age?

ANSWER: Yes. The IRS has a narrow exception that applies when an IRA owner dies before his or her required beginning date and the IRA is divided into separate accounts for the benefit of each designated beneficiary. The IRS has issued several letter rulings on what constitutes a separate account. In light of these letter rulings, it is possible that the separate account exception is available in the situation where Stuart has named Janice and Gary equally as the designated beneficiaries of his IRA and he dies before his required beginning date.

QUESTION 8.72: Is there anything that Stuart could do prior to his death that would clearly permit Gary to use his own life expectancy for purposes of calculating his required minimum distributions after Stuart's death?

ANSWER: Yes. Stuart should consider establishing two IRA's with each account having approximately $350,000 in it. He could name Janice as the designated beneficiary of IRA No. 1 and Gary as the designated beneficiary of IRA No. 2. In this instance Gary can use his life expectancy instead of Janice's life expectancy in calculating his required minimum distributions for the calendar year 2001. In 2001 Gary is age 44 and his life expectancy is 38.7 years under the IRS table shown in Appendix A. Simply by opening up two IRAs instead of one IRA, Stuart has greatly enhanced the period over which Gary may receive his required minimum distributions from 18.4 years (based upon Janice's life expectancy) to 38.7 years (based upon Gary's life expectancy), without the necessity of relying on IRS rulings. Gary would make the appropriate timely written election with the IRA institution based upon his life expectancy of 38.7 years.

QUESTION 8.73: Assume that at Stuart's death in 2000 the IRA at XYZ brokerage firm is valued at $750,000. Stuart had named his wife, Janice, and his son, Gary, as his designated beneficiaries as previously described in Question 8.68. As before, each designated beneficiary has a 50-percent interest in the IRA. Assume that Gary has not requested a letter ruling from the IRS or relied upon published IRS rulings that allow multiple beneficiaries to use their respective life expectancies for their percentage interests in the decedent's account. Gary is deemed to be his mother's age and must therefore use her life expectancy of 18 years (18.4 years rounded down to 18 years for illustrative purposes) in order to determine his required minimum distributions. Assume that the required minimum distributions are based upon a 7-percent rate of return. How much money will Gary receive over the 18-year period based upon the required minimum-distribution rules?

ANSWER: Gary will receive total required minimum distributions over the 18-year period of $775,176.43. The following schedule illustrates the computation of the required minimum distributions over an 18-year period.

Initial amount: $375,000.00 (50 percent of $750,000); earnings: 7 percent.

DISTRIBUTIONS OVER 18 YEARS

YEAR	EARNINGS AT 7 PERCENT	REQUIRED MINIMUM DISTRIBUTION	BALANCE
			$375,000.00
1	$26,250.00	$20,833.33	380,416.67
2	26,629.17	22,377.45	384,668.39
3	26,926.79	24,041.77	387,553.41 ➤

YEAR	EARNINGS AT 7 PERCENT	REQUIRED MINIMUM DISTRIBUTION	BALANCE
4	27,128.74	25,836.89	388,845.26
5	27,219.17	27,774.66	388,289.77
6	27,180.28	29,868.44	385,601.61
7	26,992.11	32,133.47	380,460.25
8	26,632.22	34,587.30	372,505.17
9	26,075.36	37,250.52	361,330.01
10	25,293.10	40,147.78	346,475.33
11	24,253.27	43,309.42	327,419.18
12	22,919.34	46,774.17	303,564.35
13	21,249.50	50,594.06	274,219.79
14	19,195.39	54,843.96	238,571.22
15	16,699.99	59,642.81	195,628.40
16	13,693.99	65,209.47	144,112.92
17	10,087.90	72,056.46	82,144.36
18	5,750.11	87,894.47	0.00
	$400,176.43	$775,176.43	

QUESTION 8.74: Assume that as in the answer to Question 8.72, Stuart has established two separate IRAs. Janice is the designated beneficiary of IRA No. 1 and Gary is the designated beneficiary of IRA No. 2. At Stuart's death in 2000, IRA No. 2 is valued

at **$375,000. In this instance, Gary, as the designated beneficiary of the separate IRA, would use his life expectancy in calculating his required minimum distributions. Gary's life expectancy is 38 years (38.7 years rounded down to 38 years for illustrative purposes) in order to determine his required minimum distributions. Assume that the required minimum distributions are based upon a 7-percent rate of return. How much money will Gary receive over the 38-year period based upon the required minimum distribution rules?**

ANSWER: Gary will receive total required minimum distributions over the 38-year period of $1,908,632.38. The following schedule illustrates the computation of the required minimum distributions over a 38-year period.

Initial amount: $375,000.00; earnings: 7 percent.

DISTRIBUTIONS OVER 38 YEARS

YEAR	EARNINGS AT 7 PERCENT	REQUIRED MINIMUM DISTRIBUTION	BALANCE
			$375,000.00
1	$26,250.00	$9,868.42	391,381.58
2	27,396.71	10,577.88	408,200.41
3	28,574.03	11,338.90	425,435.54
4	29,780.49	12,155.30	443,060.73
5	31,014.25	13,031.20	461,043.78
6	32,273.06	13,971.02	479,345.82
7	33,554.21	14,979.56	497,920.47 ➤

YEAR	EARNINGS AT 7 PERCENT	REQUIRED MINIMUM DISTRIBUTION	BALANCE
8	34,854.43	16,061.95	516,712.95
9	36,169.91	17,223.77	535,659.09
10	37,496.14	18,471.00	554,684.23
11	38,827.90	19,810.15	573,701.98
12	40,159.14	21,248.22	592,612.90
13	41,482.90	22,792.80	611,303.00
14	42,791.21	24,452.12	629,642.09
15	44,074.95	26,235.09	647,481.95
16	45,323.74	28,151.39	664,654.30
17	46,525.80	30,211.56	680,968.54
18	47,667.80	32,427.07	696,209.27
19	48,734.65	34,810.46	710,133.46
20	49,709.34	37,375.45	722,467.35
21	50,572.71	40,137.08	732,902.98
22	51,303.21	43,111.94	741,094.25
23	51,876.60	46,318.39	746,652.46
24	52,265.67	49,776.83	749,141.30
25	52,439.89	53,510.09	748,071.10
26	52,364.98	57,543.93	742,892.15
27	52,002.45	61,907.68	732,986.92

28	51,309.08	66,635.17	717,660.83
29	50,236.26	71,766.08	696,131.01
30	48,729.17	77,347.89	667,512.29
31	46,725.86	83,439.04	630,799.11
32	44,155.94	90,114.16	584,840.89
33	40,938.86	97,473.48	528,306.27
34	36,981.44	105,661.25	459,626.46
35	32,173.85	114,906.62	376,893.69
36	26,382.56	125,631.23	277,645.02
37	19,435.15	138,822.51	158,257.66
38	11,078.04	169,335.70	0.00
	$1,533,632.38	$1,908,632.38	

QUESTION 8.75: Assume that Stuart has selected his estate as a beneficiary of 50 percent of his IRA and Gary as a designated beneficiary for the other 50 percent of his IRA. Stuart dies in 2000 at age 68. May Gary elect out of the five-year rule?

ANSWER: Possibly. See the answers to Questions 8.70 and 8.71.

QUESTION 8.76: What should Stuart do if he wishes his estate to receive 50 percent of his IRA upon his death and Gary to receive the other 50 percent?

ANSWER: As previously discussed, it is best that Stuart establish two IRAs. IRA No. 1 should be payable to his estate and IRA

No. 2 should be payable to Gary. In that way Gary can definitely elect out of the five-year rule if Stuart dies before his required
beginning date. This would enable Gary to receive required minimum distributions from IRA No. 2 over his life expectancy.

MAKING A PROTECTIVE ELECTION OF THE LIFE-EXPECTANCY METHOD FOR YOUR BENEFICIARY

In certain cases, an IRA owner may want to specify the life-expectancy
distribution method for his or her beneficiary, as discussed in
Questions 8.77–8.86.

**QUESTION 8.77: Judy Clark, an IRA owner, would like to know if
she can make an election as to the distribution method that
would apply to her designated beneficiary if she dies prior to
her required beginning date. May an IRA owner elect the distribution method on behalf of his or her designated beneficiary, or
must the election decision be left to the designated beneficiary?**

ANSWER: The IRA document may permit the IRA owner to make
an election. An IRA document may permit either the IRA owner
or the designated beneficiary to elect whether the five-year rule
or the life-expectancy exception to the five-year rule will apply
in instances where the IRA owner dies prior to his required
beginning date. If the document is silent or the designated beneficiary does not exercise an option to select the method, the five-
year rule applies automatically where the designated beneficiary
is not a surviving spouse.

**QUESTION 8.78: Why would an IRA owner want to make the elec-
tion as to which distribution method should be used by his or
her designated beneficiary?**

ANSWER: An IRA owner may wish to make a protective election if,
for example, he or she is seriously ill and does not expect to live

until the required beginning date and the designated beneficiary is a minor; see Question 8.83. An IRA owner may also wish to make the election on behalf of an adult designated beneficiary if the designated beneficiary is unsophisticated in tax matters; see Question 8.80.

Keep in mind that even if the IRA owner wishes to make a protective election, the election may not be permitted under the terms of the IRA document.

Furthermore, the IRS has indicated that even if the IRA owner makes a protective election in accordance with the terms of the plan document, the election must be implemented by a timely distribution to the designated beneficiary in order to be effective. The designated beneficiary must receive the first minimum distribution figured under the life-expectancy method no later than December 31 of the calendar year following the year of the owner's death.

QUESTION 8.79: If the designated beneficiary is not sophisticated in tax matters, and the terms of the IRA document permit the IRA owner to make the election, then what type of election is recommended?

ANSWER: It is probably best to elect the life-expectancy exception to the five-year rule, thereby allowing distributions to be spread over a longer period of time.

QUESTION 8.80: Assume that Judy Clark is the IRA owner and her adult nephew, Philip Clark, is her designated beneficiary. Further assume that Judy will attain age 70^1/$_2$ during 2000. Her required beginning date is April 1, 2001. Philip is not sophisticated in tax matters and Judy wishes to make a protective election of the life-expectancy distribution method. Assuming that the terms of her IRA document allow Judy to do so, how should she make this election?

ANSWER: The IRA institution may not have a specific form for the election. In that case, Judy, as the IRA owner, would have to create her own election form. The form should be served, together with a cover letter by certified mail, return receipt requested, upon the IRA institution. The election should refer to the IRA number and should state the following:

In the event that I, Judy Clark, should die before my required beginning date of April 1, 2001, and if my designated beneficiary of this IRA account #1001 at the date of my death is my nephew, Philip Clark, and if he survives me, then the required minimum distributions of this IRA account #1001 with your institution shall be paid to Philip Clark over a period not to exceed the life expectancy of Philip Clark based upon his life expectancy under the IRS life-expectancy tables as determined in the calendar year following the year after my date of death. In the event that I, Judy Clark, should die before my required beginning date, then the first required minimum distribution shall be paid to Philip, my designated beneficiary, by no later than December 31 of the calendar year following the date of my death. Distributions shall not be paid to Philip Clark under the five-year rule. In addition, Philip Clark may accelerate distributions from this IRA after my death at any time and from time to time. This IRA title shall remain titled in my name after my death and during the entire distribution period that payments are made to Philip Clark.

Furthermore, this IRA may be directly transferred fully or partially to any other IRA institution after my death by my nephew, Philip Clark, if he is the designated beneficiary of this IRA at the date of my death and provided that the IRA is still maintained and titled in my name. This election as to the life-expectancy method shall still be applicable after any such transfer to any transferee IRA.

The election must be signed and dated by Judy Clark, the IRA owner. Additional copies of the election should be made and given to Philip Clark so that if the IRA is transferred to another IRA institution by Philip after Judy's death, there is further evidence of the fact that the life-expectancy rule rather than the five-year rule applies.

In addition to the written election by Judy, the election must be implemented by a timely distribution according to the IRS.

Philip must receive his first required minimum distribution from Judy's account under the life-expectancy method no later than December 31 of the calendar year following the year of Judy's death.

Caution: The above sample election is illustrative only. A written election should be prepared in conjunction with your professional advisor or estate planner and must be based upon the laws and rules in effect at the time the election is made. The election should be revised from time to time to reflect any changes in the law and in the IRS rules.

QUESTION 8.81: What is the advantage of having Judy make the election out of the five-year rule on behalf of her nephew, Philip?

ANSWER: If Philip is not sophisticated in tax matters then Judy's election will prevent him from defaulting into the five-year rule should Judy die before her required beginning date. In essence, Judy has given Philip a road map to guide him through the complex maze of IRS rules. Judy's election out of the five-year rule has given Philip an extended payout period while also allowing him the greatest degree of flexibility because he can always accelerate the required minimum distributions from time to time. The only disadvantage in this approach is that under the life-expectancy rule, required minimum distributions must commence to Philip by December 31 of the calendar year following Judy's year of death. Again, the election out of the five-year rule will only be required if Judy dies before her required beginning date.

QUESTION 8.82: Is there any other situation where the IRA owner would make a protective written election as to the method of payment?

ANSWER: Yes. If there is a concern that the IRA owner will not live until his or her required beginning date and the designated beneficiary is a minor, then a protective election should be made.

QUESTION 8.83: Why should the IRA owner bother making a protective written election as to a method of payment of the IRA death benefits in the event a minor is involved?

ANSWER: Based upon state law, a minor may not legally have the capacity to designate a method of payment. Therefore, the minor would probably default into the five-year rule if the IRA owner should die before his or her required beginning date. Most IRA documents provide that the default option is the five-year rule when the designated beneficiary is other than the spouse. In order to avoid this problem, and to provide an extended payout period for the minor, the IRA owner should select a method of payment based upon the minor's life expectancy that will come into play if the IRA owner should die before his or her required beginning date.

QUESTION 8.84: Assume that the designated beneficiary is a minor who may not legally elect a method of payment. What happens if the IRA document does not permit the IRA owner, prior to his or her death, to make a protective election as to a method of payment?

ANSWER: If the IRA owner dies before his or her required beginning date and the distributions are payable to a minor, then the default option is generally the five-year rule.

To avoid this default option, an IRA owner who has named a minor as a designated beneficiary should only use an IRA institution that has an IRA document that permits a protective election of the life-expectancy rule in the event that the IRA owner dies before his or her required beginning date.

QUESTION 8.85: Why can't the minor's parent make the election out of the five-year rule?

ANSWER: The parent, as the natural guardian of the minor, generally has no power under state law to make an election on behalf of the minor as to the method of payment of IRA distributions.

QUESTION 8.86: Instead of directly naming a minor as the designated beneficiary of the IRA, would it be better to select a custodian or a trust to receive the IRA assets on the minor's behalf?

ANSWER: Yes. As discussed in Chapter 5, there are advantages in naming a custodian or a trust to receive the IRA assets on the minor's behalf upon the IRA owner's death.

CHAPTER NINE

Estate Planning with Retirement Assets

Many taxpayers accumulate substantial assets in qualified plans, 403(b) annuity contracts, and Individual Retirement Accounts (IRAs). During their lifetimes these arrangements provide the vehicle for many taxpayers to live without the pressure of the need to accumulate additional wealth for retirement. However, as the aging of taxpayers in the United States takes place, many people find that their retirement-plan assets have accumulated to a point that the family is exposed to substantial tax liabilities.

Taxpayers who have accumulated substantial retirement assets must recognize that they must deal with an estate tax liability problem. Improper planning and poor advice may wipe out most of the retirement assets. The estate tax liability for purposes of this chapter is limited to the federal estate tax liability and does not consider state estate tax liabilities.

Depending on the amount of your total assets from retirement plans and other holdings, estate planning can be an involved process, requiring the expertise of an experienced tax practitioner. This chapter is designed only as an introduction to the issues that you and your advisor will face in salvaging your retirement assets for the benefit of your family.

CONSULT AN EXPERIENCED ESTATE TAX ADVISOR

Questions 9.1–9.7 introduce basic tax-planning issues related to the integration of retirement plan assets with an overall estate plan.

QUESTION 9.1: What type of advisor should I engage in order to do effective estate planning with my retirement assets?

ANSWER: The advisor that you select must be knowledgeable in estate planning. In addition, he or she must be familiar with the retirement-plan distribution rules and be able to integrate the retirement plan with the estate plan.

Ask the advisor for references and ask if he or she has had prior experience involving tax planning for clients with substantial retirement accounts.

QUESTION 9.2: Why is it difficult to find an advisor who can integrate the estate plan with the retirement plan?

ANSWER: The advisor must have a broad base of knowledge in many areas, such as the following:

a. Income taxation of estates and trusts

b. Estate taxation (federal and state)

c. State law apportionment statutes

d. State estate tax and/or state inheritance laws

e. Property law concepts

f. Pension distribution rules

g. Pension excise tax rules, i.e., penalties

h. Probate laws of the state

QUESTION 9.3: If my advisor lacks expertise in all of these areas, what should I do?

ANSWER: Ask your advisor to help you retain a knowledgeable specialist to provide assistance in developing a comprehensive estate plan that integrates your retirement assets with your overall estate plan.

QUESTION 9.4: Why should I be so concerned about integrating my retirement assets with my estate plan?

ANSWER: Retirement assets may be subject to a triple tax. If your estate is sufficiently large, the assets may be subject to estate tax; see Questions 9.5–9.7. Your beneficiaries will generally have to pay income tax on distributions from your traditional IRAs and qualified employer plan accounts. Furthermore, if a beneficiary fails to receive a required minimum distribution, then the insufficient distribution may trigger a 50-percent excise tax penalty.

QUESTION 9.5: Should I be concerned about estate planning if all of my assets, including my retirement plan assets, are payable to my spouse upon my death?

ANSWER: If you leave all of your assets to your spouse, your estate will not be subject to federal estate tax because of the unlimited marital deduction. However, when your surviving spouse subsequently dies, estate tax liability could be triggered if your spouse's taxable estate plus certain previously made gifts exceeds the estate-tax threshold applicable in the year of your spouse's death.

QUESTION 9.6: What is the threshold for subjecting an estate to federal estate tax?

ANSWER: The threshold for federal estate tax depends on the year of death. The taxable estate threshold increases annually between 1998 and 2006 under current law. For the estate of an individual dying in 1998, the taxable estate threshold was $625,000 and in 1999, $650,000. The threshold will increase to $675,000 for estates of individuals dying in 2000 and 2001; $700,000 in 2002 and 2003; $850,000 in 2004; $950,000 in 2005; and $1,000,000 in 2006 and later years.

Keep in mind that these thresholds are subject to change by Congress. Consult with your professional advisor or estate planner to keep current with any changes in the law.

QUESTION 9.7: For purposes of applying the thresholds in Question 9.6, what is the taxable estate?

ANSWER: In general, the taxable estate for federal estate-tax purposes is the gross estate minus allowable estate tax deductions such as for funeral expenses, administration expenses, debts, and bequests to a surviving spouse or to qualifying charities. If you made gifts in prior years over the applicable gift tax annual exclusion, these taxable gifts can trigger an estate tax because they are added to your taxable estate.

Keep in mind that the rules for state estate tax or state inheritance tax may be different from the federal rules. State taxes may be due even if the estate is not subject to federal estate tax.

CASE STUDY
Questions 9.8–9.18 illustrate some planning options for a family where a retirement plan account is the largest asset.

QUESTION 9.8: I am a married college professor and have two children and two grandchildren. During my teaching career I have accumulated $575,000 in my 403(b) annuity contract. In addition, I have $200,000 in life insurance that I own. My wife is the beneficiary of my 403(b) annuity contract and of my life insurance. My spouse and I jointly own a residence (tenancy by entirety) that has (net of mortgage) a value of $250,000. I have

$60,000 in a joint savings account and $50,000 in mutual funds that are jointly owned with my wife. Assume that I die first in the calendar year 2001 when the value of my 403(b) annuity contract has increased to $650,000, the savings account to 65,000, and the mutual funds to $60,000. Also assume that my wife dies shortly thereafter in 2001. Is there an estate tax liability upon my death or upon the subsequent death of my spouse?

ANSWER: While there is no federal estate tax liability on your death, there will be a federal estate tax liability upon the subsequent death of your spouse. The assets that are paid directly to your spouse upon your death qualify for the unlimited marital deduction. Therefore, there is no federal estate tax liability when you die. Upon the subsequent death of your spouse, the federal estate tax liability is approximately $207,250. The liability is computed as follows:

Retirement assets:	$650,000
Life insurance proceeds:	200,000
Residence:	250,000
Savings account:	65,000
Mutual funds:	60,000
Gross estate:	$1,225,000
Less: Expenses of administration (estimated):	(25,000)
Taxable estate:	$1,200,000
Federal estate tax before credit:	$427,800
Less: Federal unified credit:	(220,550)
Federal estate tax:	$207,250

Expenses of administration in the first estate are ignored and state estate taxes are not considered in the above example.

QUESTION 9.9: Is there anything that I can do before my death in order to eliminate the $207,250 federal estate tax liability described in Question 9.8 above?

ANSWER: Yes. There are several ways to eliminate the federal estate tax liability of $207,250. One approach is to have the life insurance proceeds payable directly to your children and to transfer the 403(b) annuity contract proceeds into two brand new IRAs if the annuity contract has a cash-out provision. One IRA could be in the amount of $335,000 and could be payable to your children, and the other IRA in the amount of $315,000 could be payable to your spouse. If the annuity contract does not have a cash-out provision, then the designated beneficiaries of the annuity contract must be split in order to accomplish the result that is desired. The split approach is complex and a professional advisor must be consulted. The split–designated beneficiary approach is not as desirable as the IRA approach under distribution payout rules. Under the split–designated beneficiary approach, the children generally are deemed to be the age of the mother. Upon the subsequent death of your spouse, her federal estate tax liability will be approximately zero. This is computed as follows:

Retirement assets:	$315,000
Life insurance proceeds:	-0-
Residence:	250,000
Savings account:	65,000
Mutual funds:	60,000
Gross estate:	$690,000

Less: Expenses of administration (estimated):	(15,000)
Taxable estate:	$675,000
Federal estate tax before credit:	$220,550
Less: Federal unified credit:	(220,550)
Federal estate tax:	$-0-

QUESTION 9.10: Could the result in Question 9.9 be accomplished by shifting other items in the estate?

ANSWER: Yes. Other assets could be partially used to accomplish the same result.

QUESTION 9.11: I thought that I could just change my will in order to avoid the estate tax liability described in Question 9.8. Doesn't that approach accomplish the same result?

ANSWER: No. A will only operates on probate assets. A will does not govern what happens to nonprobate assets. The 403(b) annuity contract payable to an individual as a beneficiary, the life insurance policy payable to an individual as a beneficiary, the jointly held assets, and the real estate held as tenancy by the entirety are not controlled by the will because they are not considered to be probate assets.

QUESTION 9.12: What is a probate asset?

ANSWER: A probate asset is an asset that is solely owned by the decedent or the proceeds of any nonprobate asset such as a life insurance policy that is payable to the estate. The executor can only control those assets that come into his possession as probate assets.

QUESTION 9.13: My wife is unhappy about the suggestions to leave the life insurance and most of the retirement assets to our children because she feels that she will not have sufficient income to live comfortably in her retirement years. Is there any other approach that will give her more financial security and still save the children a substantial amount of federal estate tax?

ANSWER: Yes. The beneficiary of the life insurance proceeds can be a trust (either revocable or irrevocable). The trust provisions could state that the trust income shall be paid to your surviving spouse during her lifetime. This would mean that your spouse receives an annual income from the trust. In addition, she may be given a 5-percent right of invasion of principal each year or $5,000, whichever is greater. The spouse generally should not be the trustee, because if she is given certain powers, it may result in the inclusion of the value of the life insurance proceeds in her estate for estate tax purposes. The children should be the trustees and should have the right in their absolute discretion to invade principal on behalf of their mother. If your spouse is a co-trustee, her powers should be limited to investment decisions and she should not have any discretionary powers over trust principal or any other discretionary powers except for investment decisions.

QUESTION 9.14: My wife still feels nervous and would like some additional security. Is there anything else that you can suggest to alleviate her anxiety?

ANSWER: Yes. Assume that the annuity contract has a cash-out provision. Upon your death as the IRA owner, the children will commence to take distributions from their inherited IRA. They may then lend the net proceeds after taxes to their mother. The loan should be evidenced by a long-term note and bear interest at the appropriate rate. The interest income and IRA payments will, of course, result in taxable income to the children, but the estate tax savings may be well in excess of the increase in the income tax liability of the children. If the annuity contract does not have a cash-out provision, the annuity contract beneficiary designations must be split between the spouse and the children. The children may then use the same loan approach as described for IRAs.

QUESTION 9.15: These steps seem to alleviate my estate tax problem if I die first. Would there be an estate tax problem if my wife died first?

ANSWER: Yes. Although there would be no federal estate tax liability if your wife died first, upon your subsequent death shortly after your wife (assuming you died during the 2001 calendar year), your estate would be subject to the same federal estate tax liability of $207,250; see the answer to Question 9.8.

QUESTION 9.16: My wife and I would like you to recommend an approach to minimize the estate tax liability if my wife is ill and it looks as though she will predecease me. Assume that I survive my wife and die shortly thereafter. Do you have any suggestions?

ANSWER: The jointly held residence (tenancy by entirety) with a net value of $250,000 should be deeded into your wife's name. The joint savings account of $65,000 should be retitled in your wife's name, as well as the mutual funds of $60,000. Your wife can then by will decide who should receive the residence, the savings account, and the mutual funds. Assume that by will she has these assets going to your children outright. On your subsequent death shortly thereafter during the calendar year 2001, your federal estate tax liability will be approximately $60,900. This liability is computed as follows:

Retirement assets:	$650,000
Life insurance proceeds:	200,000

Residence:	-0-
Savings account:	-0-
Mutual funds:	-0-
Gross estate:	$850,000
Less: Expenses of administration (estimated):	(15,000)
Taxable estate:	$835,000
Federal estate tax before credit:	$281,450
Less: Federal unified credit:	(220,550)
Federal estate tax:	$60,900

QUESTION 9.17: Assume that I am in good health. Can you suggest an approach to accomplish an even larger reduction in federal estate tax liability?

ANSWER: An approach that most estate planners suggest is that the ownership of the life insurance policy be structured in a manner that avoids including the life insurance policy in the gross estate of either spouse. Most estate planners are familiar with the concept of the irrevocable life insurance trust and can structure a transfer of the life insurance policy to an irrevocable trust for the benefit of your wife or children. Alternatively, your children can be made the owners and beneficiaries of the life insurance policy.

If you transfer the ownership of the $200,000 life insurance policy to either an irrevocable life insurance trust or to your children and survive by more than three years, then the life insurance policy is not included in your gross estate. Assume that you transfer the life insurance policy to your children on November 1, 1999, your wife predeceases you, and that you die on December 15, 2002. Also assume that your retirement assets on December 15, 2002, amount to $715,000. The federal estate tax liability of $70,150 would be reduced to zero. This is computed as follows:

Retirement assets:	$715,000
Life insurance proceeds:	-0-
Residence:	-0-
Savings account:	-0-
Mutual funds:	-0-
Gross estate:	$715,000
Less: Expenses of administration (estimated):	(15,000)
Taxable estate:	$700,000
Federal estate tax before credit:	$229,800
Less: Federal unified credit for 2002	(229,800)
Federal estate tax:	$-0-

QUESTION 9.18: I like your suggestion about transferring the life insurance policy out of my name. However, there is no guarantee that I will live for more than three years from the date of the transfer of the ownership of the life insurance policy to either an irrevocable trust or to my children. Is there anything else that I can do in order to reduce the $60,900 federal estate tax liability shown in the answer to Question 9.16?

ANSWER: You should consider making gifts to your children and to your grandchildren. Because you have two children and two grandchildren, you can make a $10,000 gift to each child and to each grandchild for a total of $40,000 of gifts in each calendar year. These gifts will not result in a reduction of your unified credit. In addition, your wife can agree to join in the gifts that you make, which will result in a doubling of the amount of gifts that you can make in each calendar year. Assume that you and

your wife agree to maximize gifts over a two-year period
because you are both in poor health. You and your wife can
each make gifts of $40,000, or your wife can consent to your
making gifts of $80,000 by filing the appropriate gift tax returns
with the necessary consents.

It is best that the $80,000 of gifts be made from your assets.
This is because you currently have substantial retirement assets
and because you will probably have to include the $200,000 of
life insurance proceeds in your gross estate because you may not
survive for the required three-year period after you transfer the
ownership of your policy. You have only one asset that lends
itself to a gift-giving program. That asset unfortunately is a
retirement asset that has never been taxed.

In order for you to net $80,000 each year (after federal and
state income taxes) you will have to withdraw approximately
$120,000 from your retirement assets on an annual basis. In
two years you will withdraw $240,000 from your retirement
assets. Assume you do this for a two-year period and then stop.
Your children have assured you that if you need the money they
will lend it to you. You agree that you will sign a note and pay a
reasonable rate of interest on the note if you need to borrow the
money from them at a later date. Assume that your wife prede-
ceases you and you die shortly thereafter, but that two years of
gifts have been consummated before your death. This can be
accomplished because you can make the $80,000 worth of gifts
in December of a calendar year and another $80,000 of gifts in
January of the subsequent calendar year. Your wife consents to
these gifts. Assume that these gifts are made in December of
1999 and January of 2000. Also assume that both you and your
spouse die in the 2001 calendar year, and as of the date of your
death, your retirement assets amount to $485,000 after consid-
ering earnings and distributions. Upon your death there is
no federal estate tax liability. This zero liability is computed as
follows:

Retirement assets:	$485,000
Life insurance proceeds:	200,000

Residence:	-0-
Savings account:	-0-
Mutual funds:	-0-
Gross estate:	$685,000
Less: Expenses of administration (estimated):	(10,000)
Taxable estate:	$675,000
Federal estate tax before credit:	$220,550
Less: Federal unified credit for 2001	(220,550)
Federal estate tax:	-0-

The above illustration assumes that the earnings from the retirement assets have been applied toward living expenses.

INCOME IN RESPECT OF A DECEDENT (IRD)

Questions 9.19–9.26 discuss the special income tax deduction that is available to nonspouse beneficiaries of retirement assets that were subject to estate tax.

QUESTION 9:19: What is income in respect of a decedent (IRD)?

ANSWER: It is an item of gross income of a decedent that was not includable in Form 1040 of the decedent prior to his/her death.

QUESTION 9:20: Can you illustrate an item of IRD?

ANSWER: Yes. Assume that Jack was entitled to a salary check of $1,000 from his employer. Jack died before receiving his salary check of $1,000 from his employer. The salary of $1,000 is IRD.

QUESTION 9:21: Can you illustrate the concept of IRD if an IRA is involved?

ANSWER: Yes. Assume that Jack owned only one IRA. As of the date of Jack's death in 1999, the IRA contained $100,000. No portion of his IRA contained any nondeductible IRA contributions. The IRA of $100,000 is IRD.

QUESTION 9:22: Assume that Jack's estate has a federal estate tax of $40,000 that is attributable to the IRA of $100,000. Also assume that his beneficiary is his brother Martin. Martin withdraws $30,000 from Jack's IRA during the year 2000. Must Martin report the $30,000 distribution from Jack's IRA during the calendar year 2000?

ANSWER: Yes. Martin must report $30,000 as ordinary income during the calendar year 2000 with respect to the distribution from Jack's IRA.

QUESTION 9.23: It seems unfair that Martin should have to pay income tax on the IRA distribution because the IRA was subject to estate tax. Is there some type of tax relief available to Martin?

ANSWER: Yes. A nonspouse beneficiary of retirement assets such as Martin is entitled to a special income tax deduction. The deduction, commonly referred to as a Section 691(c) deduction, is intended to avoid double taxation of the same item.

Martin is entitled to claim an itemized deduction of $12,000 on his Form 1040 in connection with the $30,000 IRA distribution that he received from Jack's IRA.

QUESTION 9.24: How was the $12,000 deduction in the answer to Question 9.23 computed?

ANSWER: The deduction of $12,000 is 40 percent of the $30,000 IRA distribution that he received during the calendar year 2000. Federal estate tax of $40,000 was attributable to the $100,000 IRA. The percentage ratio of the Section 691(c) amount to the IRD amount is, therefore, 40 percent ($40,000 ÷ $100,000).

QUESTION 9:25: Assume that Martin withdraws $70,000 from Jack's IRA during 2001. Is Martin entitled to an income tax deduction in his Form 1040 for the calendar year 2001 with respect to the distribution of $70,000 that he received form Jack's IRA?

ANSWER: Yes. Martin is entitled to make an itemized deduction of $28,000 on his Form 1040 in connection with the $70,000 IRA distribution that he received during the calendar year 2001. The deduction of $28,000 is 40 percent of $70,000.

QUESTION 9:26: Assume that Martin receives $10,000 from Jack's IRA during the calendar year 2002. This amount represents the growth in Jack's IRA after his date of death. Is Martin entitled to an income tax deduction for the calendar year 2002 with respect to the distribution of $10,000 from Jack's IRA?

ANSWER: No. Martin has used up his Section 691(c) deduction of $40,000 ($12,000 + $28,000) in the calendar years 2000 and 2001 respectively. He cannot deduct more than $40,000 as a Section 691(c) deduction because that is the amount of the federal estate tax that is attributable to Jack's $100,000 IRA.

QUESTION 9.27: Assume that Jack's IRA beneficiary was his wife Janet, rather than his brother Martin. If Janet withdrew $30,000 from Jack's IRA during 2000, would she be entitled to the same $12,000 income tax deduction that you said was available to Martin in the answer to Question 9.23?

ANSWER: No. The Section 691(c) deduction is intended to avoid double tax. The IRA passing from Jack to Janet would have been deducted from Jack's gross estate under the marital deduction. Because no estate tax would be attributable to the IRA, the Section 691(c) deduction would not be available to Janet when she reported distributions from Jack's IRA.

CASE STUDY

The following information letter is used by the author in his practice in order to explain the income in respect of a decedent rule to clients and is reprinted with permission from *Pension Distributions: Planning Strategies, Cases and Rulings*, Seymour Goldberg (Garden City, N.Y.: IRG Publications, 1999).

Sample Client's Letter

March 15, 2000

Mr. Robert Major
1000 Park Avenue
New York, New York 10002

Re: Income in respect of a decedent deduction

Dear Mr. Major:

As you know, the Estate of Linda Major had a federal taxable estate of $4,000,000 at the time of her death on December 1, 1999. The federal taxable estate of $4,000,000 includes an individual retirement account (IRA) of $1,000,000 that was maintained with the XYZ financial institution. The only item of "Income in Respect of Decedent" that is included in the federal estate tax return of Linda Major is the $1,000,000 IRA. You are the beneficiary of 60 percent of the IRA and your sister, Margaret Major, is beneficiary of 40 percent of the IRA.

The federal estate tax attributable to the IRA is $451,600. This amount is computed as follows:

Federal taxable estate including the IRA		$4,000,000
Federal estate tax before credits		$1,840,800
Less:		
Federal unified credit	$211,300	
State death tax credit	280,400	
Total credits		491,700
Federal estate tax after credits		$1,349,100
Federal taxable estate excluding the IRA		$3,000,000
Federal estate tax before credits		$1,290,800
Less:		
Federal unified credit	$211,300	
State death tax credit	182,000	
Total credits		393,300
Federal estate tax after credits		$897,500
Federal estate tax after credits on federal taxable estate of $4,000,000		$1,349,100
Federal estate tax after credits on federal taxable estate of $3,000,000		897,500
Federal estate tax attributable to IRA		$451,600

As I mentioned, the amount of the IRA that is determined as of the date of death of Linda Major is called "Income in Respect of a

Decedent." This is based upon the fact that the entire amount in the IRA does not contain any nondeductible IRA contributions. If, for example, Linda Major made nondeductible IRA contributions of $20,000, then only $980,000 of the IRA amount would be considered to be income in respect of a decedent. However, this is not the case in this situation. The IRA that Linda Major had at the time of her death was created as a result of a rollover distribution that she received from a qualified plan.

"Income in Respect of a Decedent" is commonly referred to as IRD. The beneficiaries of the IRA are allocated under the tax law a pro rata portion of the federal estate tax that was paid on the IRA.

The following are the calculations of the allocation of the amount of IRD that is allocable to each beneficiary as well as the amount of the federal estate tax that is allocable to each beneficiary with respect to the IRD amount:

PAYEE	IRA AMOUNT (IRD) DETERMINED AS OF THE DATE OF DEATH ON DECEMBER 1, 1999	PERCENTAGE OF IRA (IRD) ALLOCATED TO EACH BENEFICIARY
Robert Major	$600,000	60
Margaret Major	400,000	40
Total	$1,000,000	100

The amount of the federal estate tax deduction that is allocable to each beneficiary follows:

PAYEE	IRA AMOUNT (IRD) DETERMINED AS OF THE DATE OF DEATH ON DECEMBER 1, 1999	PERCENTAGE	FEDERAL ESTATE TAX ATTRIBUTABLE TO IRD AND ALLOCATED PERCENT TO EACH BENEFICIARY
Robert Major	$600,000	60	$270,960
Margaret Major	400,000	40	180,640
Total	$1,000,000	100	$451,600

The federal estate tax percentage allocated to each beneficiary is 45.16 percent. This is allocated based upon the following formula:

Robert Major

$$\frac{\text{Federal estate tax attributable to IRD and allocated to Robert Major}}{\text{Amount of IRD allocated to Robert Major}} = \frac{\$270,960}{\$600,000} = 45.16\%$$

Margaret Major

$$\frac{\text{Federal estate tax attributable to IRD and allocated to Margaret Major}}{\text{Amount of IRD allocated to Margaret Major}} = \frac{\$180,640}{\$400,000} = 45.16\%$$

In essence, Robert Major and Margaret Major take income tax deductions of $270,960 and $180,640, respectively, as they withdraw IRA (IRD) distributions from the Linda Major, deceased IRA.

It is best from a tax-planning point of view that the Linda Major IRA be divided into two IRAs that are maintained in the name of Linda Major, deceased IRA f/b/o Robert Major and Linda Major deceased IRA f/b/o Margaret Major. The Social Security number of each beneficiary should be placed on each IRA. Robert Major would have 60 percent allocated to the Linda Major deceased IRA f/b/o Robert Major. Margaret Major would have 40 percent allocated to the Linda Major deceased IRA f/b/o Margaret Major.

Assume that IRA No. 1 is the Linda Major, deceased IRA f/b/o Robert Major and IRA No. 2 is the Linda Major, deceased IRA f/b/o Margaret Major. Also assume that Robert Major withdrew $40,000 from IRA No. 1 in the calendar year 2000 and Margaret Major withdrew $20,000 from IRA No. 2 in the calendar year 2000.

Robert Major would report the $40,000 that he received in the calendar year 2000 as additional gross income. He would be entitled to an itemized deduction under IRC Sec. 691(c) of $18,064. This is determined by multiplying $40,000 by 45.16 percent.

The itemized deduction under IRC Sec. 691(c) is referred to as "Other Miscellaneous Deductions" and is called "Federal estate tax on income in respect of a decedent." It is not subject to the 2 percent of adjusted gross income limitation, but it is subject to the 3 percent of adjusted gross income limitation.

Margaret Major would report the $20,000 that she received in the calendar year 2000 as additional gross income. She would be entitled to an itemized deduction under IRC Sec. 691(c) of $9,032. This is determined by multiplying $20,000 by 45.16 percent.

The maximum itemized deduction under IRC Sec. 691(c) that may be taken by Robert Major during his lifetime with respect to the distributions that he receives as a beneficiary of the Linda Major, deceased IRA No. 1 is limited to $270,960. In addition, the maximum itemized deduction under IRC Sec. 691(c) that may be taken by Margaret Major during her lifetime with respect to the distributions that she receives as a beneficiary of the Linda Major, deceased IRA No. 2 is limited to $180,640. The calculations of IRD and the income tax returns of each beneficiary must be permanently retained so that the amount of the IRD deduction can be verified if an IRS audit takes place.

In addition, if a beneficiary should die before the allocated share of the IRC Sec. 691(c) deduction with respect to the Linda Major deceased IRA is used up, then the unused amount is available to the heirs of that deceased beneficiary. Further, if a beneficiary should die in pay status, then the heirs of that beneficiary would be entitled to a double IRC Sec. 691(c) deduction if the Linda Major IRA No. 1 or IRA No. 2, as the case may be, is in pay status and triggers a further federal estate tax in the beneficiary's estate. This would be in addition to any IRC Sec. 691(c) deduction that is allocable to the heirs of that beneficiary that is attributable to any other independent IRD items that are includable in the beneficiary's estate.

This letter should be retained by you in your permanent files. In addition, please make sure that your accountant and your potential heirs are given copies of this letter in order to protect these valuable income tax deductions for both now and in the future.

As a last point, please retain a copy of the Linda Major federal estate tax return, Form 706 in your permanent files and make sure that you advise your immediate family members and attorney where your permanent files are maintained.

A similar letter is being sent to your sister, Margaret Major, for her permanent files.

If you should have any questions, please do not hesitate to call me.

Sincerely yours,

Seymour Goldberg

CHAPTER TEN

THE ROTH IRA

The Taxpayer Relief Act of 1997 (1997 Act) created a new IRA called the Roth IRA. The IRS Restructuring and Reform Act of 1998 (1998 Act) modified the Roth IRA rules. This new Roth IRA has several interesting features that present new estate planning and income tax–planning opportunities for many taxpayers.

One of the important attributes of the Roth IRA is the fact that the Roth IRA owner is not required to receive any required distributions during his or her lifetime. This means that no matter how long the Roth IRA owner lives, he or she need not receive any required minimum distributions during his or her lifetime. Thus, substantial income tax–free growth may occur for many years.

Another key attribute of the Roth IRA is that the distributions from the Roth IRA generally are income tax–free to the recipient.

Roth IRAs may be created by making contributions or by rolling over the proceeds of traditional IRAs. Special rules apply if a traditional IRA is rolled over or converted into a Roth IRA. Roth IRAs are subject to income limitations and to a concept called "modified adjusted gross income." Traditional IRAs are subject to income limitations and are based upon a different definition of modified adjusted gross income. Modified adjusted gross income for Roth IRA purposes is discussed in this chapter.

THE ROTH IRA CREATED BY CONTRIBUTIONS

The Taxpayer Relief Act of 1997 (1997 Act) permits an individual to establish a Roth IRA by making contributions. Questions 10.1–10.27 discuss the contribution-type Roth IRA: Roth IRAs established by conversion or rollover from a traditional IRA are discussed starting at Question 10.28.

QUESTION 10.1: For what years may a Roth IRA be established?

ANSWER: A Roth IRA may be established for taxable years after December 31, 1997.

QUESTION 10.2: Assume that Jack, age 40, is single and has earned income of $35,000 and modified adjusted gross income of $42,000 during the calendar year 1999. Jack is an active participant in a qualified plan. May Jack make a $2,000 deductible contribution to a traditional IRA for the calendar year 1999?

ANSWER: No. Because Jack is single and an active participant in a qualified plan during the calendar year 1999 and has modified adjusted gross income in excess of $41,000, he may not make a deductible contribution of $2,000 to an IRA for the calendar year 1999.

QUESTION 10.3: Assume the facts in question 10.2. May Jack make a $2,000 nondeductible contribution to an IRA for the calendar year 1999?

ANSWER: Yes. The 1997 Act did not eliminate nondeductible IRA contributions. Jack may make a $2,000 nondeductible contribution to an IRA for the calendar year 1999.

QUESTION 10.4: Assume the facts in question 10.2. May Jack make a $2,000 contribution to a Roth IRA for the calendar year 1999?

ANSWER: Yes. Because Jack is single and has a modified adjusted gross income of less than $95,000, he may make a $2,000 contribution to a Roth IRA for the calendar year 1999. The fact that he is an active participant in a qualified plan does not prevent him from making a $2,000 contribution to a Roth IRA.

QUESTION 10.5: Referring to question 10.4, when must Jack make the $2,000 contribution to a Roth IRA for the calendar year 1999?

ANSWER: Jack must make the contribution to a Roth IRA for the calendar year 1999 by April 17, 2000. The contribution must be made by the initial due date of Jack's return.

QUESTION 10.6: Referring to Question 10.4, assume that Jack obtained an extension to file his 1999 tax return to August 15, 2000. May Jack make a contribution to the Roth IRA for the calendar year 1999 by August 15, 2000?

ANSWER: No. Jack must make the contribution to the Roth IRA for the calendar year 1999 by April 17, 2000, and not by August 15, 2000.

QUESTION 10.7: Assume that Jack is single and has a modified adjusted gross income of $120,000 for the calendar year 2000.

May Jack make a contribution to a Roth IRA for the calendar year 2000?

ANSWER: No. Because Jack has a modified adjusted gross income for the calendar year 2000 that is in excess of $110,000, he may not make a contribution to a Roth IRA.

QUESTION 10.8: Under the 1997 Act, up to what income levels may a single person make contributions to a Roth IRA?

ANSWER: The $2,000 maximum contribution that a single person can make to a Roth IRA is phased out for modified adjusted gross income between $95,000 and $110,000. Modified adjusted gross income is discussed in Questions 10.64–10.68.

QUESTION 10.9: Assume that John and Mary are both active participants in qualified plans. They file a joint return for the calendar year 1999. The modified adjusted gross income on their joint return is $120,000. What is the maximum amount that each may contribute to a Roth IRA for the calendar year 1999?

ANSWER: John and Mary may each contribute $2,000 to a Roth IRA for the calendar year 1999.

QUESTION 10.10: Under the 1997 Act, up to what income levels may married persons filing a joint return make contributions to Roth IRAs?

ANSWER: The maximum contributions that married persons filing a joint return can make to Roth IRAs are phased out for modified adjusted gross income between $150,000 and $160,000. See Questions 10.67–10.69 for a discussion of the concept of modified adjusted gross income.

QUESTION 10.11: Assume that Martin is a single individual who is not an active participant in a qualified plan. Martin's modified

adjusted gross income for the calendar year 1999 is $80,000. May Martin make a $2,000 deductible IRA contribution for the calendar year 1999?

ANSWER: Yes. Because Martin is not an active participant in a qualified plan, he may make a $2,000 deductible IRA contribution for the calendar year 1999.

QUESTION 10.12: Assume the facts in question 10.11. May Martin make both a $2,000 deductible IRA contribution and a $2,000 contribution to a Roth IRA for the calendar year 1999?

ANSWER: No. Martin is limited to a maximum contribution of $2,000 to all IRAs for the calendar year 1999. Thus, if Martin makes a $2,000 deductible IRA contribution for the calendar year 1999, he may not make a $2,000 contribution to a Roth IRA for the calendar year 1999.

QUESTION 10.13: Assume the facts in question 10.11. May Martin make a $2,000 contribution to a Roth IRA for the calendar year 1999 rather than make a $2,000 deductible IRA contribution for the calendar year 1999?

ANSWER: Yes. Martin has a choice as to which IRA or combination of IRAs (traditional IRA and Roth IRA) to use for the calendar year 1999. Martin could allocate his contribution for the calendar year 1999 in part to a deductible IRA and in part to a Roth IRA in any manner he wishes, as long as the aggregate contribution for the calendar year 1999 is no greater than $2,000.

QUESTION 10.14: Frank is age $70^{1}/_{2}$ in the calendar year 1999. He is single and has earned income and modified adjusted gross income of $60,000. Frank does not participate in a qualified plan. May Frank make a $2,000 deductible contribution to a traditional IRA for the calendar year 1999?

ANSWER: No. The Internal Revenue Code does not permit an individual to make a deductible IRA contribution if the individual attains age 70^1/$_2$ before the close of the taxable year. Because Frank is age 70^1/$_2$ during the calendar year 1999, he may not make a $2,000 deductible IRA contribution for the calendar year 1999.

QUESTION 10.15: Assume the facts in question 10.14. May Frank make a $2,000 contribution to a Roth IRA for the calendar year 1999?

ANSWER: Yes. Under the 1997 Act Frank may make a $2,000 Roth IRA contribution for the calendar year 1999. The Act permits an individual to make a contribution to a Roth IRA even after attaining age 70^1/$_2$.

QUESTION 10.16: Assume that Philip is age 72 in the calendar year 2000. He is single and has earned income and modified adjusted gross income of $20,000. May Philip make a contribution of $2,000 to a Roth IRA for the calendar year 2000?

ANSWER: Yes. See answer to Question 10.15.

QUESTION 10.17: Harry and Margaret are married and file a joint return for the calendar year 1999. Harry is age 74 and Margaret is age 72. The earned income shown on the return is $25,000, and the modified adjusted gross income is $30,000. May Harry and Margaret each contribute $2,000 to a Roth IRA for the calendar year 1999?

ANSWER: Yes. The 1997 Act permits each of them to make a contribution to a Roth IRA regardless of age. Harry and Margaret may each contribute $2,000 to a Roth IRA for the calendar year 1999.

QUESTION 10.18: Assume that Carol is age 65 and single, with no earned income, and interest and dividend income of $10,000 during the calendar year 1999. May Carol make a $2,000 deductible contribution to a traditional IRA for the calendar year 1999?

ANSWER: No. Carol may only make a deductible IRA contribution for the calendar year 1999 to the extent of the lesser of $2,000 or earned income. Because Carol does not have any earned income, she may not make any deductible IRA contribution for the calendar year 1999.

QUESTION 10.19: Assume the facts in question 10.18. May Carole contribute $2,000 to a Roth IRA for the calendar year 1999?

ANSWER: No. Under the 1997 Act Carol may not make a contribution to a Roth IRA unless she has earned income. Because Carol does not have any earned income she may not make a contribution to a Roth IRA for the calendar year 1999.

QUESTION 10.20: Stanley and Sally file a joint return for the calendar year 1999. Stanley earns $70,000 and Sally earns $30,000. Their earned income and modified adjusted gross income for the calendar year 1999 is $100,000. Stanley is an active participant in a simplified employee pension and Sally is an active participant in a simple retirement account. May Stanley and Sally make deductible IRA contributions for the calendar year 1999?

ANSWER: No. Because both Stanley and Sally are active participants in a simplified employee pension and a simple retirement account and have modified adjusted gross income on a joint return of an amount in excess of $61,000 for the calendar year 1999, they may not make deductible IRA contributions for the calendar year 1999.

QUESTION 10.21: Assume the facts in question 10.20. May Stanley and Sally each contribute $2,000 to a Roth IRA for the calendar year 1999?

ANSWER: Yes. Because Stanley and Sally have modified adjusted gross income of less than $150,000, each may contribute $2,000 to a Roth IRA for the calendar year 1999.

QUESTION 10.22: Assume that Gary and Janet report earned income and modified adjusted gross income of $125,000 on their joint return for the calendar year 1999. Gary is an active participant in a qualified plan. Janet is not a participant in any employer-sponsored retirement plan. May Gary make a $2,000 deductible traditional IRA contribution for the calendar year 1999?

ANSWER: No. Because the modified adjusted gross income on the joint return for the calendar year 1999 exceeds $61,000 and Gary is a participant in a qualified plan, he may not make a $2,000 deductible IRA contribution for the calendar year 1999.

QUESTION 10.23: Assume the facts in question 10.22. May Janet make a $2,000 deductible IRA contribution for the calendar year 1999?

ANSWER: Yes. Under the 1997 Act an individual is not considered to be an active participant in an employer-sponsored retirement plan merely because the individual's spouse is an active participant. In addition, under the 1997 Act the maximum deductible IRA contribution for an individual who is not an active participant but whose spouse is an active participant is phased out for taxpayers with modified adjusted gross income between $150,000 and $160,000 on their joint return. Therefore, Janet may make a $2,000 deductible IRA contribution for the calendar year 1999.

QUESTION 10.24: Assume the facts in question 10.22. May Gary make a $2,000 contribution to a Roth IRA for the calendar year 1999?

ANSWER: Yes. As previously discussed in question 10.10, the maximum contribution that can be made to a Roth IRA is phased out for married individuals filing a joint return if modified adjusted gross income is between $150,000 and $160,000. Because the modified adjusted gross income for Gary and Janet is $125,000, Gary may contribute $2,000 to a Roth IRA for the calendar year 1999.

QUESTION 10.25: What is the difference between the limitation described in your answer to question 10.10 and the limitation described in your answer to question 10.23?

ANSWER: The limitation described in the answer to question 10.10 involves the maximum contribution that can be made to a Roth IRA by married individuals filing a joint return. The limitation described in the answer to Question 10.23 involves the maximum deductible IRA contribution that can be made by an individual filing a joint return when one of the spouses is an active participant in an employer-sponsored plan.

QUESTION 10.26: Assume the facts in Question 10.22. May Janet make a contribution to a Roth IRA for the calendar year 1999 instead of a $2,000 deductible IRA contribution?

ANSWER: Yes. Janet has a choice as to which type of IRA she wishes to use for the calendar year 1999. Janet is limited to an aggregate contribution to all IRAs of $2,000 for the calendar year 1999. She may allocate a portion of the $2,000 to a deductible IRA and the balance to a Roth IRA if she wishes.

QUESTION 10.27: If a taxpayer is an active participant in an employer-sponsored retirement plan, then his or her deductible contribution

to an IRA may be limited based upon adjusted gross income. For purposes of the IRA deduction limitations, what is an employer-sponsored retirement plan?

ANSWER: An employer-sponsored retirement plan includes

1. a qualified plan,

2. a 403(a) annuity plan,

3. a governmental plan,

4. a 403(b) annuity contract,

5. a simplified employee pension, or

6. any simple retirement account.

THE ROTH IRA CREATED BY A CONVERSION

The Taxpayer Relief Act of 1997 permits an individual to establish a Roth IRA by converting a traditional IRA into a Roth IRA. A conversion includes a qualified rollover contribution (Questions 10.28–10.42) as well as a direct transfer to another trustee or to the same trustee (Questions 10.43–10.46).

QUESTION 10.28: What is a qualified rollover contribution to a Roth IRA?

ANSWER: A qualified rollover contribution to a Roth IRA is a rollover contribution from a traditional IRA. The rollover must be completed no later than the 60th day after the day on which the payment or distribution is received.

QUESTION 10.29: When may a traditional IRA be rolled over into a Roth IRA?

ANSWER: A traditional IRA may be rolled over into a Roth IRA for taxable years after December 31, 1997.

QUESTION 10.30: Once a Roth IRA is established, may it be rolled over into another Roth IRA?

ANSWER: Yes. A qualified rollover contribution to a Roth IRA includes a rollover contribution from another Roth IRA.

QUESTION 10.31: May a traditional individual retirement annuity be rolled over into a Roth IRA?

ANSWER: Yes. Any traditional individual retirement plan may be rolled over into a Roth IRA.

QUESTION 10.32: What is a traditional retirement plan?

ANSWER: A traditional individual retirement plan includes both an individual retirement account and an individual retirement annuity.

QUESTION 10.33: Are all taxpayers eligible to make a qualified rollover contribution from a traditional IRA into a Roth IRA?

ANSWER: No. Under the 1997 Act a taxpayer may not make a qualified rollover contribution from a traditional IRA to a Roth IRA if the taxpayer's modified adjusted gross income for the taxable year exceeds $100,000 or if a married taxpayer files a separate return for the taxable year.

QUESTION 10.34: Assume that Tom, age 50, files a joint return with his wife, Cathy, for the calendar year 2000. Assume that their joint return for the calendar year 2000 has a modified adjusted gross income of $80,000. Tom has a traditional IRA of $50,000.

May Tom roll over his traditional IRA of $50,000 to a Roth IRA during the calendar year 2000?

ANSWER: Yes. Tom may roll over his traditional IRA of $50,000 into a Roth IRA during the calendar year 2000.

QUESTION 10.35: Assume the facts in question 10.34, except that Tom and Cathy file separate returns for the calendar year 2000. May Tom roll over his traditional IRA into a Roth IRA during the calendar year 2000?

ANSWER: No. Tom may not roll over his traditional IRA into a Roth IRA because he is married and files a separate return.

QUESTION 10.36: Is there a special marital status rule that applies to the Roth IRA if Tom and Cathy file separate returns and live apart for the entire year?

ANSWER: Yes. Under the 1997 Act if a husband and wife file separate returns for any taxable year and live apart at all times during the taxable year, then they are not treated as married for purposes of the Roth IRA rules.

QUESTION 10.37: Assume Melvin, age 68, is single and has a modified adjusted gross income of $75,000 for the calendar year 2000. Melvin has a traditional IRA of $200,000. May he roll over his traditional IRA of $200,000 to a Roth IRA during the calendar year 2000?

ANSWER: Yes. Melvin may roll over his traditional IRA of $200,000 into a Roth IRA during the calendar year 2000.

QUESTION 10.38: Assume that the taxpayer satisfies the Roth IRA qualified rollover contribution eligibility rules. Does the 1997 Act limit the amount that may be rolled over from a traditional IRA into a Roth IRA?

ANSWER: No. The 1997 Act does not place a limitation on the amount that may be rolled over from a traditional IRA into a Roth IRA.

QUESTION 10.39: Assume that the taxpayer satisfies the Roth IRA qualified rollover contribution eligibility rules. Does the 1997 Act specify a minimum or maximum amount that may be rolled over from a traditional IRA into a Roth IRA?

ANSWER: No. The 1997 Act does not place a limitation on the minimum or maximum amount that may be rolled over from a traditional IRA into a Roth IRA.

QUESTION 10.40: Assume that the taxpayer satisfies the Roth IRA qualified rollover contribution eligibility rules. Does the 1997 Act specify a maximum age for rolling over a traditional IRA into a Roth IRA?

ANSWER: No. The 1997 Act does not specify a maximum age for rolling over a traditional IRA into a Roth IRA.

QUESTION 10.41: Assume that Margo, age 35, is single and has a modified adjusted gross income of $80,000 for the calendar year 2000. Margo has two traditional IRAs. IRA No. 1 has a value of $30,000 and IRA No. 2 has a value of $20,000. May Margo roll over IRA No. 1 to a Roth IRA during the calendar year 2000?

ANSWER: Yes. Because Margo satisfies the provisions of the 1997 Act she may roll over IRA No. 1 to a Roth IRA during the calendar year 2000. She need not rollover IRA No. 2 to a Roth IRA during the calendar year 2000.

QUESTION 10.42: Assume the facts in question 10.41. May Margo roll over both IRA No. 1 and IRA No. 2 into two separate Roth IRAs during the calendar year 2000?

ANSWER: Yes. The 1997 Act does not require Margo to roll over both of her traditional IRAs into one Roth IRA.

DIRECT TRANSFER CONVERSIONS TO A ROTH IRA: QUESTIONS 10.43–10.46

QUESTION 10.43: May an individual who satisfies the qualified rollover eligibility requirements of the 1997 Act transfer a traditional IRA directly to a Roth IRA?

ANSWER: Yes. The owner of a traditional IRA can direct the trustee to make a transfer of all or part of the account to the trustee of the Roth IRA.

QUESTION 10.44: May an individual convert amounts in a qualified plan or 403(b) contract directly to a Roth IRA?

ANSWER: No. Only amounts in a traditional IRA may be transferred to a Roth IRA.

QUESTION 10.45: May an individual who satisfies the qualified rollover eligibility requirements of the 1997 Act convert a traditional IRA to a Roth IRA at the same financial institution?

ANSWER: Yes. A trustee-to-trustee transfer is the third type of conversion recognized by the IRS, in addition to a qualified rollover contribution (see Question 10.28) and a trustee-to-trustee transfer between different institutions. If you want to transfer a traditional IRA to a Roth IRA within the same bank, mutual fund, or other institution, you can simply direct the trustee of the traditional IRA to transfer funds from the traditional IRA to a Roth IRA by submitting the proper paperwork.

QUESTION 10.46: Does the $100,000 modified adjusted gross income ceiling for qualified rollover contributions also apply to conversions made by direct transfer between different institutions or by transfer within the same IRA institution?

ANSWER: Yes, the $100,000 modified adjusted gross income ceiling applies to all three types of conversions.

The rules for determining modified adjusted gross income are discussed in Questions 10.64–10.69.

Tax Effects of a Conversion to a Roth IRA for the Calendar Year 1998

The creation of a Roth IRA as the result of a conversion, including a qualified rollover contribution, results in an income tax liability. Questions 10.47–10.63 explain the special four-year spread for conversions made for 1998.

QUESTION 10.47: Bart, age 55, is single and has a modified adjusted gross income of $60,000 during the calendar year 1998. Bart has $80,000 in a traditional IRA. He has never made any nondeductible contributions to any IRA. Bart rolls over his $80,000 traditional IRA into a Roth IRA during the calendar year 1998. What are the tax consequences of rolling over a traditional IRA into a Roth IRA during the calendar year 1998?

ANSWER: According to the 1997 Act, in the case of a rollover of a traditional IRA into a Roth IRA, the rollover triggers an income tax liability to Bart.

QUESTION 10.48: Assume the facts in question 10.47 and based upon the 1997 Act, how much must Bart report as a result of

the rollover of his $80,000 traditional IRA into a Roth IRA during the calendar year 1998?

ANSWER: According to the 1997 Act, the qualified rollover contribution is treated as if it were a distribution to Bart. If the distribution is made before January 1, 1999, any amount required to be included in gross income is included ratably over the four-taxable-year period beginning with 1998, the taxable year in which the payment or distribution is made.

QUESTION 10.49: Could Bart have elected to report the entire $80,000 amount in income in the calendar year 1998?

ANSWER: Yes. The 1998 Act (which modified the 1997 Act) is retroactive to January 1, 1998, and permitted Bart to elect to report the entire amount in the calendar year 1998.

QUESTION 10.50: Assume the facts in Question 10.47 and based upon the 1997 Act, how much would Bart have reported on his tax return for the calendar year 1998?

ANSWER: Bart would have reported $20,000 (25 percent of $80,000) on his income tax return for the calendar year 1998.

QUESTION 10.51: Assume the facts in question 10.47 and based upon the 1997 Act, how much must Bart report during the calendar years 1999, 2000, and 2001?

ANSWER: According to the 1997 Act, Bart must report $20,000 in each of the calendar years 1999, 2000, and 2001.

QUESTION 10.52: According to your answer to question 10.51, Bart must report as gross income $20,000 in each of the calendar years 1999, 2000, and 2001. What happens if Bart died during the calendar year 1999?

ANSWER: If Bart died in 1999, then the entire deferred amount of $60,000 generally is reported on Bart's Form 1040 for the calendar 1999.

QUESTION 10.53: Could the result described in your answer to Question 10.52 be avoided?

ANSWER: Yes. If Bart were married and his wife was the sole beneficiary of all his Roth IRAs, then she can elect to continue to defer the deferred income in the calendar years 2000 and 2001. In that case only $20,000 of the deferred income would be reported on Bart's final return for the calendar year 1999.

QUESTION 10.54: Assume the facts in question 10.47. Is Bart, age 55, subject to the 10-percent early-distribution penalty on the rollover of the $80,000 traditional IRA into the Roth IRA?

ANSWER: No. According to the 1997 Act, the section 72(t) 10-percent penalty does not apply to a rollover or conversion of a traditional IRA into a Roth IRA. Therefore, Bart is not subject to the 10-percent early-distribution penalty on the rollover of the $80,000 traditional IRA into the Roth IRA.

QUESTION 10.55: Michael, age 65, is single and has a modified adjusted gross income of $90,000. Over the years Michael has opened up several IRAs. He has made nondeductible IRA contributions of $20,000 during his lifetime. During the calendar year 1998 he rolled over all of his traditional IRAs (deductible and nondeductible) valued at $120,000 into a Roth IRA. What was the tax effect to Michael of the rollover of the traditional IRAs into a Roth IRA during the calendar year 1998?

ANSWER: The rollover of $120,000 of traditional IRAs into a Roth IRA results in a gross income of $100,000. This is based upon the fact that Michael had a basis of $20,000 in the traditional IRAs, attributable to the nondeductible contributions that had been made to the traditional IRAs. Because the distribution took place prior to January 1, 1999, the $100,000 is reported ratably over a four-taxable-year period commencing with the calendar year 1998, unless Michael elected to report the $100,000 amount on his 1998 return. Thus, Michael may report as gross income $25,000 in each of the calendar years 1998, 1999, 2000, and 2001.

QUESTION 10.56: Assume the facts in question 10.55, except that the $120,000 distribution from the traditional IRAs was made to Michael on December 28, 1998, and Michael rolled over the traditional IRAs of $120,000 into a Roth IRA on February 15, 1999. What is the tax effect to Michael of the rollover transaction described in this question?

ANSWER: Because the distribution was made to Michael prior to January 1, 1999, the transaction is considered to be a conversion for 1998 and not for 1999. Michael must report as gross income $25,000 in each of the calendar years 1998, 1999, 2000, and 2001.

TAX EFFECTS OF A CONVERSION TO A ROTH IRA FOR CALENDAR YEARS AFTER 1998

The tax rules for conversions after 1998 are not the same as the previously discussed rules for 1998 conversions. Questions 10.57–10.64 illustrate the tax rules for conversions in 1999 and later years.

QUESTION 10.57: Julie, age 52, and her husband Carl have modified adjusted gross income of $85,000 during the calendar year 1999. Julie has $175,000 in a traditional IRA. She never made nondeductible contributions to the account. If Julie converts her traditional IRA by making a direct transfer to a Roth IRA during 1999, what are the tax consequences?

ANSWER: Julie must report the entire $175,000 conversion amount as income on her 1999 return. She may not elect to report the conversion ratably over a four-year period. The four-year spread applicable to 1998 conversions does not apply to conversions (including qualified rollovers) after 1998.

Although Julie is under age 59$^{1}/_{2}$, she is not subject to the 10-percent early-distribution penalty; the penalty does not apply to a conversion of a traditional IRA into a Roth IRA.

QUESTION 10.58: Assume the facts in question 10.55, except that the transaction took place during the calendar year 1999. What is the tax effect to Michael of the rollover of the traditional IRAs of $120,000 into a Roth IRA during the calendar year 1999?

ANSWER: Based upon the fact that the distribution from the traditional IRAs took place during the calendar year 1999, Michael must report $100,000 as gross income on his 1999 income tax return. The four-year rule discussed in Questions 10.48–10.56 does not apply because the distribution did not take place prior to January 1, 1999.

QUESTION 10.59: Assume that Ted, age 65, is married and files a joint return with his wife, Sandra. Ted's modified adjusted gross income is $98,000 for the calendar year 1999. Ted has $80,000 in his traditional IRA. Ted has never made any nondeductible contributions to any IRA. On December 15, 1999, Ted receives a distribution of $80,000 from his traditional IRA, intending to roll over his traditional IRA into a Roth IRA. Ted dies on December 28, 1999, prior to creating the Roth IRA. May Ted's executor timely complete the rollover transaction and transfer the $80,000 proceeds of the traditional IRA into a Roth IRA in Ted's name?

ANSWER: The answer to this question will require guidance from the Internal Revenue Service.

QUESTION 10.60: In order to avoid the potential issue in Question 10.59, what should Ted have done?

ANSWER: Ted should have taken advantage of the direct transfer conversion provisions of the 1997 Act. A conversion in the form of a direct transfer from a traditional IRA into a Roth IRA avoids the potential rollover problems described in Question 10.59.

QUESTION 10.61: Assume that James, age 75, is single and has a modified adjusted gross income of $65,000 during the calendar year 2000. James has an IRA valued at $200,000. He has never made any nondeductible IRA contributions. He has been receiving required minimum distributions annually from his IRA. The $65,000 modified adjusted gross income amount includes his required minimum distributions from his IRA. May he roll over or directly transfer this traditional IRA into a Roth IRA during the calendar year 2000?

ANSWER: Yes. The 1997 Act does not have any age restriction on who can roll over or convert a traditional IRA. The fact that James must receive required minimum distributions from his IRA does not preclude him from establishing a Roth IRA by means of a rollover or conversion. He cannot, however, rollover or otherwise convert any required minimum distributions from his traditional IRA to a Roth IRA.

QUESTION 10.62: John attains age 70¹/₂ in 2000. His modified adjusted gross income for the calendar year 2000 before considering any required minimum distributions is $80,000. If he receives his required minimum distribution of $40,000 from his IRA during 2000, then his modified adjusted gross income for the calendar year 2000 would be $120,000. May John convert his traditional IRA to a Roth IRA in 2000?

ANSWER: No. According to the IRS, John's required minimum distribution of $40,000 is counted as part of his modified adjusted gross income for the calendar year 2000. Because his modified adjusted gross income exceeds the $100,000 ceiling, he is not eligible to make a conversion to a Roth IRA for the calendar year 2000. A conversion would be invalid. John would be treated as having received a taxable distribution from the traditional IRA and as making an excess contribution to the Roth IRA. Conversion would also subject John to substantial IRS penalties.

QUESTION 10.63: Assume the facts in Question 10.62 except that the transaction took place during the calendar year 2005. Would you change your answer to Question 10.62?

ANSWER: Yes. For taxable years after December 31, 2004, and solely for purposes of the $100,000 conversion eligibility ceiling, modified adjusted gross income will not include any required minimum distributions from a traditional IRA.

This rule for years after 2004 will apply only for required minimum distributions from traditional IRAs. Required minimum distributions from a qualified employer plan or a 403(b) arrangement will count toward the $100,000 ceiling in calculating modified adjusted gross income.

QUESTION 10.64: Fred attains age 70$^1/_2$ in 2000. His modified adjusted gross income for the calendar year 2000 without considering any required minimum distribution from his traditional IRA is $70,000. The required minimum distribution he must take for the calendar year 2000 is $10,000. Assume that Fred converts a $50,000 traditional IRA to a Roth IRA during 2000 before he receives the required minimum distribution of $10,000. Is the conversion subject to any IRS penalties?

ANSWER: The amount of the required minimum distribution is not eligible for conversion to a Roth IRA. In a year for which a minimum distribution is required, including the calendar year in which an individual attains age 70$^1/_2$, the individual may not convert assets of a traditional IRA to a Roth IRA to the extent that the required minimum distribution for the traditional IRA for that year has not yet been distributed.

If a required minimum distribution is contributed to a Roth IRA, it is not treated as a conversion contribution. It is treated as a taxable distribution from the traditional IRA, which is then treated as a regular contribution to the Roth IRA. Fred is subject to the 6-percent penalty for excess contributions to the Roth IRA. If Fred were under age $59^1/_2$, he would be subject to the 10-percent early-distribution penalty as well.

MODIFIED ADJUSTED GROSS INCOME AND ROTH IRAS

The contribution-type Roth IRA and the Roth IRA created by a conversion are subject to limitations that are based upon the concept of modified adjusted gross income. Questions 10.68–10.70 illustrate the computation of modified adjusted gross income when a Roth IRA is involved.

QUESTION 10.65: Robert, age 65, is single during the calendar year 2000. He has salary income of $88,000 and taxable interest income of $10,000 for the calendar year 2000. He rolls over his traditional IRA of $120,000 into a Roth IRA during the calendar year 2000. He has never made any nondeductible contributions to any IRA. Would you please determine Robert's adjusted gross income for the calendar year 2000?

ANSWER: Yes. Robert's adjusted gross income for the calendar year 2000 is $218,000.

QUESTION 10.66: Referring to Question 10.65, would you please show how Robert's adjusted gross income for the calendar year 2000 of $218,000 is determined?

ANSWER: Yes. Robert's adjusted gross income is determined as follows:

Salary income	$88,000
Interest income	10,000
Qualified rollover contribution income	120,000
Adjusted gross income	$218,000

QUESTION 10.67: Based upon the facts in Question 10.65, how is Robert's modified adjusted gross income for Roth IRA purposes different from his adjusted gross income for the calendar year 2000?

ANSWER: Robert's modified adjusted gross income for Roth IRA purposes for the calendar year 2000 is $98,000; his adjusted gross income is $218,000.

QUESTION 10.68: Would you please indicate how Robert's modified adjusted gross income for Roth IRA purposes for the calendar year 2000 is determined?

ANSWER: Yes. Robert's modified adjusted gross income for Roth IRA purposes for the calendar year 2000 is determined as follows:

Salary income	$88,000
Interest income	10,000
Qualified rollover contribution income	120,000
Adjusted gross income	$218,000
Less: Qualified rollover contribution income	(120,000)
Modified adjusted gross income	$98,000

QUESTION 10.69: Based upon the facts in Question 10.65, is Robert eligible to roll over his traditional IRA of $120,000 into a Roth IRA during the calendar year 2000?

ANSWER: Yes. Because Robert's modified adjusted gross income for the calendar year 2000 does not exceed $100,000, he may roll over his traditional IRA into a Roth IRA during the calendar year 2000.

QUESTION 10.70: Apart from subtracting the conversion amount from adjusted gross income, are there any other adjustments that must be made to adjusted gross income to determine modified adjusted gross income for Roth IRA purposes?

ANSWER: Yes. Certain deductions and exclusions from income that reduce adjusted gross income must be added back in order to determine modified adjusted gross income. If you claim a traditional IRA deduction, that deduction must be added back to adjusted gross income. You also must add back any student loan interest deduction; any foreign earned income exclusion; any foreign housing exclusion or deduction; any exclusion of Series EE savings bonds used for tuition; and any exclusion of employer-paid adoption expenses.

DISTRIBUTIONS FROM ROTH IRAS

The Taxpayer Relief Act of 1997 (1997 Act) categorizes distributions from Roth IRAs as either qualified distributions or nonqualified distributions. Questions 10.71–10.95 cover the distribution rules that apply to Roth IRAs, including mandatory distribution rules for beneficiaries of Roth IRAs.

QUESTION 10.71: When are distributions from a Roth IRA tax-free?

ANSWER: Qualified distributions (see Question 10.72) are tax-free. Nonqualified distributions are tax free to the extent they are attributable to the recovery of contributions to the Roth IRA; see Questions 10.81 and 10.82.

QUESTION 10.72: What is a qualified distribution from a Roth IRA?

ANSWER: A qualified distribution from a Roth IRA is any payment or distribution that satisfies the five-year rule (discussed in Questions 10.79 and 10.80) and also meets any one of the following conditions:

a. It is made on or after the date on which the individual attains age $59^1/2$;

b. It is made to a beneficiary (or to the estate of the individual) on or after the death of the individual;

c. It is attributable to the individual's being disabled (within the meaning of section 72(m)(7)); or

d. It is a qualified special-purpose distribution.

QUESTION 10.73: What is the definition of being disabled under section 72(m)(7) of the Internal Revenue Code?

ANSWER: According to section 72(m)(7) of the Internal Revenue Code, an individual is considered to be disabled if he or she is unable to engage in any substantial gainful activity by reason of any medically determinable or mental impairment that can be expected to result in death or to be of long-continued and indefinite duration.

QUESTION 10.74: What is a qualified special-purpose distribution?

ANSWER: A qualified special-purpose distribution is a distribution for first-time homebuyer expenses.

QUESTION 10.75: What is a distribution for first-time homebuyer expenses?

ANSWER: The 1997 Act defines a qualified first-time homebuyer distribution as any payment or distribution received by an individual to the extent it is used within 120 days to pay qualified acquisition costs for the principal residence of a first-time homebuyer who is the individual, the spouse of the individual, or any child, grandchild, or ancestor of such individual or individual's spouse.

QUESTION 10.76: Who is a first-time homebuyer?

ANSWER: A first-time homebuyer is any individual or, if married, any individual and the individual's spouse who had no interest in a principal residence during the two-year period ending on the date of acquisition of a principal residence.

QUESTION 10.77: What are "qualified acquisition costs"?

ANSWER: According to the 1997 Act, "qualified acquisition costs" are the costs of acquiring, constructing, or reconstructing a residence. The term encompasses any usual or reasonable settlement, financing, or other closing costs.

QUESTION 10.78: Is there a lifetime limitation on the amount that may be used as qualified first-time homebuyer distributions?

ANSWER: Yes. There is a lifetime limit of $10,000. The aggregate lifetime limitation on the amount that may be treated as qualified first-time homebuyer distributions is $10,000.

QUESTION 10.79: The answer to Question 10.71 indicates that for a distribution to be a tax-free qualified distribution, it must be made for any one of the reasons specified in that answer and it

also must satisfy a five-year rule. If I have a contribution-type Roth IRA, how long do I have to wait before I can receive a distribution that satisfies the five-year rule?

ANSWER: According to the 1998 Act (which modified the 1997 Act), a payment or distribution is a qualified distribution if it is made after the end of the five-taxable-year period beginning with the first day of the first taxable year for which the individual first makes a regular contribution to a Roth IRA, or, if earlier, the first day of the individual's taxable year in which the first conversion contribution is made to any Roth IRA of the individual.

QUESTION 10.80: Is the five-year rule for a Roth IRA established as a result of a conversion from a traditional IRA the same as the five-year rule for a contribution-type Roth IRA?

ANSWER: Yes. See the answer to Question 10.79.

TAX TREATMENT OF NONQUALIFED DISTRIBUTIONS: QUESTIONS 10.81–10.85

QUESTION 10.81: Assume that an individual who established a Roth IRA only through regular contributions receives a distribution that is not a qualified distribution. What is the tax effect of receiving a nonqualified distribution from his/her Roth IRA?

ANSWER: According to the 1998 Act, any distribution from a Roth IRA that is not a qualified distribution is treated as having been made from regular contributions to the Roth IRA to the extent that the distribution, when added to all previous distributions from the Roth IRA, does not exceed the aggregate amount of regular contributions to the Roth IRA.

QUESTION 10.82: Can you illustrate the point you are making in your answer to Question 10.81?

ANSWER: Yes. Assume that Jack, age 40, established a Roth IRA in the calendar year 1998 and made a $2,000 regular contribution to it. In the calendar year 1999, he withdrew $1,500 from his Roth IRA. He does not have to report the $1,500 that he withdrew from the Roth IRA during the calendar year 1999 because he has not yet recovered his prior Roth contribution of $2,000.

QUESTION 10.83: Based upon the facts in your answer to Question 10.82, is Jack subject to a 10-percent penalty with respect to the $1,500 distribution that he received in the calendar year 1999?

ANSWER: No. Under the 1998 Act the recovery of his Roth regular contribution is not subject to the 10-percent early-distribution penalty.

QUESTION 10.84: If Jack received $2,100 from his Roth IRA during 1999, would he be subject to any tax liability and/or penalty on the Roth IRA distribution?

ANSWER: Yes. He would report $100 as ordinary income because the distribution that Jack received during 1999 is not a qualified distribution. Because he recovered his $2,000 regular contribution to the Roth IRA, he must report the additional $100 as ordinary income in 1999. In addition, the $100 would be subject to a 10-percent early-distribution penalty of $10 (10 percent of $100) unless an exception applies to the early-distribution penalty.

QUESTION 10.85: What distribution rules apply if an individual has made both regular contributions to Roth IRAs and conversion contributions (including qualified rollover contributions) to Roth IRAs?

ANSWER: Under the 1998 Act, any amount from any Roth IRA is treated as made in the following order: (1) from regular contributions; (2) from conversion contributions; and (3) from earnings.

In attributing a nonqualified distribution first to regular contributions, all regular contributions to all of your Roth IRAs for all years are aggregated together. After a distribution is offset by regular contributions, it is offset by conversion contributions to all of your conversion Roth IRAs. Conversion contributions are aggregated, but distributions are allocated to conversion contributions in the order that the conversions were made. This first-in, first-out rule for conversion contributions is intended to accommodate the application of the 10-percent early-distribution penalty on conversion contributions distributed within five years as discussed in the answer to Question 10.86.

If a nonqualified distribution exceeds the total contributions attributed to both regular contributions and conversion contributions, it is then considered a taxable distribution of earnings to the extent of the excess.

QUESTION 10.86: Carl, age 50, converts his $50,000 traditional IRA to a Roth IRA in the calendar year 2000 and reports it on his Form 1040 for the calendar year 2000. He has no other Roth IRA. Assume that Carl receives $20,000 from his Roth IRA during 2001. Does Carl have to pay any taxes and/or penalties on the $20,000 distribution that he receives in the calendar year 2001?

ANSWER: The $20,000 that he received from the Roth IRA is tax-free because he reported the conversion income of $50,000 on his income tax return for the calendar year 2000. Because he did not recover the conversion contribution of $50,000 during the calendar year 2001, it is a nontaxable distribution. However, under the 1998 Act, he must pay a 10-percent early-distribution penalty of $2,000 (10 percent of $20,000) on the distribution unless an exception applies. The 10-percent early-distribution penalty applies to a nonqualified distribution to the extent it is allocable to a conversion contribution if the distribution is made within the five-taxable-year period beginning with the first day of the individual's taxable year in which the conversion contribution is made.

QUESTION 10.87: Assume the same facts in Question 10.86 but Carl receives the $20,000 during the year 2001 because he is permanently disabled in 2001. Would Carl be subject to the $2,000 early-distribution penalty described in your answer to Question 10.86?

ANSWER: No. Carl may use the permanent disability exception to avoid the 10-percent early-distribution penalty.

QUESTION 10.88: Assume Robert, age 40, converted a traditional IRA of $60,000 in 1998 and used the four-year-spread rule. He has no other Roth IRA. Assume that Robert withdraws $10,000 from his Roth IRA in the year 2000. How much does Robert report each year with respect to the Roth IRA conversion?

ANSWER: According to the 1998 Act and the IRS, Robert will report $15,000 in 1998, $15,000 in 1999, $25,000 in 2000, and $5,000 in 2001.

QUESTION 10.89: Why does Robert report conversion income of $25,000 in the year 2000?

ANSWER: According to the 1998 Act, a special income acceleration rule applies if the four-year spread was claimed for a 1998 conversion and a distribution from that conversion IRA is received before 2001. Robert must report the regular $15,000 under the four-year-spread rule for the year 2000 plus the $10,000 distribution from the Roth IRA for a total of $25,000 of conversion income. The $10,000 additional income for the year 2000 may not exceed the remaining deferred conversion income and it does not because the remaining deferred conversion income is $15,000.

QUESTION 10.90: Is Robert subject to any penalty with respect to the $10,000 distribution that he receives from the Roth IRA in the year 2000?

ANSWER: Yes. Robert is subject to a 10-percent early-distribution penalty of $1,000 (10 percent of $10,000) unless an exception applies. See answers to Questions 10.86 and 10.87.

MANDATORY DISTRIBUTIONS FOR ROTH IRA BENEFICIARIES: QUESTIONS 10.91–10.95

QUESTION 10.91: Must an individual who is the owner of a Roth IRA receive mandatory distributions from the Roth IRA during his or her lifetime?

ANSWER: No. According to the 1997 Act, the mandatory distribution rules that apply to traditional IRA owners after age $70^{1}/2$ do not apply to a Roth IRA owner while he or she is alive.

QUESTION 10.92: Do mandatory distribution rules apply to a Roth IRA after the death of the owner of the Roth IRA?

ANSWER: Yes. The Internal Revenue Service has stated that the mandatory distribution rules do apply to a Roth IRA after the death of the owner of the Roth IRA.

QUESTION 10.93: When the Roth IRA owner dies is the Roth IRA owner always deemed to have died before his required beginning date?

ANSWER: Yes. According to the IRS the Roth IRA owner is treated as if he or she died before his or her required beginning date.

QUESTION 10.94: Assume the Roth IRA owner's designated beneficiary is a child. Also assume that the child survives the Roth IRA owner. What rules apply on the death of the Roth IRA owner when a nonspouse designated beneficiary is involved?

ANSWER: See the discussion of the Five-Year Rule and the Life-Expectancy Rule in Chapter 8. The IRS has indicated that the entire amount of the Roth IRA must generally be distributed by the end of the fifth calendar year. This is to be done after the year of death unless the interest is payable to the nonspouse designated beneficiary over a period not greater than that beneficiary's life expectancy. Required minimum distributions commence to the nonspouse designated beneficiary before the end of the calendar year following the Roth IRA owner's year of death.

QUESTION 10.95: Assume that the Roth IRA owner's designated beneficiary is the spouse. Also assume that the spouse survives the Roth IRA owner. What rules apply upon the death of the Roth IRA owner?

ANSWER: If the sole beneficiary of the Roth IRA owner is the decedent's spouse, then the spouse may delay distributions until the decedent would have attained age $70^{1}/_{2}$—or may treat the Roth IRA as his or her own.

RECHARACTERIZED CONTRIBUTIONS

An individual may wish to transfer assets from a traditional IRA to a Roth IRA or transfer assets from a Roth IRA to a traditional IRA. Questions 10.96–10.109 discuss the process of transferring assets from one type of IRA to another. The IRS refers to the process as "recharacterized contributions."

QUESTION 10.96: Assume that Howard, age 40, converted a traditional IRA of $50,000 to a Roth IRA during 1998. Howard decided to reverse the 1998 transaction. Could he have transferred the assets in the Roth IRA back to a traditional IRA?

ANSWER: Yes. The 1998 Act permits Howard to reverse the transaction if he acts timely and follows the IRS rules.

QUESTION 10.97: By what date did Howard have to recharacterize his Roth IRA?

ANSWER: According to the 1998 Act he had to recharacterize the Roth IRA to a traditional IRA on or before the due date (including extensions) for filing his federal income tax return for the calendar year 1998. However, the IRS in Announcement 99-57 (June 14, 1999) allowed taxpayers who filed their 1998 federal income tax returns by April 15, 1999, to elect to recharacterize a 1998 IRA contribution, including a Roth IRA conversion, provided that appropriate corrective action occurred on or before October 15, 1999. According to IRS Announcement 99-57, to take advantage of the automatic extension a taxpayer must also file an amended federal income tax return for 1998 properly reflecting the recharacterization. The IRS did not require the amended return to be filed by October 15, 1999, but it must be filed by the normal deadline for amended returns. However, the corrective action had to be taken by October 15, 1999.

QUESTION 10.98: How does Howard recharacterize the Roth IRA?

ANSWER: Howard must arrange for a trustee-to-trustee transfer of the Roth IRA contribution including earnings to the traditional IRA. See the answer to Question 10.97 for the deadline for making the recharacterization.

QUESTION 10.99: What is the proper treatment of the net income attributable to the contribution that is being recharacterized?

ANSWER: The net income attributable to the contribution that is being recharacterized must be transferred from Howard's Roth

IRA to his traditional IRA along with the Roth IRA contribution in a trustee-to-trustee transfer.

QUESTION 10.100: Assume that Tyler converts a $50,000 traditional IRA to a Roth IRA during 1999. However, on December 15, 1999, Tyler is advised by his accountant that his modified adjusted gross income for the calendar year 1999 will exceed the $100,000 ceiling for converting to a Roth IRA. Should Tyler recharacterize the Roth IRA back to a traditional IRA?

ANSWER: Yes. Tyler should immediately recharacterize the Roth IRA back to a traditional IRA. If he does not make a timely recharacterization, he will be subject to a 6-percent penalty for excess contributions to a Roth IRA. The penalty can pyramid over several years until the excess is corrected. Tyler may also be subject to the 10-percent early-distribution penalty if he was under age 59¹/₂ when the conversion was made.

The recharacterization should be made no later than the April 17, 2000, due date, plus extensions for Tyler's 1999 return. However, if Tyler timely files his 1999 return on or before April 17, 2000, without making a recharacterization election, the IRS position as stated in Announcement 99-57 (see Question 10.97) would apparently give Tyler until October 16, 2000, to take corrective action if the recharacterization is properly reflected on a timely filed amended return for 1999.

QUESTION 10.101: If Tyler should die before he does the paperwork, may the personal representative of his estate recharacterize his Roth IRA to a traditional IRA?

ANSWER: Yes. According to the final Roth IRA regulations adopted by the IRS, dated February 3, 1999, the election to recharacterize may be made on behalf of a deceased IRA owner by his or her executor, administrator, or other person responsible for filing the final federal income tax return of the decedent under Section 6012 of the Internal Revenue Code.

QUESTION 10.102: Assume that Janet converted her traditional IRA of $150,000 to a Roth IRA in the calendar year 1999. She would like to recharacterize the Roth IRA back to a traditional IRA. What type of action must she take?

ANSWER: Janet may recharacterize the Roth IRA to a traditional IRA in a trustee-to-trustee transfer. The Roth IRA contribution of $150,000, plus the earnings thereon, generally must be transferred prior to the due date (including extensions) of Janet's Form 1040 for the calendar year 1999. However, Announcement 99-57 apparently allows Janet an automatic extension. See Question 10.100.

QUESTION 10.103: Assume that Darlene, age 40, converted a traditional IRA that was invested in mutual funds to a Roth IRA on September 15, 1998. At the time of the conversion the mutual funds were worth $60,000. Could Darlene have recharacterized the Roth IRA to a traditional IRA on October 1, 1998, even though the value had fallen to $50,000?

ANSWER: Yes. According to the IRS, if the original contribution has experienced net losses at the time of the recharacterization, the transfer of the entire original contribution less such losses generally will constitute a transfer of the entire contribution.

QUESTION 10.104: Assume the facts and the answer to Question 10.103. Could Darlene have reconverted the traditional IRA back to a Roth IRA on October 15, 1998, at the then value of $48,000?

ANSWER: Yes. According to IRS Notice 98-50, Darlene could have reconverted that amount from the traditional IRA to a Roth IRA without any problem prior to November 1, 1998.

QUESTION 10.105: Based upon your answer to question 10.104, how much conversion income must Darlene report?

ANSWER: Darlene will report conversion income of $48,000. If she uses the four-year-spread rule, then she will report $12,000 per year of conversion income for the calendar years 1998, 1999, 2000, and 2001.

QUESTION 10.106: Is there any limitation on the number of reconversions a taxpayer could have entered into during the calendar years 1998 and 1999?

ANSWER: Yes. There was no limitation on the number of reconversions that could be made prior to November 1, 1998. However, effective November 1, 1998, the IRS in Notice 98-50 allowed only one reconversion between November 1, 1998, and December 31, 1998. The one reconversion between November 1, 1998, and December 31, 1998, was in addition to any reconversions that had been made before November 1, 1998.

A one-conversion limit applies to 1999 conversions as well. If a traditional IRA is converted to a Roth IRA during 1999 and then recharacterized to a traditional IRA, it may be reconverted to a Roth IRA once during 1999.

QUESTION 10.107: Is there any limitation on the number of reconversions a taxpayer may enter into after 1999?

ANSWER: Yes. According to the final Roth IRA regulations adopted by the IRS dated February 3, 1999, a new reconversion limit rule is effective as of January 1, 2000. Effective January 1, 2000, an IRA owner who converts an amount from a traditional IRA to a Roth IRA during a taxable year and then transfers that amount back to a traditional IRA by means of a recharacterization is subject to a waiting period before he or she may reconvert that amount from the traditional IRA back to a Roth IRA. A reconversion may not be made before the *later* of: (1) the beginning of the taxable year following the taxable year that the amount was converted to a Roth IRA, or (2) the end of the 30-day period beginning on the date on which the IRA owner transfers the amount from the Roth IRA to a traditional IRA by means of a recharacterization.

If a taxpayer reconverts a contribution more than the allowable one time after December 31, 1999, the additional conversion is treated as a failed conversion. A failed conversion, if not timely recharacterized, is a taxable distribution and an excess contribution to the Roth IRA. An excess contribution is subject to substantial IRS penalties.

CASE STUDY
Questions 10.108 and 10.109 illustrate the limitation on reconversions after 1999.

QUESTION 10.108: Assume Mary converted $20,000 from a traditional IRA to a Roth IRA on July 1, 2000. On August 15, 2000, she recharacterizes that Roth IRA back to a traditional IRA. When may Mary reconvert her traditional IRA back to a Roth IRA?

ANSWER: According to the final IRS regulations, Mary may make a reconversion any time on or after January 1, 2001.

QUESTION 10.109: Assume the same facts as in Question 10.108 except that Mary recharacterizes the Roth IRA back to the traditional IRA on January 15, 2001. When may Mary reconvert her recharacterized traditional IRA back to a Roth IRA?

ANSWER: According to the final IRS regulations, Mary may make a reconversion any time on or after February 14, 2001, which is the first day after the end of the 30-day period that began on the date of the recharacterization, January 15, 2001.

APPENDIX A

LIFE-EXPECTANCY TABLES

On the following pages, we have provided life-expectancy tables from IRS Publication 590, Appendix E. They reflect the tables in section 1.72-9 of the IRS regulations. On the next page is the single life-expectancy table, Table I of Publication 590; it reflects Table V of the IRS regulations. The joint life and last survivor expectancy table that follows, Table II of Publication 590, reflects Table VI of the regulations.

On this page is the Table for Determining Applicable Divisor for MDIB (see Chapter 4 of this book), which is also from Appendix E of the IRS Publication 590.

TABLE FOR DETERMINING APPLICABLE DIVISOR FOR MDIB* (MINIMUM DISTRIBUTION INCIDENTAL BENEFIT)

Age	Applicable divisor	Age	Applicable divisor
70	26.2	93	8.8
71	25.3	94	8.3
72	24.4	95	7.8
73	23.5	96	7.3
74	22.7	97	6.9
75	21.8	98	6.5
76	20.9	99	6.1
77	20.1	100	5.7
78	19.2	101	5.3
79	18.4	102	5.0
80	17.6	103	4.7
81	16.8	104	4.4
82	16.0	105	4.1
83	15.3	106	3.8
84	14.5	107	3.6
85	13.8	108	3.3
86	13.1	109	3.1
87	12.4	110	2.8
88	11.8	111	2.6
89	11.1	112	2.4
90	10.5	113	2.2
91	9.9	114	2.0
92	9.4	115 and older	1.8

| | | TABLE I | |
| | | (Single Life Expectancy)* | |
AGE	DIVISOR	AGE	DIVISOR
35	47.3	73	13.9
36	46.4	74	13.2
37	45.4	75	12.5
38	44.4	76	11.9
39	43.5	77	11.2
40	42.5	78	10.6
41	41.5	79	10.0
42	40.6	80	9.5
43	39.6	81	8.9
44	38.7	82	8.4
45	37.7	83	7.9
46	36.8	84	7.4
47	35.9	85	6.9
48	34.9	86	6.5
49	34.0	87	6.1
50	33.1	88	5.7
51	32.2	89	5.3
52	31.3	90	5.0
53	30.4	91	4.7
54	29.5	92	4.4
55	28.6	93	4.1
56	27.7	94	3.9
57	26.8	95	3.7
58	25.9	96	3.4
59	25.0	97	3.2
60	24.2	98	3.0
61	23.3	99	2.8
62	22.5	100	2.7
63	21.6	101	2.5
64	20.8	102	2.3
65	20.0	103	2.1
66	19.2	104	1.9
67	18.4	105	1.8
68	17.6	106	1.6
69	16.8	107	1.4
70	16.0	108	1.3
71	15.3	109	1.1
72	14.6	110	1.0

* Table I does not provide for IRA owners younger than 35 years of age. For additional life expectancy tables, see Publication 939.

TABLE II
(Joint Life and Last Survivor Expectancy)*

AGES	35	36	37	38	39	40	41	42	43	44
35	54.0	53.5	53.0	52.6	52.2	51.8	51.4	51.1	50.8	50.5
36	53.5	53.0	52.5	52.0	51.6	51.2	50.8	50.4	50.1	49.8
37	53.0	52.5	52.0	51.5	51.0	50.6	50.2	49.8	49.5	49.1
38	52.6	52.0	51.5	51.0	50.5	50.0	49.6	49.2	48.8	48.5
39	52.2	51.6	51.0	50.5	50.0	49.5	49.1	48.6	48.2	47.8
40	51.8	51.2	50.6	50.0	49.5	49.0	48.5	48.1	47.6	47.2
41	51.4	50.8	50.2	49.6	49.1	48.5	48.0	47.5	47.1	46.7
42	51.1	50.4	49.8	49.2	48.6	48.1	47.5	47.0	46.6	46.1
43	50.8	50.1	49.5	48.8	48.2	47.6	47.1	46.6	46.0	45.6
44	50.5	49.8	49.1	48.5	47.8	47.2	46.7	46.1	45.6	45.1
45	50.2	49.5	48.8	48.1	47.5	46.9	46.3	45.7	45.1	44.6
46	50.0	49.2	48.5	47.8	47.2	46.5	45.9	45.3	44.7	44.1
47	49.7	49.0	48.3	47.5	46.8	46.2	45.5	44.9	44.3	43.7
48	49.5	48.8	48.0	47.3	46.6	45.9	45.2	44.5	43.9	43.3
49	49.3	48.5	47.8	47.0	46.3	45.6	44.9	44.2	43.6	42.9
50	49.2	48.4	47.6	46.8	46.0	45.3	44.6	43.9	43.2	42.6
51	49.0	48.2	47.4	46.6	45.8	45.1	44.3	43.6	42.9	42.2
52	48.8	48.0	47.2	46.4	45.6	44.8	44.1	43.3	42.6	41.9
53	48.7	47.9	47.0	46.2	45.4	44.6	43.9	43.1	42.4	41.7
54	48.6	47.7	46.9	46.0	45.2	44.4	43.6	42.9	42.1	41.4
55	48.5	47.6	46.7	45.9	45.1	44.2	43.4	42.7	41.9	41.2
56	48.3	47.5	46.6	45.8	44.9	44.1	43.3	42.5	41.7	40.9
57	48.3	47.4	46.5	45.6	44.8	43.9	43.1	42.3	41.5	40.7
58	48.2	47.3	46.4	45.5	44.7	43.8	43.0	42.1	41.3	40.5
59	48.1	47.2	46.3	45.4	44.5	43.7	42.8	42.0	41.2	40.4
60	48.0	47.1	46.2	45.3	44.4	43.6	42.7	41.9	41.0	40.2
61	47.9	47.0	46.1	45.2	44.3	43.5	42.6	41.7	40.9	40.0
62	47.9	47.0	46.0	45.1	44.2	43.4	42.5	41.6	40.8	39.9
63	47.8	46.9	46.0	45.1	44.2	43.3	42.4	41.5	40.6	39.8
64	47.8	46.8	45.9	45.0	44.1	43.2	42.3	41.4	40.5	39.7
65	47.7	46.8	45.9	44.9	44.0	43.1	42.2	41.3	40.4	39.6
66	47.7	46.7	45.8	44.9	44.0	43.1	42.2	41.3	40.4	39.5
67	47.6	46.7	45.8	44.8	43.9	43.0	42.1	41.2	40.3	39.4
68	47.6	46.7	45.7	44.8	43.9	42.9	42.0	41.1	40.2	39.3
69	47.6	46.6	45.7	44.8	43.8	42.9	42.0	41.1	40.2	39.3
70	47.5	46.6	45.7	44.7	43.8	42.9	41.9	41.0	40.1	39.2
71	47.5	46.6	45.6	44.7	43.8	42.8	41.9	41.0	40.1	39.1
72	47.5	46.6	45.6	44.7	43.7	42.8	41.9	40.9	40.0	39.1
73	47.5	46.5	45.6	44.6	43.7	42.8	41.8	40.9	40.0	39.0
74	47.5	46.5	45.6	44.6	43.7	42.7	41.8	40.9	39.9	39.0
75	47.4	46.5	45.5	44.6	43.6	42.7	41.8	40.8	39.9	39.0
76	47.4	46.5	45.5	44.6	43.6	42.7	41.7	40.8	39.9	38.9
77	47.4	46.5	45.5	44.6	43.6	42.7	41.7	40.8	39.8	38.9
78	47.4	46.4	45.5	44.5	43.6	42.6	41.7	40.7	39.8	38.9
79	47.4	46.4	45.5	44.5	43.6	42.6	41.7	40.7	39.8	38.9
80	47.4	46.4	45.5	44.5	43.6	42.6	41.7	40.7	39.8	38.8
81	47.4	46.4	45.5	44.5	43.5	42.6	41.6	40.7	39.8	38.8
82	47.4	46.4	45.4	44.5	43.5	42.6	41.6	40.7	39.7	38.8
83	47.4	46.4	45.4	44.5	43.5	42.6	41.6	40.7	39.7	38.8
84	47.4	46.4	45.4	44.5	43.5	42.6	41.6	40.7	39.7	38.8
85	47.4	46.4	45.4	44.5	43.5	42.6	41.6	40.7	39.7	38.8
86	47.3	46.4	45.4	44.5	43.5	42.5	41.6	40.6	39.7	38.8
87	47.3	46.4	45.4	44.5	43.5	42.5	41.6	40.6	39.7	38.7
88	47.3	46.4	45.4	44.5	43.5	42.5	41.6	40.6	39.7	38.7
89	47.3	46.4	45.4	44.4	43.5	42.5	41.6	40.6	39.7	38.7
90	47.3	46.4	45.4	44.4	43.5	42.5	41.6	40.6	39.7	38.7
91	47.3	46.4	45.4	44.4	43.5	42.5	41.6	40.6	39.7	38.7
92	47.3	46.4	45.4	44.4	43.5	42.5	41.6	40.6	39.7	38.7

* Table II does not provide for IRA owners or survivors younger than 35 years of age. For additional life expectancy tables, see IRS Publication 939.

				TABLE II (continued) (Joint Life and Last Survivor Expectancy)						
AGES	45	46	47	48	49	50	51	52	53	54
45	44.1	43.6	43.2	42.7	42.3	42.0	41.6	41.3	41.0	40.7
46	43.6	43.1	42.6	42.2	41.8	41.4	41.0	40.6	40.3	40.0
47	43.2	42.6	42.1	41.7	41.2	40.8	40.4	40.0	39.7	39.3
48	42.7	42.2	41.7	41.2	40.7	40.2	39.8	39.4	39.0	38.7
49	42.3	41.8	41.2	40.7	40.2	39.7	39.3	38.8	38.4	38.1
50	42.0	41.4	40.8	40.2	39.7	39.2	38.7	38.3	37.9	37.5
51	41.6	41.0	40.4	39.8	39.3	38.7	38.2	37.8	37.3	36.9
52	41.3	40.6	40.0	39.4	38.8	38.3	37.8	37.3	36.8	36.4
53	41.0	40.3	39.7	39.0	38.4	37.9	37.3	36.8	36.3	35.8
54	40.7	40.0	39.3	38.7	38.1	37.5	36.9	36.4	35.8	35.3
55	40.4	39.7	39.0	38.4	37.7	37.1	36.5	35.9	35.4	34.9
56	40.2	39.5	38.7	38.1	37.4	36.8	36.1	35.6	35.0	34.4
57	40.0	39.2	38.5	37.8	37.1	36.4	35.8	35.2	34.6	34.0
58	39.7	39.0	38.2	37.5	36.8	36.1	35.5	34.8	34.2	33.6
59	39.6	38.8	38.0	37.3	36.6	35.9	35.2	34.5	33.9	33.3
60	39.4	38.6	37.8	37.1	36.3	35.6	34.9	34.2	33.6	32.9
61	39.2	38.4	37.6	36.9	36.1	35.4	34.6	33.9	33.3	32.6
62	39.1	38.3	37.5	36.7	35.9	35.1	34.4	33.7	33.0	32.3
63	38.9	38.1	37.3	36.5	35.7	34.9	34.2	33.5	32.7	32.0
64	38.8	38.0	37.2	36.3	35.5	34.8	34.0	33.2	32.5	31.8
65	38.7	37.9	37.0	36.2	35.4	34.6	33.8	33.0	32.3	31.6
66	38.6	37.8	36.9	36.1	35.2	34.4	33.6	32.9	32.1	31.4
67	38.5	37.7	36.8	36.0	35.1	34.3	33.5	32.7	31.9	31.2
68	38.4	37.6	36.7	35.8	35.0	34.2	33.4	32.5	31.8	31.0
69	38.4	37.5	36.6	35.7	34.9	34.1	33.2	32.4	31.6	30.8
70	38.3	37.4	36.5	35.7	34.8	34.0	33.1	32.3	31.5	30.7
71	38.2	37.3	36.5	35.6	34.7	33.9	33.0	32.2	31.4	30.5
72	38.2	37.3	36.4	35.5	34.6	33.8	32.9	32.1	31.2	30.4
73	38.1	37.2	36.3	35.4	34.6	33.7	32.8	32.0	31.1	30.3
74	38.1	37.2	36.3	35.4	34.5	33.6	32.8	31.9	31.1	30.2
75	38.1	37.1	36.2	35.3	34.5	33.6	32.7	31.8	31.0	30.1
76	38.0	37.1	36.2	35.3	34.4	33.5	32.6	31.8	30.9	30.1
77	38.0	37.1	36.2	35.3	34.4	33.5	32.6	31.7	30.8	30.0
78	38.0	37.0	36.1	35.2	34.3	33.4	32.5	31.7	30.8	29.9
79	37.9	37.0	36.1	35.2	34.3	33.4	32.5	31.6	30.7	29.9
80	37.9	37.0	36.1	35.2	34.2	33.4	32.5	31.6	30.7	29.8
81	37.9	37.0	36.0	35.1	34.2	33.3	32.4	31.5	30.7	29.8
82	37.9	36.9	36.0	35.1	34.2	33.3	32.4	31.5	30.6	29.7
83	37.9	36.9	36.0	35.1	34.2	33.3	32.4	31.5	30.6	29.7
84	37.8	36.9	36.0	35.1	34.2	33.2	32.3	31.4	30.6	29.7
85	37.8	36.9	36.0	35.1	34.1	33.2	32.3	31.4	30.5	29.6
86	37.8	36.9	36.0	35.0	34.1	33.2	32.3	31.4	30.5	29.6
87	37.8	36.9	35.9	35.0	34.1	33.2	32.3	31.4	30.5	29.6
88	37.8	36.9	35.9	35.0	34.1	33.2	32.3	31.4	30.5	29.6
89	37.8	36.9	35.9	35.0	34.1	33.2	32.3	31.4	30.5	29.6
90	37.8	36.9	35.9	35.0	34.1	33.2	32.3	31.3	30.5	29.6
91	37.8	36.8	35.9	35.0	34.1	33.2	32.2	31.3	30.4	29.5
92	37.8	36.8	35.9	35.0	34.1	33.2	32.2	31.3	30.4	29.5

TABLE II (continued)
(Joint Life and Last Survivor Expectancy)

AGES	55	56	57	58	59	60	61	62	63	64	65	66	67	68	69	70	71	72	73	74
55	34.4	33.9	33.5	33.1	32.7	32.3	32.0	31.7	31.4	31.1										
56	33.9	33.4	33.0	32.5	32.1	31.7	31.4	31.0	30.7	30.4										
57	33.5	33.0	32.5	32.0	31.6	31.2	30.8	30.4	30.1	29.8										
58	33.1	32.5	32.0	31.5	31.1	30.6	30.2	29.9	29.5	29.2										
59	32.7	32.1	31.6	31.1	30.6	30.1	29.7	29.3	28.9	28.6										
60	32.3	31.7	31.2	30.6	30.1	29.7	29.2	28.8	28.4	28.0										
61	32.0	31.4	30.8	30.2	29.7	29.2	28.7	28.3	27.8	27.4										
62	31.7	31.0	30.4	29.9	29.3	28.8	28.3	27.8	27.3	26.9										
63	31.4	30.7	30.1	29.5	28.9	28.4	27.8	27.3	26.9	26.4										
64	31.1	30.4	29.8	29.2	28.6	28.0	27.4	26.9	26.4	25.9										
65	30.9	30.2	29.5	28.9	28.2	27.6	27.1	26.5	26.0	25.5	25.0	24.6	24.2	23.8	23.4	23.1	22.8	22.5	22.2	22.0
66	30.6	29.9	29.2	28.6	27.9	27.3	26.7	26.1	25.6	25.1	24.6	24.1	23.7	23.3	22.9	22.5	22.2	21.9	21.6	21.4
67	30.4	29.7	29.0	28.3	27.6	27.0	26.4	25.8	25.2	24.7	24.2	23.7	23.2	22.8	22.4	22.0	21.7	21.3	21.0	20.8
68	30.2	29.5	28.8	28.1	27.4	26.7	26.1	25.5	24.9	24.3	23.8	23.3	22.8	22.3	21.9	21.5	21.2	20.8	20.5	20.2
69	30.1	29.3	28.6	27.8	27.1	26.5	25.8	25.2	24.6	24.0	23.4	22.9	22.4	21.9	21.5	21.1	20.7	20.3	20.0	19.6
70	29.9	29.1	28.4	27.6	26.9	26.2	25.6	24.9	24.3	23.7	23.1	22.5	22.0	21.5	21.1	20.6	20.2	19.8	19.4	19.1
71	29.7	29.0	28.2	27.5	26.7	26.0	25.3	24.7	24.0	23.4	22.8	22.2	21.7	21.2	20.7	20.2	19.8	19.4	19.0	18.6
72	29.6	28.8	28.1	27.3	26.5	25.8	25.1	24.4	23.8	23.1	22.5	21.9	21.3	20.8	20.3	19.8	19.4	18.9	18.5	18.2
73	29.5	28.7	27.9	27.1	26.4	25.6	24.9	24.2	23.5	22.9	22.2	21.6	21.0	20.5	20.0	19.4	19.0	18.5	18.1	17.7
74	29.4	28.6	27.8	27.0	26.2	25.5	24.7	24.0	23.3	22.7	22.0	21.4	20.8	20.2	19.6	19.1	18.6	18.2	17.7	17.3
75	29.3	28.5	27.7	26.9	26.1	25.3	24.6	23.8	23.1	22.4	21.8	21.1	20.5	19.9	19.3	18.8	18.3	17.8	17.3	16.9
76	29.2	28.4	27.6	26.8	26.0	25.2	24.4	23.7	23.0	22.3	21.6	20.9	20.3	19.7	19.1	18.5	18.0	17.5	17.0	16.5
77	29.1	28.3	27.5	26.7	25.9	25.1	24.3	23.6	22.8	22.1	21.4	20.7	20.1	19.4	18.8	18.3	17.7	17.2	16.7	16.2
78	29.1	28.2	27.4	26.6	25.8	25.0	24.2	23.4	22.7	21.9	21.2	20.5	19.9	19.2	18.6	18.0	17.5	16.9	16.4	15.9
79	29.0	28.2	27.3	26.5	25.7	24.9	24.1	23.3	22.6	21.8	21.1	20.4	19.7	19.0	18.4	17.8	17.2	16.7	16.1	15.6
80	29.0	28.1	27.3	26.4	25.6	24.8	24.0	23.2	22.4	21.7	21.0	20.2	19.5	18.9	18.2	17.6	17.0	16.4	15.9	15.4
81	28.9	28.1	27.2	26.4	25.5	24.7	23.9	23.1	22.3	21.6	20.8	20.1	19.4	18.7	18.1	17.4	16.8	16.2	15.7	15.1
82	28.9	28.0	27.2	26.3	25.5	24.6	23.8	23.0	22.3	21.5	20.7	20.0	19.3	18.6	17.9	17.3	16.6	16.0	15.5	14.9
83	28.8	28.0	27.1	26.3	25.4	24.6	23.8	23.0	22.2	21.4	20.6	19.9	19.2	18.5	17.8	17.1	16.5	15.9	15.3	14.7
84	28.8	27.9	27.1	26.2	25.4	24.5	23.7	22.9	22.1	21.3	20.5	19.8	19.1	18.4	17.7	17.0	16.3	15.7	15.1	14.5
85	28.8	27.9	27.0	26.2	25.3	24.5	23.7	22.8	22.0	21.3	20.5	19.7	19.0	18.3	17.6	16.9	16.2	15.6	15.0	14.4
86	28.7	27.9	27.0	26.1	25.3	24.5	23.6	22.8	22.0	21.2	20.4	19.6	18.9	18.2	17.5	16.8	16.1	15.5	14.8	14.2
87	28.7	27.8	27.0	26.1	25.3	24.4	23.6	22.8	21.9	21.1	20.4	19.6	18.8	18.1	17.4	16.7	16.0	15.4	14.7	14.1
88	28.7	27.8	27.0	26.1	25.2	24.4	23.5	22.7	21.9	21.1	20.3	19.5	18.8	18.0	17.3	16.6	15.9	15.3	14.6	14.0
89	28.7	27.8	26.9	26.1	25.2	24.4	23.5	22.7	21.9	21.1	20.3	19.5	18.7	18.0	17.2	16.5	15.8	15.2	14.5	13.9
90	28.7	27.8	26.9	26.1	25.2	24.3	23.5	22.7	21.8	21.0	20.2	19.4	18.7	17.9	17.2	16.5	15.8	15.1	14.5	13.8
91	28.7	27.8	26.9	26.0	25.2	24.3	23.5	22.6	21.8	21.0	20.2	19.4	18.6	17.9	17.1	16.4	15.7	15.0	14.4	13.7
92	28.6	27.8	26.9	26.0	25.2	24.3	23.5	22.6	21.8	21.0	20.2	19.4	18.6	17.8	17.1	16.4	15.7	15.0	14.3	13.7
93	28.6	27.8	26.9	26.0	25.1	24.3	23.4	22.6	21.8	20.9	20.1	19.3	18.6	17.8	17.1	16.3	15.6	14.9	14.3	13.6
94	28.6	27.7	26.9	26.0	25.1	24.3	23.4	22.6	21.7	20.9	20.1	19.3	18.5	17.8	17.0	16.3	15.6	14.9	14.2	13.6
95	28.6	27.7	26.9	26.0	25.1	24.3	23.4	22.6	21.7	20.9	20.1	19.3	18.5	17.8	17.0	16.3	15.6	14.8	14.2	13.5
96	28.6	27.7	26.9	26.0	25.1	24.2	23.4	22.6	21.7	20.9	20.1	19.3	18.5	17.7	17.0	16.2	15.5	14.8	14.2	13.5
97	28.6	27.7	26.8	26.0	25.1	24.2	23.4	22.5	21.7	20.9	20.1	19.3	18.5	17.7	17.0	16.2	15.5	14.8	14.1	13.5
98	28.6	27.7	26.8	26.0	25.1	24.2	23.4	22.5	21.7	20.9	20.0	19.2	18.5	17.7	16.9	16.2	15.5	14.7	14.1	13.4
99	28.6	27.7	26.8	26.0	25.1	24.2	23.4	22.5	21.7	20.9	20.0	19.2	18.5	17.7	16.9	16.2	15.5	14.8	14.1	13.4
100	28.6	27.7	26.8	26.0	25.1	24.2	23.4	22.5	21.7	20.8	20.0	19.2	18.5	17.7	16.9	16.2	15.5	14.7	14.1	13.4
101	28.6	27.7	26.8	25.9	25.1	24.2	23.4	22.5	21.7	20.8	20.0	19.2	18.4	17.7	16.9	16.2	15.4	14.7	14.0	13.3
102	28.6	27.7	26.8	25.9	25.1	24.2	23.3	22.5	21.7	20.8	20.0	19.2	18.4	17.6	16.9	16.1	15.4	14.7	14.0	13.3
103	28.6	27.7	26.8	25.9	25.1	24.2	23.3	22.5	21.7	20.8	20.0	19.2	18.4	17.6	16.9	16.1	15.4	14.7	14.0	13.3
104	28.6	27.7	26.8	25.9	25.1	24.2	23.3	22.5	21.6	20.8	20.0	19.2	18.4	17.6	16.8	16.1	15.4	14.7	14.0	13.3
105	28.6	27.7	26.8	25.9	25.1	24.2	23.3	22.5	21.6	20.8	20.0	19.2	18.4	17.6	16.8	16.1	15.4	14.6	13.9	13.3
106	28.6	27.7	26.8	25.9	25.1	24.2	23.3	22.5	21.6	20.8	20.0	19.2	18.4	17.6	16.8	16.1	15.3	14.6	13.9	13.3
107	28.6	27.7	26.8	25.9	25.1	24.2	23.3	22.5	21.6	20.8	20.0	19.2	18.4	17.6	16.8	16.1	15.3	14.6	13.9	13.2
108	28.6	27.7	26.8	25.9	25.1	24.2	23.3	22.5	21.6	20.8	20.0	19.2	18.4	17.6	16.8	16.1	15.3	14.6	13.9	13.2
109	28.6	27.7	26.8	25.9	25.1	24.2	23.3	22.5	21.6	20.8	20.0	19.2	18.4	17.6	16.8	16.1	15.3	14.6	13.9	13.2
110	28.6	27.7	26.8	25.9	25.1	24.2	23.3	22.5	21.6	20.8	20.0	19.2	18.4	17.6	16.8	16.1	15.3	14.6	13.9	13.2
111	28.6	27.7	26.8	25.9	25.0	24.2	23.3	22.5	21.6	20.8	20.0	19.2	18.4	17.6	16.8	16.0	15.3	14.6	13.9	13.2
112	28.6	27.7	26.8	25.9	25.0	24.2	23.3	22.5	21.6	20.8	20.0	19.2	18.4	17.6	16.8	16.0	15.3	14.6	13.9	13.2
113	28.6	27.7	26.8	25.9	25.0	24.2	23.3	22.5	21.6	20.8	20.0	19.2	18.4	17.6	16.8	16.0	15.3	14.6	13.9	13.2
114	28.6	27.7	26.8	25.9	25.0	24.2	23.3	22.5	21.6	20.8	20.0	19.2	18.4	17.6	16.8	16.0	15.3	14.6	13.9	13.2
115	28.6	27.7	26.8	25.9	25.0	24.2	23.3	22.5	21.6	20.8	20.0	19.2	18.4	17.6	16.8	16.0	15.3	14.6	13.9	13.2

TABLE II (continued)
(Joint Life and Last Survivor Expectancy)

AGES	75	76	77	78	79	80	81	82	83	84	85	86	87	88	89	90	91	92	93	94
75	16.5	16.1	15.8	15.4	15.1	14.9	14.6	14.4	14.2	14.0										
76	16.1	15.7	15.4	15.0	14.7	14.4	14.1	13.9	13.7	13.5										
77	15.8	15.4	15.0	14.6	14.3	14.0	13.7	13.4	13.2	13.0										
78	15.4	15.0	14.6	14.2	13.9	13.5	13.2	13.0	12.7	12.5										
79	15.1	14.7	14.3	13.9	13.5	13.2	12.8	12.5	12.3	12.0										
80	14.9	14.4	14.0	13.5	13.2	12.8	12.5	12.2	11.9	11.6										
81	14.6	14.1	13.7	13.2	12.8	12.5	12.1	11.8	11.5	11.2										
82	14.4	13.9	13.4	13.0	12.5	12.2	11.8	11.5	11.1	10.9										
83	14.2	13.7	13.2	12.7	12.3	11.9	11.5	11.1	10.8	10.5										
84	14.0	13.5	13.0	12.5	12.0	11.6	11.2	10.9	10.5	10.2										
85	13.8	13.3	12.8	12.3	11.8	11.4	11.0	10.6	10.2	9.9	9.6	9.3	9.1	8.9	8.7	8.5	8.3	8.2	8.0	7.9
86	13.7	13.1	12.6	12.1	11.6	11.2	10.8	10.4	10.0	9.7	9.3	9.1	8.8	8.6	8.3	8.2	8.0	7.8	7.7	7.6
87	13.5	13.0	12.4	11.9	11.4	11.0	10.6	10.1	9.8	9.4	9.1	8.8	8.5	8.3	8.1	7.9	7.7	7.5	7.4	7.2
88	13.4	12.8	12.3	11.8	11.3	10.8	10.4	10.0	9.6	9.2	8.9	8.6	8.3	8.0	7.8	7.6	7.4	7.2	7.1	6.9
89	13.3	12.7	12.2	11.6	11.1	10.7	10.2	9.8	9.4	9.0	8.7	8.3	8.1	7.8	7.5	7.3	7.1	6.9	6.8	6.6
90	13.2	12.6	12.1	11.5	11.0	10.5	10.1	9.6	9.2	8.8	8.5	8.2	7.9	7.6	7.3	7.1	6.9	6.7	6.5	6.4
91	13.1	12.5	12.0	11.4	10.9	10.4	9.9	9.5	9.1	8.7	8.3	8.0	7.7	7.4	7.1	6.9	6.7	6.5	6.3	6.2
92	13.1	12.5	11.9	11.3	10.8	10.3	9.8	9.4	8.9	8.5	8.2	7.8	7.5	7.2	6.9	6.7	6.5	6.3	6.1	5.9
93	13.0	12.4	11.8	11.3	10.7	10.2	9.7	9.3	8.8	8.4	8.0	7.7	7.4	7.1	6.8	6.5	6.3	6.1	5.9	5.8
94	12.9	12.3	11.7	11.2	10.6	10.1	9.6	9.2	8.7	8.3	7.9	7.6	7.2	6.9	6.6	6.4	6.2	5.9	5.8	5.6
95	12.9	12.3	11.7	11.1	10.6	10.1	9.6	9.1	8.6	8.2	7.8	7.5	7.1	6.8	6.5	6.3	6.0	5.8	5.6	5.4
96	12.9	12.2	11.6	11.1	10.5	10.0	9.5	9.0	8.5	8.1	7.7	7.3	7.0	6.7	6.4	6.1	5.9	5.7	5.5	5.3
97	12.8	12.2	11.6	11.0	10.5	9.9	9.4	8.9	8.5	8.0	7.6	7.3	6.9	6.6	6.3	6.0	5.8	5.5	5.3	5.1
98	12.8	12.2	11.5	11.0	10.4	9.9	9.4	8.9	8.4	8.0	7.6	7.2	6.8	6.5	6.2	5.9	5.6	5.4	5.2	5.0
99	12.7	12.1	11.5	10.9	10.4	9.8	9.3	8.8	8.3	7.9	7.5	7.1	6.7	6.4	6.1	5.8	5.5	5.3	5.1	4.9
100	12.7	12.1	11.5	10.9	10.3	9.8	9.2	8.7	8.3	7.8	7.4	7.0	6.6	6.3	6.0	5.7	5.4	5.2	5.0	4.8
101	12.7	12.1	11.4	10.8	10.3	9.7	9.2	8.7	8.2	7.8	7.3	6.9	6.6	6.2	5.9	5.6	5.3	5.1	4.9	4.7
102	12.7	12.0	11.4	10.8	10.2	9.7	9.2	8.7	8.2	7.7	7.3	6.9	6.5	6.2	5.8	5.5	5.3	5.0	4.8	4.6
103	12.6	12.0	11.4	10.8	10.2	9.7	9.1	8.6	8.1	7.7	7.2	6.8	6.4	6.1	5.8	5.5	5.2	4.9	4.7	4.5
104	12.6	12.0	11.4	10.8	10.2	9.6	9.1	8.6	8.1	7.6	7.2	6.8	6.4	6.0	5.7	5.4	5.1	4.8	4.6	4.4
105	12.6	12.0	11.3	10.7	10.2	9.6	9.1	8.5	8.0	7.6	7.1	6.7	6.3	6.0	5.6	5.3	5.0	4.8	4.5	4.3
106	12.6	11.9	11.3	10.7	10.1	9.6	9.0	8.5	8.0	7.5	7.1	6.7	6.3	5.9	5.6	5.3	5.0	4.7	4.5	4.2
107	12.6	11.9	11.3	10.7	10.1	9.6	9.0	8.5	8.0	7.5	7.1	6.6	6.2	5.9	5.5	5.2	4.9	4.6	4.3	4.1
108	12.6	11.9	11.3	10.7	10.1	9.5	9.0	8.5	8.0	7.5	7.0	6.6	6.2	5.8	5.5	5.2	4.8	4.5	4.3	4.1
109	12.6	11.9	11.3	10.7	10.1	9.5	9.0	8.4	7.9	7.5	7.0	6.6	6.2	5.8	5.5	5.1	4.8	4.5	4.3	4.1
110	12.6	11.9	11.3	10.7	10.1	9.5	9.0	8.4	7.9	7.4	7.0	6.6	6.2	5.8	5.4	5.1	4.8	4.5	4.3	4.0
111	12.5	11.9	11.3	10.7	10.1	9.5	8.9	8.4	7.9	7.4	7.0	6.5	6.1	5.7	5.4	5.1	4.8	4.5	4.2	4.0
112	12.5	11.9	11.3	10.6	10.1	9.5	8.9	8.4	7.9	7.4	7.0	6.5	6.1	5.7	5.4	5.0	4.7	4.4	4.4	3.9
113	12.5	11.9	11.2	10.6	10.0	9.5	8.9	8.4	7.9	7.4	6.9	6.5	6.1	5.7	5.4	5.0	4.7	4.4	4.2	3.9
114	12.5	11.9	11.2	10.6	10.0	9.5	8.9	8.4	7.9	7.4	6.9	6.5	6.1	5.7	5.3	5.0	4.7	4.4	4.1	3.9
115	12.5	11.9	11.2	10.6	10.0	9.5	8.9	8.4	7.9	7.4	6.9	6.5	6.1	5.7	5.3	5.0	4.7	4.4	4.1	3.9

SAMPLE TERM-CERTAIN ELECTION WHERE SPOUSE IS THE DESIGNATED BENEFICIARY

RIDER TO INDIVIDUAL RETIREMENT ACCOUNT AGREEMENT OF JACK SMART WITH ABC INC. AS CUSTODIAN FOR IRA NUMBER 100000

I, JACK SMART, hereby elect under the existing law and IRS rules that installment payments from the above referenced Individual Retirement Account be paid out over a period certain of 26 years which period certain does not exceed the joint life expectancy of me, JACK SMART and JANE SMART, my wife, who is my designated beneficiary. The term certain of 26 years does not exceed the joint life expectancy of both me and my wife based upon our attained ages in the calendar year 1999. The calendar year 1999 is the year in which I, JACK SMART, attain age 70^1/$_2$.

Said payment shall commence no later than my required beginning date of April 1, 2000, and be paid to me, JACK SMART, for the above described 26-year period in installments and in a manner in conformity with the Internal Revenue Code and its regulations. I, JACK SMART, shall have the right to accelerate all or any part of the remaining unpaid installments of this Individual Retirement Account.

In the event that said installment payments have commenced to me and I die during the 26-year installment period and my wife, JANE SMART, survives me then in that event said installment payments shall continue to be paid to my wife, JANE SMART, in installments for the balance of the 26-year term-certain period. In such event, my wife, JANE SMART, shall have the power to accelerate all or any part of said remaining installment payments of this Individual Retirement Account to herself during her lifetime and to create a spousal IRA rollover in whole or in part to the extent permitted by law.

In the event that my wife, JANE SMART, survives me and dies during the 26-year installment payment period, then the remaining installment payments shall be continued and shall be paid to the estate of my wife, JANE SMART, for the remainder of the 26-year installment payment period unless JANE SMART has created a spousal IRA rollover.

In addition, in the event that my wife, JANE SMART, survives me and dies during the 26-year installment payment period and fails to create a spousal IRA rollover, then in that event her Executor may in his sole and absolute discretion assign the rights of said payments from my wife's estate to the beneficiary of her estate.

In the event that installment payments have commenced to me, JACK SMART, and my wife, JANE SMART, has predeceased me and I should then die during the installment payment period, then any remaining installments shall be paid to my contingent beneficiary(s) in installments over the remaining installment period.

Notwithstanding anything contained herein to the contrary, any estate or beneficiary of any estate entitled to the remaining unpaid installment payments described herein shall have the right to accelerate all or any part of the remaining unpaid installments of this Individual Retirement Account.

In the event that any contingency occurs wherein the installment payments under this agreement are in violation of any provision of the Internal Revenue Code and its regulations, then the beneficiary of the remaining unpaid installments including any estate or individual, as the case may be, shall have the right to increase the amount and increase the frequency of the payments in order to comply with the Internal Revenue Code and its regulations.

It is further agreed that all installment payments shall be paid annually or at more frequent intervals.

Notwithstanding anything contained herein to the contrary, it shall be the obligation of the individual or entity entitled to payment from this Individual Retirement Account to compute and direct ABC Inc., as to both the amount and date of any payment with respect to this Individual Retirement Account. ABC, Inc. shall have no obligation with respect to computing the amount and date of any payment from this Individual Retirement Account.

This election shall not preclude an expansion of the period certain if at a subsequent date the law and IRS rules are changed and the period certain may be expanded in a manner provided for under the law and IRS rules.

I irrevocably elect that there shall be no recalculation of my life expectancy or the life expectancy of my wife, JANE SMART, with respect to distributions from this Individual Retirement Account for the calendar year 1998 or any subsequent calendar year.

Dated: December 1, 1999
Jack Smart

Sample Term-Certain Election Where Child Is the Designated Beneficiary

RIDER TO THE INDIVIDUAL RETIREMENT ACCOUNT AGREEMENT OF ALBERT TAYLOR WITH XYZ, INC. AS CUSTODIAN FOR IRA NUMBER 200000

I.   Designation of Beneficiary

I, ALBERT TAYLOR, the owner of the Individual Retirement Account No. 200000 with XYZ, INC. as Custodian for said account hereby designate the following as the designated beneficiary of the death benefits of this Individual Retirement Account:

Primary Beneficiary:

Mark Taylor

Contingent Beneficiary:

Janet Smart

II.   Designation of Maximum Period of Distributions

A.   Death of ALBERT TAYLOR prior to April 1, 2000

In the event that I, ALBERT TAYLOR, die before my required beginning date of April 1, 2000, and I am survived by MARK TAYLOR and the designated beneficiary at the date of my death is still MARK TAYLOR, then I request that MARK TAYLOR shall make the appropriate timely written election with the Custodian of this

Individual Retirement Account as to the period of time over which payments of required minimum distributions from this Individual Retirement Account shall be paid to MARK TAYLOR. This written election as to the time period that is made by MARK TAYLOR as described shall not preclude the designated beneficiary from accelerating distributions from this Individual Retirement Account at any time and from time to time on or after the date of death of ALBERT TAYLOR.

B. Lifetime distribution to ALBERT TAYLOR on or after April 1, 2000; Death of ALBERT TAYLOR on or after April 1, 2000

I, ALBERT TAYLOR, hereby elect under the existing law and IRS rules to utilize to the extent described below my life expectancy and the life expectancy of MARK TAYLOR in determining the amount of required minimum distributions that I, ALBERT TAYLOR, must receive from this Individual Retirement Account during my lifetime commencing on or after my required beginning date of April 1, 2000.

I, ALBERT TAYLOR, hereby elect to utilize to the extent described below my life expectancy and the life expectancy of MARK TAYLOR in determining the amount of required minimum distributions that my designated beneficiary must receive from this Individual Retirement Account in the event of my death on or after my required beginning date of April 1, 2000.

I, ALBERT TAYLOR, may consider my life expectancy and the life expectancy of MARK TAYLOR provided that as of my required beginning date of April 1, 2000, MARK TAYLOR is still the designated beneficiary of this Individual Retirement Account and MARK TAYLOR is alive as of April 1, 2000.

I, ALBERT TAYLOR, hereby elect that the required minimum distributions from this Individual Retirement Account be paid out over a period certain of thirty-eight (38) years which period certain does not exceed the joint life expectancy of me ALBERT TAYLOR and MARK TAYLOR, based upon our attained ages in the calendar year 1999. The calendar year 1999 is the year in which I, ALBERT TAYLOR, attained age $70^{1}/_{2}$. The payments over the thirty-eight (38) year term-certain period shall be subject to the acceleration rights described in this agreement and the Minimum Distribution Incidental Benefit Requirement described in this Agreement.

The fact that I, ALBERT TAYLOR, have elected that required

minimum distribution payments from this Individual Retirement Account be paid over a period of thirty-eight (38) years shall not preclude me from accelerating distributions from this Individual Retirement Account during my lifetime at any time and from time to time.

In addition, the fact that I, ALBERT TAYLOR, have elected that payments from this Individual Retirement Account be paid over a period of thirty-eight (38) years shall not preclude my designated beneficiary from accelerating distributions from this Individual Retirement Account after the date of my death at any time and from time to time.

I, ALBERT TAYLOR, recognize that during my lifetime and on or after April 1, 2000, that I, ALBERT TAYLOR, am subject to the Minimum Distribution Incidental Benefit Requirement (MDIB Requirement) based upon the Internal Revenue Code and its regulations and that this will require me to take my required minimum distributions from this Individual Retirement Account in a manner that requires me to utilize the "Applicable Divisor" as that term is described in the IRS regulations and IRS publications instead of the thirty-eight (38) year period described above.

I, ALBERT TAYLOR, recognize that the MDIB Requirement does not apply to distributions that are made to my designated beneficiary in years after the date of my death and that my designated beneficiary in those years shall receive the required minimum distributions over the original period certain of thirty-eight (38) years (subject to acceleration rights described in this rider) that I, ALBERT TAYLOR, elected but reduced by one year for each distribution calendar year or portion of distribution calendar year beginning with the calendar year 1999 that has elapsed while I, ALBERT TAYLOR, was alive. The fact that I, ALBERT TAYLOR, elected that required minimum distributions from this Individual Retirement Account be paid over a period of thirty-eight (38) years shall not preclude my designated beneficiary after the date of my death from accelerating distributions from this Individual Retirement Account at any time and from time to time.

Notwithstanding anything contained herein to the contrary, it shall be the obligation of the individual or entity entitled to payment from this Individual Retirement Account to compute and direct XYZ, INC., as to both the amount and date of any payment with respect to this Individual Retirement Account. XYZ, INC., shall have no obligation with respect to computing the amount and date of any payment from this Individual Retirement Account.

This election shall not preclude an expansion of the period certain if at a subsequent date the law and IRS rules are changed and the period certain may be expanded in a manner provided for under the law and IRS rules.

I irrevocably elect that there shall be no recalculation of my life expectancy with respect to distributions from this Individual Retirement Account for the calendar year 1999 or any subsequent calendar year.

Dated: December 1, 1999
Albert Taylor

SAMPLE IRA DESIGNATION OF BENEFICIARY FORM

JASON S. GOLDBERG
80 Kings Road
Southampton, New York 11530
Social Security No.: 785-11-2204
Date of Birth: 02/08/40
IRA Number: 10987654321

PRIMARY BENEFICIARY

NAME/RELATIONSHIP	DATE OF BIRTH	SOCIAL SECURITY	PERCENT
JENNIFER L. GOLDBERG/ WIFE	12/11/45	123-45-6789	100%

CONTINGENT BENEFICIARIES

NAME/RELATIONSHIP	DATE OF BIRTH	SOCIAL SECURITY	PERCENT
*MARK GOLDBERG/SON	02/22/64	234-56-7891	$33^1/_3\%$
*ERIC GOLDBERG/SON	11/05/66	345-67-8910	$33^1/_3\%$
*JILL GOLDBERG/DAUGHTER	04/17/68	456-78-9101	$33^1/_3\%$

In the event that any of my children shall predecease me, then in that event said deceased child's share shall be paid to the issue of such deceased child, per stirpes. In the event that a child shall predecease me leaving no issue, then in that event said deceased child's share shall be paid to my issue, per stirpes. In the event that any beneficiary entitled to receive benefits is a minor, then in that event said minor beneficiary's share shall be paid to a custodian under the Uniform Transfers to Minors Act or similar act for the benefit of such minor beneficiary until the maximum age permitted by law and thereafter directly to such beneficiary. The custodian shall be designated by the executor or administrator of my estate, as the case may be, to the extent permitted by law.

Dated: December 1, 1999
Jason S. Goldberg

INDEX